Many Are Chosen

....

DIVINE ELECTION AND
WESTERN NATIONALISM

Edited By

William R. Hutchison and Hartmut Lehmann

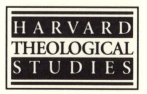

HARVARD
THEOLOGICAL
STUDIES

Fortress Press
Minneapolis

Many Are Chosen
Divine Election and Western Nationalism

Harvard Theological Studies 38

Book design and typesetting: the staff of *Harvard Theological Review*
Managing Editor: Tamar Duke-Cohan
Editorial Assistants: Ellen B. Aitken and Laura Nasrallah
Cover Photo: H. Armstrong Roberts
Cover Design: McCormick Creative
Harvard Theological Studies Series Editors: John B. Carman, David D. Hall, Helmut Koester, Jon D. Levenson, Francis Schüssler Fiorenza, Ronald F. Thiemann

Library of Congress Cataloging-in-Publication data

Many are chosen : divine election and Western nationalism /
edited by William R. Hutchison and Hartmut Lehmann.
    p.   cm. — (Harvard theological studies; no. 38)
    Includes bibliographical references and index.
    ISBN 0-8006-7091-4 (alk. paper) :
    1. Nationalism—Religious aspects—Congresses. I.
Hutchison, William R. II. Lehmann, Hartmut, 1936–
III. Series: Harvard theological studies.
BL65.N3M26   1994
291.1'77—dc20   94-16621
                                                          CIP

The paper used in this publication meets the minimum requirements of American National Standard for Information Sciences—Permanence of paper for Printed Library Materials, ANSI Z329.48-1984. (∞)™

Manufactured in the U.S.A.
98 97 96 95 94   1   2   3   4   5   6   7   8   9   10

CONTENTS

Acknowledgments

The editors are grateful to the Gerda Henkel Foundation of Düsseldorf and the German Historical Institute in Washington for their help in staging the conference from which this book has grown. The Lilly Endowment of Indianapolis and its Vice President for Religion, Craig Dykstra, provided support both for the conference and for subsequent editorial and promotional expenses.

We also acknowledge the very helpful participation, in the Conference on Religion and Nationalism, of Professors Hana Gaifman of New York University, Reinhard R. Doerries of Erlangen-Nürnberg, and Robert Trisco of the Catholic University of America. Richard H. Seager served as coordinator for the conference, and Missy Daniel was executive assistant for our volume in the early stages of its preparation. We are deeply indebted to both of them, as we are to Tamar Duke-Cohan and the editorial staff of Harvard Theological Studies and to Michael West, Senior Editor of Fortress Press.

Two contributors to the volume, Professors Robert P. Ericksen and Robert T. Handy, deserve special mention. Both came to our aid with critiques of particular essays even though they had not participated in the conference.

W. R. H.
H. L.

Standing among men and women who do not hide the intensity of their feelings, I understand what nationalism really is: the dream that a whole nation could be like a congregation—singing the same hymns, listening to the same gospel, sharing the same emotions, linked not only to each other but to the dead buried beneath their feet.

— MICHAEL IGNATIEFF

Introduction

William R. Hutchison[*]

William R. Hutchison[*]

In late June 1991, the *Times* of London carried an article headed by an exasperated query: "Why Do Some Nations Still See Themselves as the Chosen People?" The article's author, Conor Cruise O'Brien, had just returned to Ireland after attending the historical conference for which these essays were first written. His question, like Michael Ignatieff's reflections on his experience of a cathedral service in Ukraine, quoted in the epigraph to this volume, identified contemporary concerns that undoubtedly had helped to prompt our inquiry.[1]

---

[*]William R. Hutchison is Charles Warren Professor of the History of Religion in America at Harvard Divinity School.
[1]Conor Cruise O'Brien, "Why Do Some Nations Still See Themselves as the Chosen People?" *Times* (London) 25 June 1991, 14. Michael Ignatieff, *Blood and Belonging: Journeys into the New Nationalism* (New York: Farrar, Strauss & Giroux, 1994) 127.

O'Brien and the other conference participants had spent most of their time, however, on certain "previous questions" more within our area of competence. One of these questions was historical, the other historiographic: First, in what ways have chosen people ideas—whether couched in this or equivalent terminology—figured historically in the dialogue between religion and nationalism? and second, given the evident interest today in the real or suspected interactions between these two massive forces—nationalism and religion—how is it that historians have paid so little attention to the rich heritage (or burdensome baggage) of their past relationships?

This second question depended obviously on an assumption that earlier relationships between religion and modern nationalism have been neglected. I think that it is possible to show that they have been, at least as a matter of broad historical analysis. To be sure, with respect to particular nations, cultures, and subcultures, the topic has received intensive and often brilliant treatment; had that not been the case, we could not have located scholars prepared and willing to launch into the rougher seas of comparative analysis. Because of the genuine and well-known difficulties in cross-cultural ventures, however, and because historians have taken religious determinants less seriously than, say, economic ones, we did not have an appreciable body of relevant comparative history upon which to build.

For the same reasons, it made sense to focus on a particular set of ideas—ideas of national "divine election" derived from Jewish and Christian traditions. Since, moreover, the history and prehistory of those conceptions, even in their modern forms, reaches back at least into the seventeenth-century world of Gustavus Adolphus and Oliver Cromwell, we thought it well to give most of our attention to a brief but crucially important span of years: the decades often called the high imperial era.

Our further limiting of the investigation to a small number of national or protonational examples was mostly the result of what we hope is well-informed design. It was also affected, however, by such accidents as our success or failure in the search for scholars, working in or near this subject matter, who could fit our project into their schedules.

Comparative History and the General Study of Nationalism

Preliminary or stage-setting ventures like the one published here ought not to pose as full-fledged comparative analyses. They can, however, keep the objectives of such analysis in view and be shaped by them; in fact they will make little contribution unless they do so. In the present instance, we have been attentive to the two most common reasons for launching comparative studies in history. The first of these is the need to expand and enrich understanding of such general phenomena as modern nationalism or the influence in the West of Judaism and Christianity.

The other most usual motive for cross-cultural studies is a concern about the insularity of much that scholars teach and write about particular societies. This motive leads, for example, to the use of consciously comparative methods to test generalizations or national stereotypes that are already (but often quite unconsciously) comparative in nature. Louis L. Snyder, in one of the articles for his *Encyclopedia of Nationalism*, complains that "people throughout the world believe [that] all Scotsmen are thrifty, all Germans hopelessly belligerent, all Frenchmen amourous, all Swedes cold, and all Americans naive and aggressive."[2] In turning this perhaps exaggerated charge into questions for research, one asks not merely whether Scots and Swedes fit these stereotypes—and other more important ones—but also who else does or does not exemplify them. Are Americans, as commonly reported, enormously idealistic and at the same time grossly materialistic? The crucial response ought to be something like that of the woman who was asked routinely, "How's your husband?" and whose riposte was "Compared to what?"

This need to look behind national stereotypes was not the principal rationale for our conference and book, but it did serve as an important starting point. It was a natural place to begin simply because so much has been said and written about a single chosen people ideology—that of the Americans. The vast literature documenting the importance of these conceptions in American cultural development has

[2]Louis L. Snyder, *Encyclopedia of Nationalism* (Chicago: St. James, 1990) 235–36.

established a genre as well as posed what should be compelling comparative questions.

Our book clearly is not about American history. Indeed, it purports indeed not to take the American example as normative or archetypal. Although unacknowledged assumptions about what *is* normative are quite likely to lurk in anyone's research design, such preconceptions are the very ghosts the comparativist hopes to exorcise or at least bring into plain view. In any case, this initiatory look at chosen people ideologies, while it does raise some questions about conventional national stereotypes, addresses principally the first objective of comparative history mentioned above: the elucidation of a theme or relationship.

In the broadest terms, this means that we hope to contribute to the continuing study of the place of religion in historical development. We would agree, surely, with the position stated by Theodore Rabb and Robert Rotberg in introducing their own recent symposium on history and religion. They write that these disciplines, in spite of their long relationship, "still have much to gain from explicit. . . explorations of their interdependence."[3] Rabb and Rotberg in their turn would probably agree that studies of nationalism, together with such related phenomena as civil religion and imperialism, stand out as significant items on any encompassing history-and-religion agenda.

Here, however, the historiographic questions recur and deserve to be addressed. Has the subject of "religion and nationalism" really been slighted? If so, why? That it has at least been "not much explored" seems clear if one consults standard bibliographies of the literature on modern nationalism. Koppel Pinson in 1935 found five "religion" items to list in a total of 431, and Karl Deutsch, two decades later, could add only twenty-five more. These "religion" entries, moreover, on the whole were not remarkable either for breadth or for their seriousness as scholarship. Most of the writings that one might classify as cross-cultural or international in scope dealt with the Roman Catholic church in its struggles with this particular aspect of

---

[3]Theodore K. Rabb and Robert I. Rotberg, "History and Religion: Interpretation and Illumination," *Journal of Interdisciplinary History* 23 (1993) 448.

modernity. Other entries were lectures or popular essays—for example, articles from American religious periodicals on the churches' relations to war or racism—that would not qualify as historical monographs and had not been so intended. Newer listings in the late 1960s and at the start of the present decade made it clear that, with respect to broad interpretation of the topic, very little had changed.[4]

Hans Kohn's classic *Idea of Nationalism*, first published in 1945, revealed in one pivotal statement why he and many others saw little point in pursuing "religious dimensions" once the watershed of the French Revolutionary era had been crossed: "In the new age nationalism, taking the place of religion, [was] as diversified in its manifestations and aspirations, in its form and even in its substance as religion itself."[5] Although religion had perhaps not disappeared, it had lost its dominant "place" and therefore, in Kohn's view, retained little explanatory usefulness in the chronicling of post-Revolutionary nationalism.

The notion of "nationalism *as* religion," which was not incompatible with that of institutional and intellectual displacement, was implicit in Kohn's work and explicit in the writings of the other prolific contributor in Kohn's generation to this field of study, Carlton J. H. Hayes. But Hayes and Salo W. Baron (who in 1944 published

---

[4]Koppel Pinson, *Bibliographical Introduction to Nationalism* (New York: Columbia University Press, 1935); Karl W. Deutsch, *Interdisciplinary Bibliography of Nationalism, 1935–1953* (Cambridge, MA: Technology, 1956). In 1968, Hans Kohn's brief bibliography for the "Nationalism" article in the *International Encyclopedia of the Social Sciences* [ed. David L. Sills; 16 vols.; New York: Macmillan and Free Press, 1968] 11. 69–70) was entirely silent on religious factors, whether general or local. Louis Snyder, in 1990, found six books or articles on religion and nationalism worthy of mention in a bibliography of over two hundred items. On historians' obliviousness to religion in their analyses of nationalism, see Gertrude Himmelfarb, "The Dark and Bloody Crossroads Where Nationalism and Religion Meet," *The National Interest* 32 (1993) 56–57.

[5]Hans Kohn, *The Idea of Nationalism: A Study in Its Origins and Background* (New York: Macmillan, 1945) 574. Similarily, Boyd C. Shafer, ten years later, treated nineteenth-century nationalism as a successor to religion and the principal substitute for it. See Shafer, *Nationalism, Myth and Reality* (New York: Harcourt, Brace, 1955).

Rauschenbusch Lectures on *Modern Nationalism and Religion*), were almost alone in treating religious thought and institutions, in their more usual definitions, as independent variables in nationalist discourse and actions or even as representing popular interests that policymakers still had to take into account. Religion was seen as an important predecessor to nationalism and then as its frequent challenger (particularly in the form of Roman Catholicism). Except for those functions, in nearly all general treatments of nineteenth-century European nationalism religion figured as little more than reminiscence or false consciousness.[6]

I have not tried to avoid entirely the use of terms like "neglect" to characterize the thinness of scholarship and analysis in relation to these subjects. To do so would be disingenuous. None of the participants in this symposium, however, would rule out the possibility that religion and religious language did lose any independent significance, in the post-Revolutionary West, as a component of nationalist enthusiasms and advocacy. Far from being a question we consider settled, it is one that we are intent upon exploring.

Comparative History and the Question of American Exceptionalism

Some time in the late 1970s, taking my turn as presenter in a faculty seminar at Harvard, I talked about my own inquiries into American ideas of religious and national mission. Probably my remarks were shot through with assumptions about Americans' allegedly singular proclivity to see themselves and their society as divinely chosen redeemers of a fallen humanity. A foreign-born colleague, the New Testament scholar Krister Stendahl, while he shared my impatience with nationalist pretensions, nonetheless questioned the

---

[6]Carlton J. H. Hayes, *Nationalism: A Religion* (New York: Macmillan, 1960); Salo W. Baron, *Modern Nationalism and Religion* (New York: Harper, 1947); Kohn, "Nationalism." Snyder's *Encyclopedia* includes substantial entries for such relationships as "Music and Nationalism" and "Language and Nationalism," but none for "Religion and Nationalism." While Snyder devotes four paragraphs to "Nationalism as a Religion," these constitute a nod to Carlton Hayes and amount to less coverage than that given to "Languedoc Particularism" and "Magyar Diaspora Nationalism."

"exceptionalist" premise. "It's just like you Americans," he observed wryly, "to suppose you've been Number One in guilt."

Stendahl's suspicions—that historians who chide the exceptionalist illusions of their predecessors may well be caught in the same trap—were only partially justified in this case. Students of American culture had been voicing concern about their own possible parochialism at least since the controversies following Frederick Jackson Turner's announcement of a "frontier thesis" in the 1890s. A minority among them had been trying with greater intensity to combat these tendencies since the blossoming of an American studies movement in more recent decades. Most major works on American ideas of chosenness and national mission, in the same recent period, had carried warning labels that eschewed parochialism and in effect made a case for comparative studies.

Albert K. Weinberg's pioneering work of 1935, *Manifest Destiny*, had referred to the American experience as "an excellent *laboratory* for the study of expansionist ideology" (my emphasis).[7] Ralph Gabriel's later and even more influential survey of American thought, although it had featured the belief in national mission as a tenet in what he called the American Democratic Faith, had also acknowledged that this and other tenets "were old and were borrowed"; Gabriel had regarded the American idea of mission as one exemplification of "that sense of superiority which an in-group normally feels with respect to out-groups."[8] In 1966, Russel B. Nye's *This Almost Chosen People* had stated flatly that "all nations. . . have long agreed that they are chosen peoples; the idea of special destiny is as old as nationalism itself."[9]

---

[7]Albert K. Weinberg, *Manifest Destiny: A Study of Nationalist Expansionism in American History* (Baltimore: Johns Hopkins University Press, 1935) 8.

[8]Ralph H. Gabriel, *The Course of American Democratic Thought: An Intellectual History Since 1815* (New York: Ronald, 1940) 13, 24.

[9]Russel B. Nye, *This Almost Chosen People: Essays in the History of American Ideas* (East Lansing: Michigan State University Press, 1966) 164. See also, on this point, Conrad Cherry's introduction to his documentary collection, *God's New Israel: Religious Interpretations of American Destiny* (Englewood Cliffs, NJ: Prentice-Hall, 1971) 21–22.

This kind of caveat had not, however, gone much beyond the stage of ritual incantation.[10] One may wish to place the blame for this nonfeasance, this failure to follow through, not just on parochialism but on sheer laziness. Paraphrasing Robert Maynard Hutchins on the subject of exercise, we may want to suggest that Americanists have proven their love for comparative studies by lying right down and thinking about them. It would be well, however, before we indulge that judgment, to consider two points that are of some importance in themselves. One is that, when it comes to modern convictions and expressions about chosenness, the prima facie case for American singularity is indeed uncommonly strong. A second and more extenuating point is that until quite recently neither American nor other historians could have gone much farther than they did in the direction of cross-cultural analysis. Before about 1980, the groundwork, in the form of studies of other chosen people ideologies and their religious ramifications, was more fragmentary, even less in place, than it is now.

"Only One Applicant for Canonization"

Prima facie cases, of course, by definition are not conclusive. Investigators may find not only that, as the present collection of essays amply confirms, others besides the Americans have harbored these ideas, but also that other societies—perhaps the British in our period, or Slavophile Russians in a somewhat earlier one—have maintained such self-estimations with a similar degree of passion and consistency. For the time being, however, we can say that scholarly and popular fixation on the American case is at least understandable.

---

[10]The most extensive comparative treatment, so far as I know, had been an intriguing couple of pages in Edward McNall Burns's *American Idea of Mission* (New Brunswick: Rutgers University Press, 1957) 4–5. "From time immemorial," Burns wrote, "nations have conceived of themselves as superior and as endowed with a mission to dominate other peoples or to lead the rest of the world into paths of light." Whether one listened to Hebrews, Greeks, and Confucianist Chinese, nineteenth-century Western Europeans and Slavophiles, or those in Nehru's India who were discovering and embellishing a glorious past, one would detect a longing "to assume a white man's or a brown or yellow man's supremacy over weak and retarded peoples."

Ralph Gabriel, having acknowledged the long pedigree of ideas about national mission and the generic similarities among them, could still argue that the American configuration had been unique. "National religions are, perforce, unique because they have utilities which are limited to the group which practices them."[11] About fifty years later, Conor Cruise O'Brien, nearly in shock after reading the hyperbolic American self-congratulations recorded in Ernest Tuveson's *Redeemer Nation*, found the American configuration not merely unique in Gabriel's sense, but truly exceptional—unmatched—when viewed against the background of others to which O'Brien had given his attention earlier. All peoples, he wrote, have been guilty of heinous crimes, and some besides the Americans—for example, the English Puritans—have fancied themselves essentially pure. "The idea of American innocence," O'Brien admitted, "was not invented in America." He added, however, that "I must stick to the case in hand. Only one nation has submitted a case for canonization."[12]

Most of O'Brien's historical colleagues, American and other, would probably find that contrast a bit too sharp. Not only would they suppose that the dualism of "innocent nation, wicked world" can be found in other national ideologies; they would also emphasize that, along with the theme of America's innocence, contrapuntal themes of national guilt and failure can be detected if one listens closely. Those who have chronicled the American sense of mission have in fact confirmed that my Swedish colleague was on to something: In their own special ways Americans have indeed wanted to be Number One in guilt as well as innocence.

But not, of course, at the same time; what historians like Nye have discussed, and writers such as Arthur Miller have found reflected in the life experience of Americans, is a tendency toward self-flagellation that these observers see as one response to the failure of unrealistic moral aspirations. Edward McNall Burns made this a cardinal

[11]Gabriel, *Democratic Thought*, 13.
[12]Conor Cruise O'Brien, "Innocent Nation, Wicked World," *Harper's*, April 1980, 32. The magazine's "department heading," a surely intentional *double entendre* placed above O'Brien's article, was "Purely American." See also Ernest Tuveson, *Redeemer Nation: The Idea of America's Millennial Role* (Chicago: University of Chicago Press, 1968).

point. Americans, he suggested, had done about as well as any other people in the fulfillment of stated ideals—which is to say not very well. (Reviewing a standard list of goals that included "highest standard of living," he found that only this not-too-exalted ideal had actually been fulfilled.) Burns found no fault with the ideals. He did, however, deplore the "swagger, conceit, and sense of superiority" with which nations too often advertise their purposes. His discussion conveyed a certain sadness (rather than denunciation) about the fact that Americans had believed their own sometimes swaggering rhetoric and had therefore suffered acutely whenever the real world made its inevitable appearance.[13]

As Nye wrote in expanding this point several years later, Americans from Jefferson to Eisenhower had been obsessed with the problem of defining and redefining ideals. Nye was willing to treat this particular obsession as exceptional. "It is probable," he wrote, "that only in the United States would a national body, appointed by the head of the state, embark on a study of the national purpose, as President Eisenhower's Commission on National Goals did in 1959."[14] Even though Nye, more than other interpreters, credited Americans with being "aware. . . of the impossibility of attaining perfection," he did not think this awareness in any way diminished their nagging sense of failure. Quite the contrary, "The American lives with a constant compromise of his dreams." Americans, he thought,

---

[13]Burns, *Idea of Mission*, viii, 350–58. In the program notes for Arthur Miller's "The Last Yankee," which began a London run in January 1993, Christopher Bigsby remarked on this persistent theme in Miller's work, "America was born out of a belief in perfection. . . . It follows that the burden of a failed utopia falls on those who feel they have not realised its promise. To fail [in America] is to acknowledge some deep flaw in the self, for responsibility cannot lie with a society whose promise of happiness and possibility [is] its reason for being." Among earlier critiques, the most relevant, perhaps, would be those of writers like D. H. Lawrence, George Santayana, and the young Van Wyck Brooks, all of whom saw excessive idealism as issuing perversely in materialism and, as a consequence, in guilt and repression. The classic statement is Van Wyck Brooks, *America's Coming-of-Age* (New York: Dutton, 1915).

[14]Nye, *Almost Chosen People*, 167.

must continue to attempt to meet their own high standards, and
suffer when they do not; they are no doubt the only people in
the world who blame themselves for not having finally created
the perfect society, and who submit themselves to constant self-
examination to determine why they have not. . . . No other
nation has quite the same sense of guilt over its [own] failures.[15]

"No Major Collective Research Has Been Undertaken"

The extensiveness of what I am calling the prima facie case regarding American ideas of chosenness—the sheer profuseness of the
evidence—is such that it is a difficult point to which to do justice,
not only in a few paragraphs here, but in entire books. Nye, for
example, found no space even to quote from the "hundreds of statements about America's destiny, mission, and function in the congress
of nations" that Charles Sumner collected for the American centenary
celebrations of 1876. Nye had too many other "mission of America"
documents to deal with. He could only mention Sumner's anthology
and exclaim about it.[16] A mound of compelling evidence, however,
should not inhibit, and I think is not what has inhibited, comparative
investigation. If Americans have seemingly established world records
for both idealism and self-flagellation, this dubious achievement en-
hances the need for comparison and contrast; certainly it does not
lessen it. The better reason for reticence has been a perfectly respectable realism about the research prerequisites for any wide-ranging
comparative judgments.

Hans Kohn, in his 1968 encyclopedia article, suggested both the
pressing need for comparison and the procedure required for meeting
this need. He wrote that "only a comparative historical study of the
various forms of nationalism can do justice to any one of them" and
lamented that, up to that time, "no major collective research effort
has yet been undertaken in this field, in spite of its vital importance
for an understanding of the contemporary world."[17]

---

[15]Ibid., 204.

[16]Ibid., 171. Charles Sumner's book is *Prophetic Voices Concerning America:
A Monograph* (Boston: Lee & Shepard, 1874).

[17]Kohn, "Nationalism," 64. As late as 1983, Ernest Gellner put a sharper
point on this by paraphrasing Eric Hobsbawm's wry comment on "the dispro-

Although that challenge still has not been met, considerable ground-work was laid during the succeeding quarter century. During the 1980s especially, analysis of nationalism and other forms of group identity developed with unusual rapidity, and on a number of disciplinary and ideological fronts. Benedict Anderson exclaimed in 1991 that the study of nationalism had been "startlingly transformed" in the dozen years since he had presented his own definition of nationalities as "imag-ined communities." The scholarship in that short time had expanded "in method, scale, sophistication, and sheer quantity."[18]

The kind of elaboration to which Anderson referred owed a great deal, in turn, to forms of inquiry that invited attention—whether or not they themselves gave explicit attention—to the place and possible importance of religion. This was true, for example, of the work of those social psychologists, historians, and students of international affairs who examined the formation or disruption of various forms of collective identity or who explored the presumed relationships be-tween any of these forms and individual experience. The new analysts of group identity adverted readily to myths of origin and vehicles of group cohesion that often were religious in nature and that they found operative in Western as well as non-Western societies.[19]

Scholarship after 1970 also produced a few systematic attempts (although still surprisingly few) to do "collective research" on given elements within the phenomenon of nationalism—imperialism, for

---

portion between the importance of nationalism and the amount of thought given to it"; see Ernest Gellner, *Nations and Nationalism* (Ithaca: Cornell University Press, 1983) 124.

[18]Benedict Anderson, *Imagined Communities: Reflections on the Origin and Spread of Nationalism* (rev. ed.; London/New York, Verso, 1991) xii. For further and more current references to the relevant historical work, see Himmelfarb, "Dark and Bloody Crossroads."

[19]Edwin E. Sampson, "The Challenge of Social Change for Psychology: Globalization and Psychology's Theory of the Person," *American Psycholo-gist* 44 (1989) 914–21; William Bloom, *Personal Identity, National Identity, and International Relations* (Cambridge: Cambridge University Press, 1990); Nicholas Canny and Anthony Pagden, eds., *Colonial Identity in the Atlantic World, 1500–1800* (Princeton: Princeton University Press, 1987); and Samuel P. Huntington, "The Clash of Civilizations?" *Foreign Affairs* 72 (1993) 22–49.

example, or the ideologies and activities of Christian missionaries. In at least one of the latter volumes, *Missionary Ideologies in the Imperialist Era*, published in the early 1980s, the theme of national chosenness came up repeatedly. With it, of course, came questions concerning the biblical and other religious sources or rationales for such convictions.[20]

During the 1980s, also, individual scholars who were pursuing agendas in religious history and political thought began to scrutinize the chosen people ideologies, other than those of white Americans, that informed particular nationalist or protonationalist formulations.[21] In other words, by the end of the decade "way had been opened," as the Quakers would say, for collaborative effort on a pancultural phenomenon—ideas of chosenness and national mission—that in truth now seemed ready for some fraction of the attention previously lavished on the Americans.

"Many are Chosen": The Conference and the Book

In 1990, therefore, after preliminary consultations and one small-scale presentation at the annual meeting of the American Society of Church History in December 1988, the editors put several questions to scholars who had agreed to write brief papers for a June 1991

---

[20]Michael Twaddle, ed., *Imperialism, the State, and the Third World* (London: British Academic Press, 1992); John K. Fairbank, ed., *The Missionary Enterprise in China and America* (Cambridge, MA: Harvard University Press, 1974); Torben Christensen and William R. Hutchison, eds., *Missionary Ideologies in the Imperialist Era* (Aarhus: Forlaget Aros, 1982).

[21]Hartmut Lehmann, "Pietism and Nationalism: The Relationship of Protestant Revivalism and National Renewal in Nineteenth Century Germany," *Church History* 51 (1982) 39–53; Albert J. Raboteau, "'Ethiopia Shall Soon Stretch Forth Her Hands': Black Destiny in Nineteenth-Century America" (University Lecture in Religion; Tempe: Arizona State University, 1983). For André du Toit's writings of this period, see notes 2 and 3 for his article in the present volume. O'Brien, at the end of the decade, published a study focused on American ideology that offered comparative observations. See Conor Cruise O'Brien, *God Land: Reflections on Religion and Nationalism* (Cambridge, MA: Harvard University Press, 1988). A later, highly impressive addition to the literature was Donald H. Akenson, *God's People: Covenant and Land in South Africa, Israel, and Ulster* (Ithaca: Cornell University Press, 1992).

conference on "Chosen People Themes in Western Nationalist Movements." The questions, to be addressed "in no particular sequence, and with the understanding that responses to some queries may render others 'Not Applicable,'" were the following:

(1) Was some notion of national or ethnic chosenness operative in this particular society or group during the period under discussion?

(2) If so, what form(s) did this take?

(3) To what extent was the "Old Testament" covenant transferred and used as a model for describing a modern "chosen people" proceeding under a new (or continuing, or revised) covenant?

(4) Which social and political groups utilized or supported this chosen people rhetoric, and what were the means by which it was propagated?

(5) If a concept of chosenness is not evident in this case, or not important, what sort of rhetoric *was* used, or *was* primary?

By and large, the contributors to this book have answered our first query in the affirmative. In each of the several cases—Swiss, Afrikaner, and Zionist—in which an author has questioned the existence or solidity of the idea of chosenness in a given national experience, the responder has been inclined to disagree. As far as our still-limited set of examples can tell us, therefore, previous writers on chosen people themes were justified in supposing that most peoples who have thought of themselves as "nations" at all have at some points considered themselves divinely chosen to a special destiny.

One must be wary, of course, about a certain preselection that could contribute to this near unanimity in our results. Because we were aware of this potential biasing of the discussion, but also because of the intrinsic interest attaching to counterexamples, the organizers did attempt to give more of a hearing to the latter than the reader will find in our volume.[22]

---

[22]We tried, for example, to enlist the help of Sacvan Bercovitch, the prominent interpreter of American culture, who in various writings has remarked on the resistance among his Canadian compatriots to any idea of national chosenness. See, for example, Bercovitch's title essay in Rob Kroes, ed., *The American Identity: Fusion and Fragmentation* (Amsterdam: Dutch American Studies Association, 1980) 19–45. Bercovitch was one of several appropriate and interested persons who could not participate in the project at this stage.

As scholars go forward with studies that we hope this preliminary effort will encourage, such suspected cases of dissent should be pursued. It seems likely, however, that the title of our own volume will turn out to be, if anything, a bit moderate; not just "many" Western societies, but perhaps most of them, have found divine appointment a natural component of nationalist enthusiasms. In any case, these essays give more attention to our second and third questions, those that queried the forms of chosen people rhetoric or assumptions, and that addressed the complex matter of biblical sources and their use, transformation, or displacement.

The contributors, besides giving more attention to these questions, have offered more varied answers for them. The findings in these areas are in fact disparate enough that grouping the essays was not a simple procedure. In the end, we embraced a distinction between those instances in which chosenness and nationalist expansionism appear to have been conjoined and those in which one or both of those elements were missing. To make use of such a distinction is to recognize that the place of religion or religious rhetoric in the expansive variety of nationalism is a topic in itself, one that can best be addressed by placing these examples side by side—or end to end. Far from privileging that important relationship, however, this way of subdividing the topic also serves to underline the point that variant patterns exist and are important. In particular, the identification of a nonexpansionist version of chosenness certifies that such myths may perform what Robert Ericksen in his essay for this volume calls "nonmalignant" functions.

Weary Titans and Upstart Enthusiasts

Even within the expansionist category, the concept of chosenness rarely took the unreservedly smug or arrogant forms that tend to be extracted for anthologies and, fairly enough, denounced in critiques of imperialism. "The idea of chosenness," as Conor Cruise O'Brien pointed out in the his Massey Lectures of 1987, "contains within itself not only national pride, but also humiliation, anquish, fear, and guilt. . . . The chosen people can rightly be punished. . . God, having chosen one people, can simply drop it for another."[23] Among the least an-

---

[23]O'Brien, *God Land*, 41.

guished, moreover—and here the Americans seem by any measure to claim the prize—universal concerns and humanitarian aspirations played an especially strong role. Whether genuine or a mere cover for baser motives, universalist ideals appear to have been as much a part of chosen people rhetoric as were flamboyant utterances about national destiny.

Certainly flamboyant nationalism, or at least a seemingly illogical claim to nearly exclusive divine favor, rears its head in each of these five instances. We find J. G. Greenhough, in Andrew Walls's account, assuring fellow Baptists that God has granted power and prosperity to the British in order "that we should be more than all others God's messengers of light and truth." At the same time, according to Hartmut Lehmann, God was the special "old ally" of the Germans because "no people had understood the biblical message as well as the German people and no people had given expression to the biblical message as well as they had." In France, Thomas Kselman finds royalists and republicans, although bitterly at odds, agreeing that "France would not perish because it had a unique mission in the world." James Moorhead quotes an American cleric who, outdoing the Reverend Josiah Strong, argued "that the United States was the final world kingdom foretold in Daniel 2." Even among the Afrikaners, whom André du Toit depicts as speaking principally within wider discourses of European imperialism and Christian mission, the Anglo-Boer conflict at the turn of the century elicited more particularistic claims: "God has fought on our side. . . . The Lord Himself planted us in South Africa and let us flourish. . . . He will not let us perish."

Yet in nearly all these expansionist cases, the claims to special divine favor were accompanied not only by universal and humanitarian protestations of which we may well be suspicious, but also by the sort of anguish to which O'Brien referred. This is not merely the relatively superficial annoyance about the white man's burden—about the ingratitude and impoliteness of those for whom Europeans are giving their hearts' blood. The anguish is a deeper and more generalized sense of the burden and frustration of empire. It is the *fin de siècle* mood that pervaded numerous literary renderings of the era and that Aaron Friedberg and others have found best expressed in Joseph

Chamberlain's poignant estimate of imperial England as a "weary titan."[24]

The more theological, or at least theologized, form of this ambivalence concerning empire appears in the humility, the sense of divine judgment, that in Rudyard Kipling's writings and elsewhere came packaged so grotesquely with bluster and condescension. If, "drunk with sight of power," we begin to rave like the Gentiles and the "lesser breeds," please, dear God, remain with us! The French and German formulations, as rendered in this book by Kselman and Lehmann, pick up the same *motifs*, but in these instances we hear notes not merely, in the words of the much-later American song, of warning but of danger: God will abandon this favored people if they ignore the need for personal and collective regeneration; but he may already have abandoned them.[25]

Among the Afrikaners, on the other hand, the kind of ambivalence that du Toit finds most salient for his story relates not to God's favor, or its feared withdrawal, but to God's initial intentions. The disclaimer voiced by the agnostic J. M. B. Hertzog—"Although I have my belief, I say that neither you nor I know in the least what is the finger of God!"—was seconded in more reverential contexts: "Faith [means] 'Lord, *Thy* will be done—not *my* will to be the victor.'"

Even though each of these forms of humility can doubtless be found somewhere in the literature of the various expansionist exemplars, it seems to be scarce indeed in American nationalist rhetoric. James H. Moorhead's account supports O'Brien's classification of the

---

[24] Aaron Friedberg, *The Weary Titan: Britain and the Experience of Relative Decline* (Princeton: Princeton University Press, 1988). Matthew Arnold's earlier use of the phrase, along with other literary expressions of the mood, is noted in James Morris's chapter "The Wearying Titan," in idem, *Farewell the Trumpets: An Imperial Retreat* (London: Faber & Faber, 1978) 91 and 91–104. See also, especially for its bibliography, Robert Giddings, ed., *Literature and Imperialism* (London: Macmillan, 1991).

[25] As American readers are bound to know, the song referred to is a plea for social justice composed in 1949 by Lee Hays and Pete Seeger: "If I had a hammer. . . I'd hammer out danger, I'd hammer out warning, I'd hammer out love between my brothers and my sisters. . . . "

Americans, through much of their history, as not just a chosen people but a holy nation, a "chosen people with tenure."[26] Moorhead's essay is perhaps the only one in this book that does not record significant reservations about national chosenness. Such doubts do not appear to assail the opponents of the late-blooming American imperialism, to say nothing of its proponents.

I think that, difficult as it is to prove a negative, any of us who have tried to compare such expressions as those in British and American hymns and national songs would find it hard to disagree with Moorhead. Americans of this period may occasionally have sung Kipling's "Recessional," William Blake's "Jerusalem," or G. K. Chesterton's scathing "God of Earth and Altar" ("Our earthly rulers falter, Our people drift and die"), but Americans themselves contributed nothing quite comparable to Anglophone hymnology. Although American writers such as Herman Melville had long since depicted America's own dark, satanic mills,[27] these do not appear in the hymnology even of the Protestant social gospel. In the patriotic hymnology of this era, which was the very era of record-breaking urbanization and of sweat shops, tropes like those we find in Katherine Lee Bates's "America the Beautiful" were more the norm: "Thine alabaster cities gleam, undimmed by human tears." (In the only "alabaster" city I can picture except that of the 1893 Columbian Exposition Bates had just visited, United States congressmen carried guns when they went out at night.) One may propose, not entirely in jest, that if the Americans had had a queen it would not have occurred to them that she was in need of "saving."

In certain crucial areas, in other words, we must indeed "score one" for American exceptionalism, and also for later critics of American liberal optimism. For this newest and initially most reluctant of the imperialist societies, perfervid nationalism was filtered through universalist idealism, but not noticeably dimmed by shadows of divine judgment.

[26]O'Brien, *God Land*, 42.
[27]Herman Melville, "The Paradise of Bachelors and the Tartarus of Maids," in Jay Leyda, ed., *The Complete Stories of Herman Melville* (New York: Random House, 1949) 185–211.

Counterpoint: Suffering Servants and Unchosen People

Among our four other examples, none—with the probable exception of the Swiss—managed to avoid all participation in the Western expansionism of the era. Zionists most of the time, and African Americans some of the time, looked to a homeland on the African continent; and American blacks, in partial concert with white Westerners, looked upon Africa as a field for evangelizing and "civilizing" efforts. In Sweden, influential minority movements sought to reinstate some elements of a glorious expansionist past.

All four of these cases, however, serve primarily to provide counterpoint to the preceding five. Early Zionism, as Paul Mendes-Flohr interprets it, sought vigorously to distance itself from Western hegemonic impulses that had meant little but oppression and suppression for the Jewish people. If chosenness connoted what so-called Christian societies seemed to assume, Zionists wanted no part of it. From that perspective, the Jewish case is, remarkably, the principal counterexample in this collection. Mendes-Flohr's answer to our initial chosenness question, while it not only acknowledges but highlights complexity, is fundamentally negative. He insists that if one is talking about intentional or at least conscious forms of discourse, this is one discourse that most early Zionists intended not to utilize.

In the Swiss instance, the dissent from patterns of chosenness is configured quite differently. To be sure, Ulrich Gäbler uncovers in Swiss intellectual history and patriotic expression some elements of chosen people thinking. He finds, for example, powerful expressions of confidence in God's special solicitude for the Confederation, coupled with warnings that God's favor was conditioned upon individual and national virtue. If, as Gäbler argues, this thinking did not form until quite recently into chosen people typologies, it was because the Swiss, unlike the Americans, recognized their nation as a historical and geographic construct; they did not conceive of it as having been brought into being for God's special purposes. The notion of chosenness had little resonance for those who could only with intense effort think of themselves as a "people" at all.

The Swedes, according to Stephen Mitchell and Alf Tergel, experienced little such hesitation; chosenness, at least in the sense of special vocation, was never in doubt. Swedes in this era, however, did exhibit a divided consciousness—conflicting notions of what the Lord required of them. If things had gone as younger militants (secular as well as religious) wanted them to, Sweden would have played with the big boys in the nationalist game, if only on the second team, and if only on defense. As it was, the pacific and internationalist interpretations of the national vocation not only remained potent, but rather quickly reasserted their dominance, and did so with eloquence and force. The original watchword of the nationalistic Young Church Movement, "The People of Sweden—A People of God," had been somewhat modest as such slogans go. A later leadership, nonetheless, preferred a different emphasis: "The Nations—God's Peoples." The claim to special vocation was not relinquished, but the Swedes were saying that all godly vocations are created equal.

African Americans were dissenters in somewhat similar ways. A strong, long-sustained ideology of chosenness seems as evident here as it is in the Swedish case or in those of, say, the English people and their American cousins. Specific metaphors relating to chosen status would seem, in fact, to have been more persistently in use in the American black communities of this period than in any of the other eight societies treated in this book. The biblical metaphors that Albert Raboteau finds most prevalent, however, all went against the grain of the Euroamerican formulations. Although racial messianism can be seen as drawing upon such white Christian conceptions as Anglo-Saxonism, black mythologies of Exodus and Ethiopianism entirely denied or subverted those conceptions.

It was still true, decades after "emancipation," that African Americans as a chosen people were wandering in the wilderness. To many black thinkers it was clear, still and always, that despite this painful reality the world's destiny lay in the hands not of Europeans but of Africans.

The Use and Disuse of Biblical Language

The African American instance is striking also in the degree to which it is set off from others by blacks' use of unsecularized biblical language. In general, these essays reveal strong convictions of national chosenness in which the identification with ancient Israel comes up sporadically or casually if it comes up at all.

This was not usually a matter of radical rejection. It may have been such in the case of Zionists intent on normalizing Jewish national aspirations; one thinks, moreover, of those American evangelical Protestants who defended a Jewish right-in-perpetuity to the Israelite heritage and who thereby renounced any claims of their own. Such exceptions aside, the chosen peoples of this era were not intent on denying their own connections to the experience of Israel.

They were also, however, not obsessed or even greatly reliant upon that model. If it is true, as Gäbler remarks in passing, that "the *motif* of the chosen people nearly always goes along with an identification with Israel," it seems also to be true that such identification, by our period, had been reduced to the status of what du Toit aptly calls an available discourse.

As such, moreover, it was one discourse among several. The Afrikaners, for example, once they began flooding their national rhetoric with the language of chosenness, were not preoccupied with the imagery of Exodus and covenant; it seems they were just as likely to call upon the psalmist ("Perhaps it is His will to lead [us] through the valley of the shadow of death") or to cite God's favoring interventions in the national history ("Our battlefields testify to the powerful miracles which God has wrought"). For the French, chosen protectors of Christ's Church, the most readily available discourses were those related to the Sacred Heart of Jesus, Mary the Mother of God, and the story and symbolism of Joan of Arc.

White Americans, too, had reached a stage in which the relevant images came more from the Book of Revelation and the New Testament than from the experience of Israel. Americans in this perspective were a people who, having long since survived the perils of an exodus, had been assigned the sort of responsibility identified in H. Richard Niebuhr's analysis of this era's public theology: a responsibility to lead the world in recognizing "the reality of the reign of Christ," and to guide the world in performing those human tasks essential to "the manifestation in power" of Christ's kingdom on earth.[28]

---

[28]Helmut Richard Niebuhr, *The Kingdom of God in America* (New York: Harper, 1937) 126, 127.

Regions and Subcultures: the Question of Internal Variation

This leaves our fourth question to be considered. "What social and political groups utilized or supported. . . chosen people rhetoric, and what were the means by which it was propagated?"

Although it made sense to remind our investigators, by means of this question, to watch for variations relating to class, gender, region, political ideology, and other forms of group identity, it would not have been reasonable to expect extended or systematic treatment of these matters. Authors needed to search out "dominant" ideologies in each of these communities, and they had their hands full pursuing that part of the assignment.

Perhaps we should be content with the fact that the terminology and frequently holistic assumptions of "national character" studies are not controlling in any of these essays or commentaries. (I believe it is correct to say that the term "national character" is not used.) The authors do, of course, attempt to identify expressions that can be shown to have enjoyed popular support and that, partly for this reason, held the attention of policymakers. None of the essayists, however, forecloses the rich possibilities in more differentiated treatments of the society under discussion.

It would be surprising if any of them did, since much of the discussion at the 1991 conference—perhaps a fourth of it—involved these internal variations and the problems raised for the analyst of any given nationalism until such issues can be explored. The participants were especially concerned, as the organizers of the conference had been, to recruit principal investigators who would be able and willing to deal with gender as a category of analysis. This was a special concern not because gender seemed more likely to be determinative than ethnicity or region, but simply because the relatively new field of women's studies was considerably less well represented among our conferees than were the other forms of differentiation.

Our efforts on this front were unsuccessful, as were the attempts to add articles on Slavic, Celtic, and Southern European instances. The most we can claim to have gathered, therefore, is a number of potentially instructive hints about social class and other internal variations, as well as about various means of propagation.

By my count, at least six of the essays, plus several of the responses, offer informed judgments about interactions between elite and popular expressions, or between intellectuals on the one hand, and a working class or middle class on the other. In most although not all of these cases, what is suggested is a high degree of interdependence. Americanists might well be reminded, as they read these essays, of Gabriel's insight about the popular sources (or at least analogues) of pragmatism: "When William James made the creative individual the center of his philosophy, he pushed his canoe into the main current of American thought. When he urged in America the importance of activism, he sought with his paddle to give the Mississippi a push toward the sea."[29]

Anyone who wishes to extend these studies and ask additional questions must, however, look more closely than we have done at the sort of internal differentiation that is so visible in the American case between blacks and whites and between expansionists and their opponents; or in the Swedish case among those who were bitterly at odds, not about launching canoes in some Mississippi, but about launching submarines in the Baltic.

As for means of propagation, certainly a scan of these essays would reveal a heavy reliance on the printed word—the book or article, the treatise, the poem—plus the kind of public proclamation that may originally have been oral. There is sufficient reference, however, brief or extended, to hymns, spirituals, and sermons to confirm that these are sources deserving further attention. Among resources surely worth mining, but no more than briefly alluded to here (for example in Lehmann's use of his grandfather's diaries), the most obvious are personal papers. Again, we hope the way has been opened for more intense and more targeted studies.

Conclusion

These essays show that a rhetoric of chosenness was still very much in use during the high imperial era; that it appeared in religious, secularized, and imperfectly secularized forms; and that it was not the exclusive property of imperialist nations nor, certainly, of

---

[29]Gabriel, *Democratic Thought*, 287.

elites within any nation. What the essays cannot show, but perhaps can suggest, is that beliefs about chosenness made a difference—that they played a role, along with other forces, in the adventures and misadventures of Western nationalism.

Although much remains to be studied, the evidence so far surely makes it possible to say that religious ideologies of this kind did make a difference in the nineteenth- and early-twentieth century West, if only because public policy was forced to take account of them and because the policymakers often willingly exploited them. The more difficult question is whether it is possible to say more. Can we venture beyond a minimalist recognition of religious ideas and tropes as vehicles for possibly cynical manipulation of a populace?

Not many analysts of these historical issues, even in the 1990s, have been prepared to go as far as Donald Akenson does: "Ideas count. And. . . the ideas that count most are religious."[30] Most interpreters, however, and by something more than a slim majority, have been ready to concede that religious ideas and motives have exerted genuine influence, in almost all times and places, upon the formation and maintenance of communities. By the middle years of the decade, language such as Francis Fukuyama's did not seem strange, "Communities sharing 'languages of good and evil' are. . . likely to be held together by a stronger glue than those based merely on shared self-interest."[31]

I have used the phrase "*almost* all times and places" because so many recent interpreters, including relatively conservative ones, who have stressed the importance of religion to nationalism have persisted in making an exception for nineteenth-century Europe. There, most of them have continued to argue, nationalism did take the place of religion, just as (or approximately as) Hans Kohn's generation had thought.

This nineteenth-century exception, however, was being honored in more qualified tones than before.[32] Why the new equivocation? It

---

[30]Akenson, *God's Peoples*, 353.

[31]Francis Fukuyama, *The End of History and the Last Man* (New York: Free Press, 1992) 325.

[32]See Anderson, *Imagined Communities*, 11–12; Fukuyama, *End of History*, 270–71 esp. n. 11; William Pfaff, *The Wrath of Nations: Civilization and the Furies of Nationalism* (New York: Simon & Schuster, 1993) 56–57.

took a Marxist historian to provide a clue. Eric Hobsbawm, in the course of asserting a generic relationship between religion and nationalism, observed in 1990 that this relationship is closer when nationalism has become a "mass force" than when nationalism is a minority ideology.[33]

This perception made perfect sense, but it was not clear that its implications had yet been considered in relation to the conventional wisdom concerning nineteenth-century nationalism. Even though this conventional wisdom had laid enormous stress upon popular sentiment, assertions about the alleged displacement of religion had relied almost exclusively upon references to intellectuals and reformers.[34]

It was entirely possible, in other words, that the traditional paradigm of displacement had been based upon a too-traditional conception of intellectual life in which social history played either a small or a nonexistent role. Perhaps the idea of an utterly secularized nationalism, like the perception of secularization itself, had relied upon a limited historical vision (limited, that is, to elites and their ideologies), and consequently upon a methodology that many or most historians no longer consider adequate.

In the case before us, appeals to popular ideas of chosenness, whether these were offered by literary figures or by politicians, probably cannot be dismissed out of hand as cynical constructions. The evidence suggests, instead, that policymakers in nineteenth-century Europe and America, like their successors in various world societies of today, were dependent for some of their support on religiously derived beliefs that they did not need to construct—beliefs that, for good or ill, were really there.

[33]Eric J. Hobsbawm, *Nations and Nationalism since 1780: Programme, Myth, Reality* (Cambridge: Cambridge University Press, 1990) 67–68.
[34]For Kohn's insistence upon "popular sovereignty" as the defining element in modern nationalism, see his *Idea of Nationalism*, 3–18. For a recent, striking example of the tendency to forget about popular thought when one is discussing religion's alleged "displacement," see Himmelfarb, "Dark and Bloody Crossroads," 57–58.

Part One

·············

C H O S E N   I M P E R I A L I S T S

Carrying the White Man's Burden:
Some British Views of National Vocation in the Imperial Era

A. F. Walls[*]

Rudyard Kipling the Secular Theologian

Said England unto Pharaoh, "I must make a man of you,
That will stand upon his feet and play the game;
That will Maxim his oppressor as a Christian ought to do,"
And she sent old Pharaoh Sergeant Whatsisname.

Said England to the Sergeant, "You can let my people go"
(England used 'em cheap and nasty from the start)

---

[*]Professor A. F. Walls is Director of the Centre for the Study of Christianity in the Non-Western World at the University of Edinburgh.

And they entered 'em in battle on a most astonished foe
But the Sergeant he had hardened Pharaoh's heart.[1]

"**P**haraoh" is the Egypt of Khedive Ismail; "the Sergeant" repre-
sents the British military instructors sent to the Egyptian army
for the Sudan campaign. As the story develops, "Pharaoh," under the
Sergeant's tutelage, produces quite unexpected vigor and resilience;
this "Pharaoh" swarms desert, river, and railway "like Israelites from
bondage":

'Tween the clouds o' dust and fire to the land of his desire,
And his Moses, it was Sergeant Whatsisname![2]

The poem is typical Kipling. The rich fund of biblical allusion is
detached from any conventional framework of Christian doctrine, with
even a touch of cynicism ("that will Maxim his oppressor as a Christian ought to do"). The glory in Empire is tempered by *Schadenfreude*,
the ultimate betrayal of Empire by easygoing metropolitan indiffer-
ence. Empire is Destiny, British destiny; but it is a lonely, burdensome business, with no more tangible rewards than the consciousness
of duty done and manhood proven.

It is natural to begin with Kipling, for no one more clearly articu-
lates the British consciousness of chosenness in the high imperial
period, and no one perhaps has ever spoken more comprehensively to
the British soul. No major writer since Shakespeare has more sharply
reflected the reactions of the ordinary soldier. At the same time,
Kipling's vision of the world, his sense of history, and his interpretation of East and West gave him something of prophetic status; his
wealth of biblical imagery and his capacity to weave it into narrative
or sentiment made him a sort of honorary lay theologian. The fact
that Kipling's intellectual schema was far from classical Christian
theology did not prevent preachers and theologians from drawing on

[1]Rudyard Kipling, "Pharaoh and the Sergeant," in idem, *The Collected
Works of Rudyard Kipling* (28 vols.; New York: AMS Press, 1970) 26. 224–
26.
[2]Ibid.

him, nor did it prevent his reaching quasi-canonical status in Christian hymnody. "Almost since the beginning of his career I have read every word he wrote," said John Watson, the popular preacher who wrote still more popular idylls of Christian Scotland under the name of Ian Maclaren; Watson designated Kipling the "real poet laureate" of England.[3] Hugh Price Hughes, Methodist orator and social activist, so antimilitarist that he would shudder on viewing a military parade from the top of an omnibus[4] and devote five whole sermons to a single foolish outburst from a field marshal,[5] was equally anxious to appropriate Kipling. His daughter assures us that he greeted the appearance in *The Times* of the poem "Recessional" "with rapture," and that he attributed the poem to Kipling's partly Methodist background.[6]

Clearly, therefore, Kipling offered to many reflective contemporaries (as well as to those to whom reflection came less naturally) an interpretation of the British role in the world with which they instinctively identified. This interpretation is famously made explicit in "The White Man's Burden."[7] Although the poem was originally written to encourage the Americans to annex the Philippine Islands, the "burden" was preeminently that of the British white man, going out to bring peace and equity to a new-found empire.

[3]W. Robertson Nicoll, *Ian Maclaren: Life of the Rev. John Watson, D.D.* (London: Hodder & Stoughton, 1908) 324.

[4]Dorothea Price Hughes, *The Life of Hugh Price Hughes* (London: Hodder & Stoughton, 1907) 562.

[5]Hugh Price Hughes, Sermons 5–9, in idem, *The Philanthropy of God Described and Illustrated in a Series of Sermons* (London: Hodder & Stoughton, 1890). Lord Wolseley had complained about "people who object to a barrier between nations upon religious grounds," since "I cannot for one moment believe that the strong instinct which has been given to me, and I dare say to most of you, of love of country, and of intense nationality, can be in any way opposed to the teachings of religion" (quoted in ibid., 79–80).

[6]D. P. Hughes, *The Life of Hugh Price Hughes*, 562. Not surprisingly, Charles Gore was more astringent. "One gets weary of [Kipling's] eternal diablerie," he wrote during a visit to India soon after the appearance of *Lux Mundi*, "and his morality seems as lax as his creed. But he is certainly brilliant" (George Leonard Prestige, *The Life of Charles Gore, Great Englishman* [London: Heinemann, 1935] 112).

[7]Rudyard Kipling, "The White Man's Burden," in idem, *Collected Works*, 26. 221–23.

> Send forth the best ye breed—
> Go bind your sons to exile
> To serve your captives' need.[8]

As the poem portrays it, this will be slow, hard, repetitive, wearying work, but essentially vicarious and altruistic.

> To seek another's profit,
> And work another's gain.

Above all, it will be unpopular. The "captives" ("half-devil and half-child") will be sullen; their idleness and folly will endlessly wreck the work of their benefactors. The reward of service will be

> The blame of those ye better,
> The hate of those ye guard.

The "ye" is deliberately reminiscent of biblical injunction, and the point is soon made explicit: the hosts whom the high-souled administrator is slowly humoring toward the light cry:

> Why brought ye us from bondage,
> Our loved Egyptian night?

The White Man's Burden laid upon British shoulders—whether as viceroys of India[9] or as sergeant-instructors in Egypt—involved playing Moses to a stiff-necked people, leading them into a land of promise and getting no thanks for it. The people will be watching Moses narrowly:

---

[8]This quotation and those that follow in sequence are found in ibid.

[9]See Rudyard Kipling, "One Viceroy Resigns," in idem, *Collected Works,* 25. 137–43. An imaginary conversation between Dufferin and Lansdowne occurs: "And all the while commend you to Fate's hand (Here at the top one loses sight o' God)" (p. 140). A later parenthesis states, "God help you, if there be a God (There must be one to startle Gladstone's soul)" (p. 141).

The silent, sullen peoples
Shall weigh your Gods and you.

Kipling's cosmology would allow him neither the use of the singular of the divine name here nor the use of lower case for "Gods." Many of his readers concurred. Aware of Darwin and of the newly opened mysteries of Eastern thought, they could no longer make *ex animo* the old Christian doctrinal affirmations. Their moral code, however, was still shaped by their Christian inheritance. They could recognize the voice of duty and the transcendent sanctions attached to eternal values. They could recognize destiny, and they expected this destiny to involve moral choice. If heaven and hell no longer conditioned their responses, they still expected the path of duty, as of old, to be strenuous and the rewards of this path to be intangible. The gate leading to life was still a strait one, as it was for the earnest evangelical Christian.

Even orthodox Christians, however, could heartily identify with Kipling's "Recessional," written for the Queen's Diamond Jubilee in 1897. Each verse is addressed to the Lord God of Hosts, the Judge of the Nations, who is also "God of our fathers, known of old" and the lord of the far-flung British battle line. God takes ultimate responsibility for the British Empire from Canada to the tropics.

Beneath whose awful Hand we hold
Dominion over palm and pine.

Lo, all our pomp of yesterday
Is one with Nineveh and Tyre!

"Recessional" recognizes the transitory nature of imperial glory. It also accepts as the national requirement the Psalmist's sacrifice of the humble and contrite heart.[10] It recognizes the danger of becoming drunk with power and the futility of trust in armaments ("reeking tube and iron shard").

[10]Ps 51:17.

Conscientious preachers also insisted on all these things. No wonder Hugh Price Hughes was enraptured; he too called for national humility, national responsibility, and a sense of God's sovereignty and judgment. If all these pieties left the Empire intact, so, generally speaking, did the preachers. Better behavior was to be demanded and expected of Britain than of other imperial nations:

> If, drunk with sight of power, we loose
> Wild tongues that have not thee in awe
> Such boasting as the Gentiles use
> Or lesser breeds without the Law.

It took some knowledge of biblical exegesis to pick up the full implications of "Gentiles," "lesser breeds," and "without the Law" (again the capitalization is important), and it was not necessary to say aloud that these terms really referred to the Germans. All this, however, hammers home the point underlying the whole poem: Britain is God's people, heir to the privileges and the responsibilities of special relationship.

In "The Reformers," the imperial vocation requires a dedicated life that breaks from the easy luxury to which it has been bred. This is the rhetoric of many appeals for missionary recruits and was perhaps influenced by them. Kipling then takes the biblical language where Christian orthodoxy would fear to tread. The imperial devotee becomes a Christ figure and even a propitiatory, atoning sacrifice for his sleek, indolent nation.

> Virtue shall go out of him:
> Example profiting his peers.[11]
>
> Who is his Nation's sacrifice
> To turn the judgment from his race.[12]

In other words, he is the Suffering Servant.[13]

---

[11]The reference is to Mark 5:30 (*KJV*) and its parallels; Jesus is touched by a woman seeking healing and feels that "virtue" has gone out of him.

[12]Rudyard Kipling, "The Reformers," in *Collected Works*, 26. 254–55.

[13]The last verse refers to victory being demonstrated in the children and

The experiences of the Anglo-Boer War gave the idea of imperial destiny a jolt and gave the preachers a text as well. Kipling's answer was that "it was our fault, and our very great fault and *not* the judgment of Heaven."[14] Not only the military, but politicians, clergy, and clerisy ("Council and Creed and College"), stifled as they were by "obese, unchallenged old things," must take this "imperial lesson" to heart.[15]

There were other poets of imperialism. Sir Henry Newbolt in particular produced some influential pieces,[16] as did a whole clutch of novelists of imperialism. It was Kipling, however, who most moved the imagination. Part of the appeal lay in his discreet, but nonetheless pervasive, view of the special chosenness of Britain, the vision of a beneficent, worldwide British Empire of free, consenting partners revealed as part of the emerging purpose of history.

The ambiguity in Kipling's own religious position was helpful here. His discourse was so thoroughly biblical that a knowledge of the English Bible was needed for its elucidation; earnest Christians could identify with so much of it that many were prepared to take their chance with the odd worrying application or pagan reference. It was not necessary, however, to make a Christian affirmation in order to appropriate his biblical allusions; and post-Christian readers influenced by the new comparative religion could identify with his views on God made in man's image, his dislike for judgmental exponents of "the narrow way," his assertion of the need to recognize that "the wildest dreams of Kew are the facts of Khatmandhu,"[17] and his conviction

---

grandchildren. Kipling probably has Isaiah 53 in mind, especially verse 10, where the servant is made a sin offering but afterwards "sees his seed."

[14]Rudyard Kipling, "The Lesson (1899–1902)," in idem, *Collected Works,* 26. 248–49.

[15]Ibid.

[16]One line of "Vitaï Lampada," which links crises on the public school cricket ground and the desert battlefield, long furnished one of the few poetic quotations that "everybody" knew: "Play up! play up! and play the game!" See Henry Newbolt, *Poems: New and Old* (London: John Murray, 1915) 78–79.

[17]See Rudyard Kipling, "Buddha at Kamakura" in idem, *Collected Works,* 26. 219–20.

that "there are nine and sixty ways of constructing tribal lays / And every single one of them is right!"[18]

He was thus accessible to all but the most punctilious Christians (and even they could, if necessary, treat him as reflecting an "Old Testament" position). He was also ideally suited to a rising post-Christian generation that retained the memory and influence of its biblical education.

There was no real theology—nor much ideology—attached to Kipling's idea of chosenness. It involved the application to Britain of a series of images of old Israel, but they were still manifestly poetic images, metaphors at most, into which a wide range of theology or ideology could be imported.

> Fair is our lot—goodly is our heritage!
> (Humble ye, my people, and be fearful in your mirth!)
> For the Lord and God Most High
> He hath made the deep as dry
> He hath made for us a pathway to the ends of all the earth![19]

Imperial Religion

Watts and Wesley—not to mention the apostle Paul—had already used the Exodus motif as a figure of Christ's redemption. Kipling used the same figure to describe the preordination of the Empire on which the sun never set; from the point of view of classical theology, this represented a secularization, even a degradation. Classical theology, however, was less fashionable in the era of high imperialism than in earlier generations, and some of the pious may have found Kipling's exhortations to humility, self-sacrifice, and moral exertion an acceptable substitute. From the point of view of many earnest post-Christians for whom the old theology held no meaning, such words offered a resacralization of the biblical narrative and gave a transcendent dimension to a code of duty, patriotism, and service to

---

[18]Rudyard Kipling, "In the Neolithic Age," in idem, *Collected Works*, 26. 86–87.

[19]Rudyard Kipling, "A Song of the English," in idem, *Collected Works*, 26. 3–13.

the nation. From muscular Christianity to muscular devotion to duty was not such a great leap.

Elsewhere I have offered a comment on John Hargreaves's contention that "imperialist religion" in the late nineteenth century produced a consensus among exponents of secular rationalism, evangelical piety, and broad Christian humanism, and that outstanding examples of each are to be found among the great proconsuls.[20] I suggested that an examination of the sort of sermons delivered to Britain missionary bodies in the 1880–1920 period tends to support Hargreaves's observation; many offer some clues to account for this new consensus. The sermons took the Empire and its essential beneficence for granted; by contrast with earlier evangelicalism, they represented a spiritualizing of the gospel and its detachment from social context. The secular sphere was thus the concern of someone else, namely, the colonial government. Preoccupied with the responsibility of the West, they were relatively unaware of the existence of indigenous churches in Africa and Asia. In contrast to the midcentury, they saw missions as embattled at home, surrounded by hostile forces of the spirit of the age.

It seems reasonable in considering British concepts of chosenness in this period to look again at preachers who dealt with missionary themes. From the 1880s onward, ideas of British chosenness inevitably have to do with Empire. Before that time they had more to do with insularity—with seagirt security, with freedom from invasion and warfare, and with the defense of true religion and the Protestant faith. There is, as we shall see, certainly some continuity with these ideas in the later nineteenth century, but the principal perceptions of Great Britain's distinctiveness centered on its world role. Even the function of the sea changed;[21] it was no longer a bulwark for defense, but a

[20]Andrew F. Walls, "'Such boasting as the Gentiles use. . .' Some Thoughts on Imperialist Religion," in Roy C. Bridges, ed., *An African Miscellany for John Hargreaves* (Aberdeen: Aberdeen University African Studies Group, 1983) 109–16.

[21]Sir John Seeley did most to supply a historical theory for British imperialism. He argued (*The Expansion of England* [London: Macmillan, 1883]) that Britain was, unlike Norway, not a *naturally* maritime country; England had become a maritime country only in the time of Elizabeth.

path to worlds beyond. As John Watson put it to a Wesleyan audience,

> Are any man's eyes so blind that he cannot see the mission of England? Have we not been surrounded by the seas and our national character formed for purposes that we can recognize? What nation has ever planted so many colonies, explored so many unknown lands, made such practical contributions to civilization, set such an illustrious example of liberty?[22]

Or, as Kipling phrased it, God has made the sea a path for Britain to the ends of the earth.[23] The Empire was believed to be the result of essentially peaceful expansion that brought peace in its train. Hugh Price Hughes decried militaristic and bombastic utterances from politicians and press, but he did so on basically imperialist grounds. The colonial Empire, he urged, had been built up not by military operations, but in spite of them. British traders, British explorers, and British missionaries were responsible for the peaceable establishment of Empire. All the military had done was to lose America.[24] Even when force was used, it was for peaceful ends, as it had been in Egypt (Kipling's sergeant-instructors, for example). How liberating it was for these timid Egyptian fellows to learn to charge and fight on horseback against dervishes![25]

Naturally, therefore, Britain and the colonies were clasped together in a close family community that foreigners could not understand. For Watson,

> A covenant has been made between England and her Colonies, and the covenant has been sealed with blood, and today England and the colonies are one. They reviled us, those nations of Europe. . . but it does not matter what the outside world says if your own family is true.[26]

[22]Nicoll, *Life of the Rev. John Watson*, 266–67.
[23]Kipling, "Song of the English," 26. 3.
[24]H. P. Hughes, *The Philanthropy of God*, 74–75, 96.
[25]D. P. Hughes, *The Life of Hugh Price Hughes*, 555.
[26]Nicoll, *Life of the Rev. John Watson*, 267.

Here is Kipling's family of queens; each daughter is in her English mother's house as well as the mistress in her own.[27]

Hughes and Watson, and the preachers generally, took for granted both that Britain had a God-given civilizing mission to its Empire, and that, generally speaking, the effect of the Empire had been a beneficently civilizing one.[28] In one sense this continued an older tradition of evangelical and missionary apologetic. There were important differences and new emphases, however. Thomas Fowell Buxton, for instance, had thought of Britain's civilizing mission in the 1830s and 1840s in terms of reparation for wrongs done to Africa by Britain; he had no idea of effecting it by British overseas acquisition and rule.[29] By the 1880s an important change in perception had taken place. Buxton had seen "civilization," in Greco-Roman terms, as the answer to "barbarism"; civilization was a self-evidently desirable state that was to be commended to the barbarians, who were nonetheless regarded as responsible beings. A later age, influenced by evolutionary thought, saw these same peoples as languishing at low stages of development ("half-devil and half-child," in Kipling's extreme terms[30]). The term "child races" passed into common currency among those who supported missions.[31] The historic role of Britain thus became transmuted into that of the kind but firm tutor whose guidance was essential for the eventual maturity of the "children" committed to its care.

[27]Rudyard Kipling, "Our Lady of the Snows," in idem, *Collected Works,* 26. 227–28. Canada is the Queen of the North, who sends word to the Queens of the East and the South—partners in a single imperial destiny, united when "the world's war trumpet blows" (p. 228).

[28]See Watson (Nicoll, *Life of the Rev. John Watson,* 266): "England, if one can make anything of history, has been God's instrument in spreading civilization and administering justice among savage or oppressed peoples."

[29]See Andrew F. Walls, "The Legacy of Thomas Fowell Buxton," *International Bulletin of Missionary Research* 15 (1991) 74–78.

[30]Kipling, "White Man's Burden," 26. 221.

[31]See, for example, Henry Hutchison Montgomery, ed., *Mankind and the Church, Being an Attempt to Estimate the Contribution of Great Races to Fulness of the Church of God* (London: Longmans, Green, 1907); J. N. Ogilvie, *Our Empire's Debt to Missions* (London: Hodder & Stoughton, 1923) chap. 3.

When this role was linked to a missionary vocation, Kipling's themes were introduced into territory where Kipling himself could not go. Evangelical Christians might agree that civilization was a desirable and regular accompaniment of Christianity, but they did not believe that the two were the same thing. They did believe, however, that Britain's past history and present situation demonstrated its unique role in the worldwide proclamation of the gospel. "We are elect by all signs and proofs to be the great missionary nation," announced the Baptist preacher J. G. Greenhough to the 1896 meeting of the Baptist Missionary Society.[32]

Greenhough's rhetoric, while claiming to abjure the "boastful jingoism of the music hall" in favor of "the humbler patriotism of the sanctuary," often came close to the language of the former. He asked, however, "Have we got all this glory by our own might and power, or is it because He has 'beset us behind and before' and laid His hand upon us?"[33] Greenhough would have recognized, as many other preachers did, the same sentiment expressed in Kipling's "Recessional," which appeared a year later. Like Kipling, he did not forget "the Gentiles" who, like old Babylon, boast in themselves. (He also made it quite clear that he saw no signs of authentic Christian vitality outside the areas where the English language was used.[34]) The analogy with Israel went further:

> Was [British power and prosperity] not especially with this intent—that we should be more than all others God's messengers of light and truth to the nations that sit in darkness? In all this God's voice has been calling us. God's consecrating hands have been laid on our heads. Thus saith the Lord: "In the shadow of My hand have I hid thee, and made thee a polished shaft, and in the day of salvation have I helped thee, that thou mayest say to the prisoners: 'Go forth.'"[35]

[32]J. G. Greenough, in *Missionary Sermons. A Selection from the Discourses Delivered on Behalf of the Baptist Missionary Society on Various Occasions* (London: Carey, 1924) 265.
[33]Ibid., 265.
[34]Ibid., 209.
[35]Ibid., 265.

The Uncertain Boundaries of Chosenness

Britain's election as the missionary nation was not evident to all who accepted the necessity of taking up the White Man's Burden. This fact was to cause endless disappointment within the British missionary movement, and it was the source of the embattled note among the preachers as they encountered the post-Christian nature of much British intellectual life. They realized that the British Empire had become the world's largest Islamic power and far more efficient at excluding missionaries than was the Turkish sultan. The potency of the imperial idea of chosenness, which distinguished it from earlier ideas of national election or responsibility, lay in its compatibility with a variety of theologies and ideologies.

For the same reason, there seems to be no agreed body of biblical exegesis behind Christian appropriations of the chosenness motif. The contemporaneous stress on the necessity for historical exegesis as well as the reaction against the older typological methods would have rendered such a thing unlikely in any case. British Israelism, which used exegetical methods to prove that Britain was the legitimate heir of the prophetic promises to Israel and provided etymologies to match, never touched more than a narrow fringe of those who held some belief in national chosenness.[36] At the Baptist Missionary Society meeting of 1897, a Wesleyan minister, W. L. Watkinson, came as close to such a formulation as a mainstream preacher could come. Referring explicitly to the situation in Isa 19:23–25, he sustained a parallel between this text and the position of Britain:

> England stands much in the same position that Israel did. It is the spiritual centre of the world. As Palestine came between Egypt and Assyria, so this island comes in a wonderful manner between the old world and the new. God gave spiritual gifts in a remarkable degree to Israel; the revelation of Himself, the knowledge of His law, the sense of eternity. . . . God in His

---

[36]One highly popular writer at the end of the period, the versifier Patience Strong, held British Israelite views; probably only a small minority of those who responded to her homely mass-circulation doggerel, however, realized the nature of these notions.

government has also given to us special powers for the diffusion
of the Gospel.[37]

These special powers included the English language and literature, the
spirit of adventure, the gift of colonization, and "a capacity of universality."[38] The preachers invariably insisted that these privileges brought
responsibility and should call forth humble gratitude and unstinting
service.

At certain points, nonetheless, the missionary tradition sat uneasily
with the new version of British national chosenness. Most obviously
and basically, by the later part of the nineteenth century North America
was manifestly becoming quite as important as Britain in missionary
effort. Even Greenhough, sure of Britain's election as the great missionary nation, implicitly set America—alone among foreign nations—
with Britain among the righteous. ("In nearly all Protestant lands save
where our language is spoken religion is feeble or apathetic."[39]) George
C. Lorimer, preaching to the Baptist Missionary Society in 1898, announced,

> The united energies, faith and wealth of Great Britain and the
> United States, if intelligently directed, should be able in a few
> years to conquer heathen darkness. . . . As the flags of the two
> living nations blend together, let us bathe them in the splendour
> of the Cross of Christ; and as they move together about the
> globe let us see to it that between them, and over them gleams
> the Cross; and then shall follow the sublime resurrection of the
> nations and then the angels' song of goodwill to men.[40]

A decade earlier, James Johnston, the secretary of the Centenary
Missionary Conference, had noted the extent to which the work of
evangelization devolved on the Saxon race. He also announced the
decline of the Latin race, the great colonizers of ancient times, under

---

[37]W. L. Watkinson, in *Missionary Sermons*, 209.
[38]Ibid., 209–10.
[39]Greenhough, in *Missionary Sermons*, 264.
[40]George C. Lorimer, in *Missionary Sermons*, 182.

Roman Catholic domination: "It is to the race which is sending the blessings of Christianity to the heathen to which God is giving success as the colonisers and conquerors of the world."[41] The latter sentiment, however, does not quite agree with the rest of this section of the report, which highlights the importance of the missions of other northern countries, not all of which had the same colonial success. It was hard to talk of vocation to mission without recognizing that other nations shared with Britain in this vocation.

When the focus was turned from the activity of sending missionaries to the life of the mission church, another set of factors came into play. Roland Allen, with his stress on the transitoriness of the missionary function and the primacy of the indigenous church, is a minority voice within the period, but a significant one.[42] The liberal Bernard Lucas saw the British Empire as only a dim, broken pointer toward a far grander empire of Christ in which the hidden glory of India would be revealed.[43] Other missionary thinkers who stressed the catholicity of the Church emphasized that each "race" had its own contribution to the fullness of the body; none was complete in itself. This view was another brake on the idea of "chosenness," since in Christ all races were "chosen." In *Mankind and the Church*, a symposium by high church Anglicans, the secretary of the Society for the Propagation of the Gospel drew a portrait of the English character showing the limitations that could be corrected only by Asia (and, no doubt, in due time, by Africa).[44]

Singing New Songs

So much for the preachers. Preaching, however, is not the only source of religious impressions, and it seems appropriate to give some

---

[41]James Johnston, ed., *Report of the Centenary Conference on the Protestant Missions of the World Held in Exeter Hall, June 9–19, London, 1888* (2 vols.; London: Nisbet, 1889) 1. xvi.

[42]See Roland Allen, *Missionary Methods, St. Paul's or Ours?* (London: Scott, 1912).

[43]Bernard Lucas, *The Empire of Christ: Being a Study of the Missionary Enterprise in the Light of Modern Religious Thought* (London: Macmillan, 1907).

[44]Montgomery, *Mankind and the Church*, xxxiv–xxxv.

consideration to a particularly important source for the British religious consciousness: the hymn book.

Only during the high imperial period did a special section devoted to the nation first appear in British hymn books. The 1864 edition of *Hymns Ancient and Modern*,[45] which marked the final acknowledgment by official Anglicanism that the hymn had become an acceptable and regular part of the service, contained no such section; neither did the supplement to Wesley's hymns that was authorized by the Wesleyan Conference of 1876.[46] One hymn in the latter collection was a prayer for the monarch, but this was an old Wesley hymn, clearly written with George III in mind. The Free Church of Scotland hymn book, commissioned in 1878, did not have topical sections at all, but included an index of subjects that identified two hymns as suitable for "National Fast and Thanksgiving."[47] In *Psalms and Hymns*, published for Baptist churches in 1883, the last hymn in the book was headed "Prayer for Our Country."[48] This hymn was W. R. Hickson's christianized version of the national anthem "God Bless Our Native Land." The first hymn book to devote a section explicitly to national hymns may have been the Bible Christian hymn book of 1889.[49] It was the final section, except for benedictions and doxologies, and it contained no fewer than seventeen hymns, beginning with the national anthem. None of the hymn books mentioned above included this feature. Among the other hymns were several that rejoiced in Britain's chosenness, including a spectacular rouser by Thomas Hornblower Gill, which began "Lift thy song among the nations /

[45]*Hymns Ancient and Modern* (ed. Henry Hutchison; London: Clowes & Sons, 1864).

[46]*A Collection of Hymns for the People called Methodists by the Rev. John Wesley. . . with a new supplement* (London: Methodist Book Room, 1876).

[47]*The Free Church Hymn Book* (Edinburgh: Free Church of Scotland, n.d. [1882]). Of the two hymns in question, no. 93 would have been suitable for a national fast, no. 325 equally suitable for a national thanksgiving or a church anniversary.

[48]*Psalms and Hymns with Supplement for Public, Social and Private Worship; prepared for the use of the Baptist Denomination* (London: Haddon for the Trustees, 1883).

[49]*Bible Christian Hymns* (London: Bible Christian Book Room, 1889).

England of the Lord beloved!" and recounted the past discomfitures of invaders, tyrants, and popery. The hymn went on to describe the sword of the Lord gleaming in the hands of British heroes, freedom's fire remaining "where it first did burn and shine." Eventually the congregation recognizes that the Lord still provides for England "boundless realms and tasks divine."[50]

The last hymn in the section was by Isaac Watts. It was one of those updated paraphrases of the psalms in which he endeavored to make David "speak the common sense of a Christian."[51] Late Victorian Bible Christians, humble in station for the most part, invested the late-period Puritan psalm "Shine, Mighty God, on Britain Shine" with a significance Watts could not have contemplated:

> Sing to the Lord, ye distant lands
> Sing loud, with solemn voice,
> While British tongues exalt his praise
> And British hearts rejoice.[52]

The early twentieth century saw a multiplication of new books and supplements, including new books for the Wesleyan, English Presbyterian, and Baptist churches; a *Church Hymnary* (1905) for the main Presbyterian churches in and beyond Scotland, the high Anglican *English Hymnal* (1906), and the quirky Anglican *Songs of Praise* (1925). All of these had sections of national hymns. All included the national anthem; all except one included Kipling's "Recessional." Hickson's verses appeared in most, and some had Kipling's lines for children, "Land of our birth we pledge to thee." The cry of Ebenezer Elliott, the Corn Law rhymer, "When wilt thou save the people?" was usually present (interestingly it was the Wesleyans, not the Anglicans, who modified his language in the interests of social order). Also a

[50]Ibid., no. 994 (1924 ed.).

[51]See the preface to Isaac Watts, *The Psalms of David Imitated in New Testament Language together with Hymns and Spiritual Songs* (London: n.p., 1719); and the discussion in Bernard L. Manning, *The Hymns of Wesley and Watts* (London, Epworth, 1942) chap. 4.

[52]*Bible Christian Hymns*, no. 996 (1924 ed.).

common entry, although not always placed in this section, was Henry Scott Holland's prayer for national purgation, "Judge Eternal Throned in Splendour," which included the lines, "Cleanse the body of this empire / Through the glory of the Lord."[53]

In including hymns reflecting the sense of national chosenness, the Presbyterian *Church Hymnary* was the most restrained; it did not even include Kipling's "Recessional" in its first edition. The *English Hymnal* included a hymn by an Eton schoolmaster, A. C. Ainger, with the significant opening, "God of our fathers," which gave thanks "for eastern realms, for western coasts / For islands washed by every sea" and clearly expected "our fame to wax through coming days."[54]

The Wesleyans included a hymn based on one originally composed for the official celebrations of the Queen's Golden Jubilee in 1887. It reflected a vision of the British Empire as God's gift to the world:

> Our bounds of empire thou hast set in many a distant isle
> And in the shadow of our throne the desert places smile
> For in our laws and in our faith it's thine own light they see
> The truth that brings to captive souls the wider liberty.[55]

The Baptists were the most rumbustiously patriotic of all, with one of their own members, Nathaniel Barnaby, designer of battleships for the Royal Navy and Sunday School superintendent, contributing such strong rhymes as

> God bless our motherland! Cradled in ocean
> Nursed into greatness by storm and by sea

[53]Henry Scott Holland, "Judge Eternal Throned in Splendour."

[54]*The English Hymnal* (London: Oxford University Press, n.d. [1906]) no. 559.

[55]*The Methodist Hymn-Book* (London: Wesleyan Conference Office, n.d. [1904]) no. 995. The author was a Wesleyan minister, Dr. Henry Burton (see John Telford, *The Methodist Hymnbook Illustrated* [2d ed.; London: Culley, 1909] 165). This hymn was a by-product of Queen Victoria's Golden Jubilee (1887) and was a response to a request by the composer, Sir John Stainer, for "a patriotic hymn" to a tune of his own (Telford, *Methodist Hymnbook Illustrated*, 489).

Out on the stormy winds, and in war's commotion
She had no helper, Jehovah, but Thee![56]

All of these pale, however, before the uninhibited flag waving of *Hoyle's Hymns*, popular in the Band of Hope Union and other temperance societies. Band of Hope meetings were, of course, not normal services, but their predominantly working class companies seem to have been happy to join in such rhapsodies as "Oh proudly stand, my Fatherland, the envy of the world!"[57]

Some of these effusions were pleas on patriotic grounds for the removal of the curse of drink, but there is little sign in this cheerful little collection of national humility, whether in Henry Scott Holland's sense or Kipling's. It is the Band of Hope Union, above all, that celebrates Empire without tears.

Two important points are suggested by this sampling of hymn books as a whole. First, the most uninhibited assertions of British chosenness were to be found where lay and working class influence was strongest. Second, the specifically "missionary" sections of all the books are remarkably free from imperial and national allusions. Some deep-rooted instinct kept the idea of God-given Empire in a different sphere from the kingdom of God.

Conclusion

National election was not a new theme among English writers. John Milton (who was prepared to believe that Pythagoras and the Magi learned their lore from the Druids of Britain) found the evidence for national chosenness in Wycliffe's ministry: "Why else was this nation chosen before any other, that out of her, as out of Sion, should be proclaimed and sounded forth the first tiding and trumpet

---

[56]The hymn survives in the *Baptist Church Hymnal Revised* (London: Psalms and Hymns Trust, 1933) no. 698. On Sir Nathaniel Barnaby (1829–1915), see *Dictionary of National Biography* (22 vols.; New York: Macmillan and London: Smith, Elder & Co., 1908).

[57]*Hoyle's Hymns and Songs for Temperance Societies and Bands of Hope. 275 Gems of Song* (London: Partridge and National Temperance Publications Depot, n.d.).

of reformation to all Europe?"[58] Although episcopal perverseness had in this case inhibited England's primacy and made necessary the ministrations of the foreigners John Hus and Martin Luther, the signs were that "God is decreeing to begin some new and great period in his church," and "what does he then but reveal himself to his servants, and as his manner is, first to Englishmen?"[59]

Conscious participation in a pioneering political and religious revolution ("even to the reforming of reformation itself"[60]) and the sight of a nationwide new dawn in learning, science, and education[61] provoked such thoughts in anyone with a strong sense of providence. The position of imperial Britain in the late nineteenth century was equally suggestive of reflections on national history. The happy gift for peaceable progress struck many observers, and, as we have seen, imperial expansion itself could be viewed as a manifestation of peaceful progress. Providentialist historiography was no longer in vogue; but if historical meditations were now secular in tone, they were by no means materialist. For John Richard Green, "in England, more than elsewhere, constitutional progress has been the result of social development," and he believed the part played by war in English history was smaller than in any of the European nations.[62]

Such views did not demand providentialist convictions, but did not forbid them either. Providentialists continued to find their links with the seventeenth-century revolutions. George Smith, former India journalist addressing the Student Volunteer Missionary Union, could call attention to Oliver Cromwell's new statue in Parliament Square and link him both with Livingstone and (as one of the few English statesmen genuinely interested in overseas missions) with Gladstone—people with "the imperial instinct to recognize missions as the purest handmaid of statesmanship and of geographical expansion."[63]

[58]John Milton, "Areopagitica" (1644).
[59]Ibid.
[60]Ibid.
[61]See R. Hooykaas, *Religion and the Rise of Modern Science* (Edinburgh: Scottish Academic Press, 1972) 141–42.
[62]John Richard Green, *A Short History of the English People* (London: Macmillan, 1876) v–vii.
[63]George Smith, *Students and the Missionary Problem. Addresses Delivered at the International Student Missionary Conference* (London: Student Voluntary Mission Union, 1900) 95. Gladstone and Cromwell are also brought

A new form of the idea of British chosenness based on the Empire appeared in the period after 1880. It drew on biblical motifs, but part of its strength lay in the way in which it could receive assent both from committed Christians and from those who were in the process of parting with Christianity and had already abandoned its traditional forms and classical doctrines. For this very reason it was somewhat imprecisely formulated; it represented exactly that combination of sentiment and ethical rigor, "morality tinged with emotion," that Matthew Arnold—John the Baptist to the age—saw as the heart of religion. It needed a climate of theological imprecision in which to develop among Christians. The new idea of chosenness would have had a harder task amid the old certainties and the old formulations about election, judgment, and covenant.

When Charles Haddon Spurgeon, preaching to the Baptist Missionary Society in 1858, said that "the Holy Spirit must be poured on England, and then shall it go to the utmost borders of the habitable earth,"[64] his audience knew well that he meant the *churches* in England, and specifically the Baptist churches. Forty years later, however, the words had a different ring, as Greenhough's 1896 sermon to the same constituency shows. In 1858, moreover, a year after the Indian Mutiny, Spurgeon had cheerfully looked forward to the day when Lord Nelson's statue would be hauled from its column to make way for one of George Whitefield and when John Wesley would replace Sir Charles Napier, conqueror in India, in Trafalgar Square: "We shall say about these men, 'They were very respectable men in the days of our forefathers, who did not know better than to kill one another, but we do not care for them now!'"[65] Had they been delivered in the 1890s, such words would have seemed almost profane.

The Scottish dimension is also worth considering. The erosion of the old discourse and the old certainties, along with the arrival of a new imperial consciousness, tended to reduce the traditional difference between English and Scottish perceptions. It is hard to identify any specifically Scottish dimension of chosenness in relation to Em-

---

together as ideal figures by John Clifford in *Typical Christian Leaders* (London: Marshall, 1898) 7.

[64]Charles Haddon Spurgeon, in *Missionary Sermons*, 17.

[65]Ibid., 11.

pire during the period in question. This is especially interesting in view of the importance of the covenant idea in Scottish history. Historically, Scotland was a nation bound by covenant and at times torn apart over covenants. No theological theme was more identifiably Scottish than that of the Crown Rights of the Redeemer as applied to the nation. It underlay the idea of the "godly commonwealth" envisaged by Thomas Chalmers and a broad band of Scottish churchmen in the first half of the century. We hear little of these matters, however, in relation to the imperial age. Covenant rhetoric remained, but it was rhetoric rather than theology and was often transferred to the political sphere.

In 1911, D. S. Cairns, the Scottish theologian most clearly identified with the student movement, addressed Scottish students in a book entitled *The Vocation of Scotland in View of Her Religious Heritage.* He identified the determining elements in this heritage as the kingdom of God ("the central stream of Scottish religious life is theocratic"), the importance of the Church (as distinct from "freelances" of the Spirit), and the acceptance of a strong theology.[66] These traditional Scottish emphases were not exactly hospitable to the new version of imperial chosenness, and it is noteworthy that they were not applied to it. Watson was not the only Scot of the period content to call Britain "England," as the Scots, too, clad themselves in the robes of Empire.[67]

---

[66]D. S. Cairns, *The Vocation of Scotland in View of Her Religious Heritage* (London: Student Christian Movement, 1911).

[67]The stress here has been on the omissions from contemporary theological discourse. How far contemporary biblical studies actually assisted the notion of chosenness would need further study. It is interesting to note the influence of Sir William Ramsay's stress on the essentially imperial outlook of Paul and how this affected early gentile Christianity. See especially William M. Ramsay, *St. Paul the Traveller and Roman Citizen* (London: Hodder & Stoughton, 1895). Lucas eagerly seized on this aspect of Paul in an appendix to *The Empire of Christ*, 149–51.

Response

*W. R. Ward**

A ndrew Walls's discussion of British messianism has, despite its competence and grace, left one issue unaddressed. If the context of the discussion is extended somewhat in time and space, it becomes apparent that some nations—including, among those treated in this volume, Sweden, Switzerland, and England—did not develop full-blooded messianic characteristics. The reasons for this deserve investigation.

A peculiarly pure form of political messianism is to be found in old Russia. Moscow was not merely the Third Rome; the czar was a sacred ruler, imagined as Christlike and merciful and as casting a golden glow over the soil of Russia. In this sacred vocation, the people, Holy Russia, participated with such effect that when czarist rule became unbearable, the people themselves could assume the messianic role, establishing their credentials by their capacity to suffer. Fyodor Dostoyevsky described them as "the only god-bearing people on earth, destined to regenerate and save the world."[1] When the communists claimed to have achieved all this on a secular basis, they still presented the story as the triumph of a saving people over a corrupt regime. By this time, the vocation of the sacred monarch had divided into rival messianisms, triumphalist and suffering, and the story is confused by the delusions sustained on both sides. Peasants convinced themselves that the czar really suffered, bearing the burdens of state amid the crooked intrigues of the court. The survival of this frame of mind was revealed in 1991 as televised pictures of a procession to reopen a Moscow cathedral showed not only Romanov emblems being carried but also men in the uniforms of the old imperial army. On the

*W. R. Ward is Professor of Modern History Emeritus at the University of Durham.
[1]Fyodor Dostoyevsky, *The Possessed* (2 vols.; London: Everyman Library, 1931) 1. 227.

other side, it was necessary for the czars, like all political messiahs, to claim that their mission was one of universal benefit. Even the spokesmen of suffering messianism could be appallingly triumphalist: Dostoyevsky, after drawing comfort from the defeats of Russia in the Crimean War (which at least saved an over-mighty Russia from being confronted by a Grand Alliance) wrote in his diary that

> very soon—perhaps in the immediate future—Russia will prove stronger than any nation in Europe. . . . Yes, the Golden Horn and Constantinople, they will be ours. . . . This would not be. . . political usurpation and violence. . . . No, this would be a new exaltation of Christ's Cross.[2]

Of course, as was to be shown often enough in the West, it was perfectly possible for the sacred people to absorb the sacred mission of the sacred king.

It is true that at the end of our period, the Swiss religious socialists and Karl Barth believed that the messianic role of the church had been assumed by the organized socialist working class; but a Barth who claimed to adhere to the two-and-a-half International was hardly giving a clarion call to the latter-day glory. Of course, Switzerland lacked all the basic components of a messianic mission as we have observed them in Russia. There had never been a sacred king; indeed, Swiss independence had been wrested from the Holy Roman Emperor. Nor could there be a sacred people or a sacred land where citizens were so profoundly divided by language and religion and where they were abandoning the land—sacred or otherwise—in huge numbers in the hope of obtaining larger farmsteads in the southwest of the empire or in the American colonies. What Switzerland needed was a civic religion, and what it needed most of all in the twentieth century was to keep out the foreign messianisms that threatened to tear the country apart exactly as foreign confessional conflicts had intruded on its domestic frictions down to the eighteenth century.

---

[2]Fyodor Dostoyevsky, *Diary of a Writer* (New York: Scribner's, 1949) 1. 364–65. On the whole subject, see Josef Bohatec, *Der Imperialismusgedanke und die Lebensphilosophie Dostojweskijs* (Graz/Cologne: Böhlaus, 1951).

What then of England, which Ulrich Gäbler, later in this volume, depicts as the prime early example of national messianism? Here I must admit to an interest. I was raised in the purest school of Little Englandism, and while frequently grieved at the complacency, inefficiency, and amateurism of my fellow English, I have not often found them aggressively nationalistic or suffering from an overdose of messianic elan. When, following Walls, I came to consult my ancestral hymn book, *The Primitive Methodist Hymnal* (1889), I found that its puny section of eleven national hymns contained, besides the national anthem and "God Bless Our Native Land," a couple of missionary hymns and some perfectly proper prayers to be spared the judgment due. No wonder the Primitives could be generous even to Parnell! The Americans Moody and Sankey, who provided the final culture of that whole popular milieu, have virtually nothing of a national character. Their characteristic eschatological note is that of Sankey's collaborator Philip Bliss: "Only a few more years, only a few more cares. . . Only a few more wrongs. . . Only a few more prayers, Only a few more earthly songs, Only a few goodbyes. . . Then an eternal glorious day. Then an eternal song." This might have made an anthem for a suffering messianism, but it is a testimony to the real feebleness of English messianism that there has never been an English suffering messianism, Protestant or socialist.

At an earlier stage, of course, there were many Englishmen who thought that God was English, but the foundations of English messianism were steadily undermined. One king by divine right lost his head in the Civil War, and the reigning head of the dynasty ran away in 1689. Meanwhile those who saw church membership primarily in terms of election had been beaten by the royalist violence into a minority so small as to be unable to set a political fashion. The succession to the Stuarts was acquired first by a Dutch Reformed ruler and then by a line of Hanoverian Lutheran monarchs so unpopular with the pacesetters among the Anglican clergy as to turn many of the latter into disgruntled proto-revolutionaries, entirely unwilling to sacralize the state. In any case the Union with Scotland required the monarch to be a Presbyterian north of the border; it also plunged the Church of Scotland into an agonized concern that its mission to smash episcopalianism and popery in Scotland was being undermined

by subtle forces of assimilation working through patronage and manipulated from the South. The Kirk did at least succeed in its own
mission of assimilation, winning the Highlands for Lowland religion
and the English Bible. At the same time, the Church of England
failed in its mission of assimilation both in Wales and in the American colonies, and never got properly started in Ireland. After these
failures of the English establishment, it is not altogether surprising
that England suffered more religious fragmentation than any other
country; the Religious Census of 1851 made it clear that a majority
of the minority who were in church on the census day were not
Anglicans.

Anglican hymn books might contain verses commencing, "Bulwark
of a mighty nation, see the Church of England stands," but those
whose main interest in the church had been its sanctifying public
order turned wholesale to other things. As Walls has shown, Kipling
did well to sound like a Christian while actually not being a Christian
at all. A correspondent in the *Times* on 3 June 1991 recalled that

> as a piping treble in a school choir in the early days of World
> War I (in words translated, I think, from the Greek) [i.e., pre-
> sumably classical not Christian Greek] I joined in singing:
>   War comes well to a lad,
>   'Tis well that he should be foremost
>   While in his hair are entwined
>   Blossoms and flowers of spring.

He added, "I forget whether mothers of the choristers applauded."

What made this kind of Kiplingesque nonsense seductive to the
religious dissenters who ought to have been most resistant to it was
that the brief triumph of liberalism in the 1870s and 1880s induced
in many of them a sense of having "arrived" at last. At its worst this
sense was represented by the opening of the dissenters' Mansfield
College at Oxford. Mansfield's stained glass windows bore the pre-
posterous claim that its creators were the principal and rightful heirs
to the entire Christian and cultural heritage; meanwhile its Principal,
A. N. Fairbairn, boasted that the Puritan and evangelical traditions
"reared the men that expanded our Empire, founded our colonies,

created the will, the spirit, the education, the foresight and the faith that, in spite of all the forces of misrule thrown by wild and outcast Europe on her shores, still hold the splendid West in happy and progressive peace. . . . We belong to the larger and greater Church of England."[3]

This was indeed a foretaste of the frame of mind of the present-day spokesmen for the United Reformed Church (a union of English Presbyterians and Congregationalists) who seem incapable of dissenting from anything but their own past. The only things that made it plausible at the time were the large vested interest the evangelical denominations had in colonial missions and the extraordinary success the political establishment had in pushing off the cost of the Indian Empire onto the Indian people. If the cost of the Indian enterprise had been an annual matter of parliamentary conflict in the way that Irish issues actually were, the notion that the British imperial greatness rested on consensus or on Fairbairn's "education, foresight, and faith" could never have obtained the hold it did.

When all has been said, however, English messianism, as Walls has shown, often had a somewhat defensive and embattled sound, and it left almost no mark on the growth of English historical studies, which were overwhelmingly devoted to tracing the superior merits of the English constitution. Indeed, English undergraduates found it almost as difficult to get any instruction in the history of the Empire, as they still do in the history of Scotland. English messianism was indeed so feeble that when the time came to lay down the claims to empire after the Second World War, there was hardly a whimper. Alas! The pretense that the burden of the messianic vocation was altruistically borne for the sake of some greater good reinforced the complacency that is an English vice. This was exemplified in the 1960 book *The End of Empire* by the upper-crust former Marxist,

---

[3]*Mansfield College, Oxford: Its Origin and Opening* (London: n.p., 1890) 133–34, quoted in Clyde Binfield, "'We Claim Our Part in the Great Inheritance': The Message of Four Congregational Buildings," in Keith Robbins, ed., *Protestant Evnagelism: Britain, Ireland, Germany and America c. 1750–c. 1950: Essays in Honour of W. R. Ward* (Oxford/New York: Blackwell, 1990) 212.

John Strachey. He declared that the only "ideal high enough, difficult enough of attainment, and therefore inspiring enough to fire the national imagination" was "to help the underdeveloped world"; this would be building upon one of Britain's "deepest national traditions."[4]

An imperial messianism that could not even complain at the surrender of empire was of course far too weak to generate a suffering messianism in its own image, and it encountered one mainly in Ireland. It is worth noting, however, that, just after our allotted period was over, the British Foreign Office encountered persistent trouble with the old biblical messianic hope in its Zionist form. This elicited from the Foreign Office a persistent anti-Semitism that is still with us. The moves that led ultimately to the establishment of the state of Israel showed that there remained people in the world who believed that God had promised that land to them. Neither imperial messianism nor the assumption unquestioned in the churches for so long that the covenant of God's promises had been transferred from the old Israel to the new provided the intellectual mechanism to cope with a claim of this kind. Nor did ecumenism or other fashions dominant in the church do so. One Anglican clergyman, James Parkes, wrote extensively on the need for a Christian reassessment of Jewish messianism, and he was nearly unique. Such a focus of interest was, to say the least, extremely unfashionable.[5]

---

[4]John Strachey, *The End of Empire* (New York: Random House, 1960) 244–45.

[5]On James Parkes and the literature, see John S. Conway, "Christian-Jewish Relations during the 'Fifties," *Kirchliche Zeitgeschichte* 3 (1990) 22.

Religion and French Identity:
The Origins of the *Union Sacreé*

Thomas Kselman*

The identification of France as a nation chosen by God to be his special instrument in history can be traced to the late thirteenth century and the reign of Philip the Fair (1285–1314). Although previous kings, including Saint Louis (1226–1270) had referred to themselves as "most Christian" kings, it was during Philip's reign that writers such as Guillaume de Nogaret, the Keeper of the Seals, began to transfer the attributes of piety and devotion from king to kingdom and to make the French a chosen people. This association became such an essential element in French national consciousness that by 1429 Joan of Arc, a peasant girl from Lorraine, "believed as firmly in the sacred king and his holy kingdom as she did in God and the

*Thomas Kselman is Professor in the Department of History at the University of Notre Dame.

saints."[1] Colette Beaune has argued that the early development of this sense of chosenness inspired France, more than other nations, "to draw its worth from its faith and its conformity to divine will.... Little by little the title ['most Christian'] developed into a reason for their glory and pride, justified their very being, and brought with it the calming certainty that France would always play an important role in God's plan for the order of the world."[2]

It is an enormous leap from the fourteenth to the nineteenth century, and much happened in the interim to shape national consciousness. The absolute state created by the Bourbons of the seventeenth century (legitimized by Bishop Bossuet's ideas of divine right monarchy) tightened the ideological links between God and France. The French Revolution threatened for a time to de-Christianize France, but although many of the revolutionaries detested Catholicism as a tool of the monarch, they adopted in a secularized form the idea of France as a chosen people, charged with carrying freedom to the world. The Napoleonic Concordat of 1801 reestablished Catholicism as the religion of the majority of the French, but it did little to resolve the political and religious divisions generated by the Revolution, which continued to divide France throughout the nineteenth century.

Eugen Weber has identified the last decades of the nineteenth century and the prewar period as a crucial stage in the formation of French national consciousness.[3] France's defeat in the Franco-Prussian

---

[1]Joseph R. Strayer, "France, the Holy Land, the Chosen People, and the Most Christian King," in Theodore Rabb and Jerrold Seigel, eds., *Action and Conviction in Early Modern Europe—Essays in Memory of E. H. Harbison* (Princeton: Princeton University Press, 1969) 3–16.

[2]Colette Beaune, *The Birth of an Ideology—Myths and Symbols of Nation in Late-Medieval France* (trans. Susan Ross Huston; Berkeley: University of California Press, 1991) 192–93.

[3]Eugen Weber, *Peasants into Frenchmen: The Modernization of Rural France* (Stanford: Stanford University Press, 1976). For general background on this period, see Jean-Marie Mayeur and Madeleine Rebérioux, *The Third Republic from its Origins to the Great War* (Cambridge: Cambridge University Press, 1984). For a brief account of the role religion played in the politics of the day, see John McManners, *Church and State in France, 1870–1914* (New York: Harper & Row, 1972).

War (1870–1871) was a traumatic event that led to the collapse of the Second Empire of Napoleon III and a struggle between monarchists and republicans about the nature of the regime that should replace it. Although a republican majority succeeded in establishing the Third Republic by the late 1870s, relations between republicans and their opponents, many of whom were Catholics as well as monarchists, were generally hostile throughout the period of 1870 to 1914. During the same period, however, the republican regime worked hard to provide schools, roads, and national military service as a way to break down regional isolation and provide the French with the basis for a common outlook. This process of modernization built on the older traditions of religious and secular patriotism and resulted in a common devotion to France and a general conviction that the nation had a unique mission in the world. Political and religious leaders argued about who (or what) had assigned France its role in world history, who should carry it out, and how this might be done. They shared enough common ground, however, to form the basis of an alliance over France's role in World War I. That they agreed to call this coalition a *union sacrée*—a sacred union—suggests that there was a religious dimension to the nationalist consensus.[4]

French foreign policy under Charles de Gaulle and François Mitterrand has been informed by a national consensus about France's place in the world, and American tourists and politicians alike have been known to grumble about French pride, which is well displayed in cafés and at conference tables.[5] French self-consciousness about their nation, its qualities, and its mission is a complicated historical problem, and national identity did not emerge at once and in a single era. I shall suggest, however, that the political and religious debates of the late nineteenth and early twentieth century contributed to a sense of mission which informed French attitudes during World War I and still finds echoes in contemporary life.

[4]Jean-Jacques Becker, *1914: Comment les Français sont entrés dans la guerre* (Paris: Presses de la Fondation Nationale des Sciences Politiques, 1977).
[5]Mort Rosenblum, *Mission to Civilize—The French Way* (New York: Doubleday, 1988).

Catholic France: The Eldest Daughter of the Church

During the early 1870s, a religious revival brought thousands of French men and women to Catholic shrines throughout the country. At Lourdes, La Salette, Paray-le-Monial, and elsewhere, the clergy preached repentance as the necessary response to the trauma of military defeat and occupation, the collapse of the Second Empire, and the civil war over the Paris Commune. This call to repent was frequently embedded in a prophetic framework that had its origins in the Middle Ages and persisted throughout the nineteenth century, fueled by political revolution, social conflict, and war.[6]

The prophetic messages that circulated widely in the 1870s were part of a propaganda campaign designed to restore a Bourbon monarch to the French throne and forge an alliance between France and the pope that would result in his recovery of Rome, lost to the Italian state when French troops withdrew their forces during the Franco-Prussian War. Collections of prophecies edited by clergy included texts and warnings that had first appeared at the time of the French Revolution and resurfaced in subsequent political crises.[7] Although they differed in detail, these prophecies shared a basic pattern: a period of turmoil would be followed by the coming to the throne of a great king who would cooperate with an angelic pope to usher in an age of universal peace.

Popular devotions as well as prophecies contributed to the sense of mission in which royalism and Catholicism were explicitly linked. The cult of the Sacred Heart of Jesus was among the most prominent devotions in nineteenth-century France, and it exemplified the royalist character of the French ideology of chosenness as this was expressed

---

[6]For a more extended discussion of the prophetic tradition of the nineteenth century and the religious revival of the 1870s, see Thomas Kselman, *Miracles and Prophecies in Nineteenth-Century France* (New Brunswick, NJ: Rutgers University Press, 1983) 60–83, 113–40. For a treatment that emphasizes popular prophetic traditions, see Judith Devlin, *The Superstitious Mind: French Peasants and the Supernatural in the Nineteenth Century* (New Haven: Yale University Press, 1987) 140–64.

[7]Abbé Chabauty, *Lettres sur les prophéties modernes* (Poitiers: Oudin, 1871); idem, *Les prophéties modernes vengées* (Paris: Palmé and Poitiers: Oudin, 1874); Abbé Curicque, *Voix prophétiques* (2 vols.; 5th ed.; Paris: Palmé, 1872).

by Catholics in the 1870s. Devotion to the Sacred Heart was based on a series of apparitions experienced by Marguerite Marie Alacoque, a sister in the Visitation convent at Paray-le-Monial from 1671 to 1690.[8] In 1689 Jesus revealed to Marguerite Marie that he would reign over France if Louis XIV would build a temple to honor the Sacred Heart and consecrate himself and his court to this image. On the basis of this revelation devotees believed that the troubles of France were the result of the king's failure to honor the Sacred Heart. The crisis of 1870–1871 was another occasion for recalling this covenant, and in March 1873 the French Assembly agreed, after a heated discussion, to build the church of Sacré-Coeur that still overlooks Paris from its site on the hill of Montmartre. This decision demonstrated the strength of royalist support in the Assembly and a desire to fulfill the terms of a divine contract. The pilgrimage of fifty deputies to Paray-le-Monial on 29 June 1873, where the royalist politician the baron de Belcastel consecrated France to the Sacred Heart, was read by Catholics as yet another sign that a restoration of the Bourbons to France was about to occur.[9]

According to the prophetic texts, political and social order in France depended on restoring the king. Prophecies also insisted that France could not be content with a mission that was exclusively internal, but must concern itself with the fate of the pope and his Church. This association with the Church gave to France a task of universal significance that was a source of enormous pride on the part of French Catholics. In the history that students learned in Catholic schools, France's success in the world corresponded precisely to those periods when she took up her mission to defend the Church.[10] The Bourbon

[8]Michel Cinquin, "Paray-le-Monial," in Philippe Boutry and Michel Cinquin, *Deux pèlerinages au XIXe siècle: Ars et Paray-le-Monial* (Paris: Beaushesne, 1980) 174–75.

[9]Ibid., 179–84, 206–10; Kselman, *Miracles and Prophecies*, 125–27.

[10]Abbé Courval, *Histoire contemporaine à l'usage de la jeunesse* (8th ed.; Paris: Poussielgue, 1895) 314. See also Charles Vandepitte, *Petite histoire de l'église depuis Jésus-Christ jusqu'a nos jours* (5th ed.; Cambrai: Deligne, 1911) 55, where the author describes the conversion of Clovis following a military victory. This story suggests a pact in which the French are offered military victory over the Germans in exchange for religious loyalty, an appar-

pretender the count of Chambord, in a public letter of May 1871, explicitly recognized the French obligation to the pope, as did pilgrims to Paray-le-Monial, who prayed and sang that God would "save Rome and France / Through your Sacred Heart."[11]

It is impossible to know how many people read and believed the prophecies of a return of the king and the salvation of the pope.[12] But the pilgrimage movement and the royalist campaign, which almost succeeded in bringing a Bourbon back to the throne, were infused with a similar sense of mission that was both religious and political. France was called on by God to return to its faith, restore the king, and defend the pope. None of this happened. Chambord's refusal to accept the tricolor made him unacceptable to a majority that included some monarchists. German pressure on the French to restrain public expression of support for the papacy was increasingly successful; in the aftermath of their defeat, French politicians—even those sympathetic to the Bourbons—became unwilling to risk what were viewed as unnecessarily provocative actions.[13]

The failure of the Restoration movement had important consequences for the French Right, which struggled for the rest of the century to formulate a political alternative to royalism. One of the major difficulties the Right faced was its historic suspicion of the "people," for since the Revolution of 1789 this term had been associated with vio-

---

ent appeal to the anti-German sentiment so important during the Third Republic. Even the republican historian Ernest Lavisse (*Histoire de France—Cours Elémentaire* [New York: Heath, 1919] 14–15) emphasized the close relationship between France and the Church.

[11]"Lettre de M. le comte de Chambord," *Rosier de Marie*, 17 June 1871, 510–11. See also Cinquin, "Paray-le-Monial," 291–92.

[12]Prophecies troubled Church officials who feared they made excessive claims. See Monseigneur Félix Dupanloup, "Lettre sur les prophéties publiées dans ces derniers temps," *Le Correspondant*, 25 March 1874, 1097–121; and Jean-Marie Mayeur, "Mgr Dupanloup et Louis Veuillot devant les prophéties contemporaines en 1874," *Revue d'histoire de la spiritualité* 48 (1972) 193–204.

[13]Allan Mitchell, *Victors and Vanquished—The German Influence on Army and Church after 1870* (Chapel Hill: University of North Carolina Press, 1984) 159–69.

lence and disorder.[14] *La Croix*, the widely distributed Catholic newspaper of the Assumptionist fathers, expressed this suspicion of popular sovereignty and majority rule in 1883 when an anonymous editorial writer known as "the monk" distinguished the "true people," who recognized the sovereignty of God, from a mere majority of electors.[15] An emphasis on royalty as the agent of God's will, along with a suspicion of the people, resulted in a political rhetoric that created a distance between the French people and their God; this distance had to be bridged in the political realm by a king, just as the clergy served as intermediaries in the spiritual realm. As we shall see, the republicans linked people and nation directly in a construction of the French mission that competed with the Catholic prophetic tradition. Whereas revolutionary events and rhetoric had rendered any appeal to the concept of "people" suspect for those on the Right, republicans and anticlericals were not so constrained.

In their search for a popular constituency, some former royalists were willing to support the Boulangist movement of the 1880s. Although General Boulanger's supporters failed in their efforts to put into place an authoritarian regime, the movement represented an important step by the Right, which sought through the general to draw popular support on the basis of nationalist sentiment and class resentment.[16] Anti-Semitism represented another political message that the Right began using in the 1880s as a means for generating popular support, one that was to have explosive consequences during the Dreyfus Affair at the turn of the century.[17] In its search for a con-

[14]See Simon Schama, *Citizens—A Chronicle of the French Revolution* (New York: Knopf, 1989) 300–304, for examples of the revolutionary use of "people."

[15]"Suffragiens," *La Croix*, 15 August 1883, 1b.

[16]See William Irvine, *The Boulanger Affair Reconsidered: Royalism, Boulangism, and the Origins of the Radical Right in France* (New York: Oxford University Press, 1989); Michael Burns, *Rural Society and French Politics: Boulangism and the Dreyfus Affair, 1886–1900* (Princeton: Princeton University Press, 1984); Zeev Sternhell, *La droite révolutionnaire, 1885–1914: Les origines françaises du fascisme* (Paris: Seuil, 1978) 33–60; Patrick Hutton, "Popular Boulangism and the Advent of Mass Politics in France, 1886–1890," *Journal of Contemporary History* 11 (1976) 85–106.

[17]Sternhell, *La droite révolutionnaire*, 177–244; Stephen Wilson, *Ideology and Experience: Antisemitism in France at the Time of the Dreyfus Affair*

stituency in the closing decades of the nineteenth century, the Right redefined its political agenda by claiming to defend the French people against German domination from beyond the border and Jewish influence from within. Some of the polemicists conjured up a fantasy world in which Germans, Jews, Freemasons, and Protestants merged into a single diabolical conspiracy aimed at dominating the French people.[18]

Those who sought to increase the Church's political influence did not, however, rely exclusively on Boulangism and anti-Semitic rhetoric. During the 1890s, in a movement known as the *ralliement*, they made an effort to reconcile Catholicism and republicanism. The movement began with a toast to the government at a dinner for naval officers held by Cardinal Lavigerie of Algiers in 1890. In February 1892, Pope Leo XIII pushed the *ralliement* further along when he issued the encyclical "Au Milieu des solicitudes," which defended the legitimacy of the Republic and called on Catholics to work for legislative reforms, but not for change in the political system.[19] In this search for reconciliation Catholics and republicans groped for a common symbol that could link them in common devotion to France. Joan of Arc, the peasant girl from Lorraine who became a national heroine in the fifteenth century, was for a time able to appeal to the French across their political differences.[20] For both Catholics and republicans

---

(Rutherford, NJ: Fairleigh Dickinson University Press, 1982); Pierre Sorlin, *La Croix et les juifs (1880–1899), contribution à l'histoire de l'antisémitisme contemporain* (Paris: Grasset, 1967); Nancy Fitch, "Mass Culture, Mass Parliamentary Politics, and Modern Anti-Semitism: The Dreyfus Affair in Rural France," *AHR* 97 (1992) 55–95.

[18]Eugen Weber, *Satan franc-maçon* (Paris: Gallimard, 1964).

[19]Alexander Sedgwick, *The Ralliement in French Politics, 1890–1898* (Cambridge, MA: Harvard University Press, 1965).

[20]Rosemonde Sanson, "La 'fête de Jeanne d'Arc' en 1894: controverse et célébration," *Revue d'histoire moderne et contemporaine* 20 (1973) 444–63; Thomas Worcester, "Religion et Patrie: Joan of Arc and the Ideological Grounding of Church/State Relations in France, 1889–1920," (paper prepared for Professor William Hutchison's seminar on American Religious Thought in Western Context, Harvard Divinity School, 1989). For a brief review of how Joan of Arc was reinterpreted in the nineteenth century, see Maria Warner, *Joan of Arc: The Image of Female Heroism* (New York: Knopf, 1981) 255–75.

Joan of Arc's victory over the English in 1429 at Orléans represented the liberation of French soil from an invading army, an exemplary model for those concerned about the German seizure of Alsace and Lorraine.

Devotion to Joan of Arc was not an innovation of the 1890s. In 1853, the historian Jules Michelet published a popular biography praising Joan's patriotism and playing down the supernatural elements in her story, an emphasis that helped her attract a following from republicans.[21] Catholic devotion to Joan led the bishop of Orléans, Félix Dupanloup, to request in 1869 that Rome declare her a saint. In 1874, when monarchists still controlled the National Assembly, an equestrian statue of Joan was raised at the Place des Pyramides and soon became a site for pilgrimages in her honor. The appeal of Joan of Arc to both Catholics and republicans led Joseph Fabre, a republican deputy from Aveyron, to introduce in the French Chamber of 1884 a bill that would create a national feast day in her honor. Fabre hoped that a holiday in honor of Joan would bring together believers and freethinkers and permit them to celebrate the nation with a similar enthusiasm.

Fabre's initiative of 1884 fit perfectly with the *ralliement* of the 1890s, when moderate Catholics and republicans worked hard to define Joan as a figure who, in her loyalty to France, transcended political differences. When his bill was reintroduced in 1894, the same year in which Joan was declared Venerable by Leo XIII, it attracted majority support in the French Senate. Catholic acceptance of republican France, mediated by Joan of Arc, can be seen in a number of the panegyrics preached in the cathedral of Orléans on Joan's feast day, the eighth of May, between 1889 and 1898. All of the preachers drew parallels between France and ancient Israel; Joan of Arc exemplified how God intervened miraculously in history to save France, just as he acted in ancient times to save Israel. None of the sermons, however, embraced royalism, and several took pains to distance themselves from the close association between the monarchy and France. Monseigneur Jean-Pierre Pagis, the bishop of Verdun, who delivered

[21]Jules Michelet, *Jeanne d'Arc (1412–1432)* (Paris: Hachette, 1853). For another biographical work in the republican tradition, see Henri Martin, *Jeanne d'Arc* (Paris: Furne, 1857).

the Orléans panegyric in 1898, proposed that whether France was a republic or a monarchy was a secondary matter. For Pagis, however, it was essential that France, whatever the form of its government, remain faithful to its Christian vocation. This mission involved defending the Church and carrying Christianity to the world, a mission that could be carried out as easily by a republican as a monarchical government.[22]

The *ralliement* and the move to create a national holiday to honor Joan of Arc foundered despite the good intentions of the moderates in both republican and Catholic camps. Royalists on the right and anticlerical republicans on the left insisted instead that Joan be understood in narrowly partisan terms. Charles Maurras, the leader of Action Française, condemned those who ignored Joan's loyalty to the king and dismissed the divine origins of her mission. Joan's royalism was not a secondary matter for Maurras; it was her principal message, as relevant in the modern age as it was in medieval times.[23] On the left, anticlericals working within the tradition of Jules Michelet pointed out how King Charles VII had abandoned her to the English, who in 1431 had burned her at the stake for heresy, an observation that also allowed them to condemn the Church for fanaticism and hypocrisy.[24] The politicization of Joan led the French Chamber to reject the initiative of the Senate in 1894. Subsequently, the divisions provoked by the Dreyfus Affair—between Right and Left, Catholics and anticlericals—for a time destroyed her usefulness as a unifying symbol.

A broad-based devotion to Joan of Arc reappeared, however, as a result of the *union sacrée* forged during World War I. In the panegyric to Joan the Liberator preached at Notre Dame in Paris in 1915, Monseigneur Alfred Baudrillart compared the crisis of 1429 with that of the current war; he described the French victory on the Marne that stopped the German invaders as a "miracle" attributable to Joan's intervention. This event had been preceded, however, by another equally significant miracle, the "instantaneous reawakening and the

[22]Worcester, "Religion et Patrie," 18–30.

[23]Charles Maurras, *La Politique de Jeanne d'Arc* (Paris: Editions de "La Seule France," n.d.).

[24]Sanson, "La 'fête de Jeanne d'Arc' en 1894," 451–52.

common effort of all of the profound forces of the French soul."[25] The sense of national unity generated by World War I led the French Chamber in 1920 finally to approve the Senate proposal that the Third Republic celebrate her feast every second Sunday in May, the anniversary of the liberation of Orléans.

The sermons preached on Joan of Arc at Orléans suggest that in the 1890s some of the Catholic clergy sought to distance themselves from royalism, even while they remained nationalistic. A similar shift can be seen in Catholic devotional life; even the cult of the Sacred Heart, which was tied so intimately to the Bourbons, was increasingly presented by its official spokesmen as a call to the French rather than to the king. Félix de Rosnay, who published a devotional history of Paray-le-Monial in 1900, made no reference to the Bourbons and their claim on the throne. The devotion to the Sacred Heart and the shrine at Paray-le-Monial were nonetheless interpreted as destined to play a major role in history; they were seen as the source of a religious conversion that would sweep the world in the twentieth century. De Rosnay was naturally proud of this mission, which he saw as part of a providential plan in which France played a determining role.

Paray-le-Monial, in Rosnay's account, stands for a universal destiny. There is no doubt that this destiny includes an entirely legitimate predominance for France. "The Sacred Heart was revealed on French soil to a French virgin, and it made a particularly pressing appeal to the French soul. As the first invited, this soul should be the first and most eager to respond to the divine call. Paray is a Jerusalem, the Zion of modern times, the royal citadel that from its heights dominates the entire history of the world."[26]

Rosnay's devotional text, like the prophetic literature of the 1870s, charged France with a national mission to reshape the history of the world. For believing Catholics, the series of Marian apparitions that began in Paris in 1830 and that inaugurated major shrines at La Salette

---

[25]Monseigneur Baudrillart, *Jeanne la Libératrice, 1429–1915* (Paris: Beauchesne, 1915) 26. For a brief review of public opinion toward Catholicism during the war, see Jean-Jacques Becker, *The Great War and the French People* (trans. Arnold Pomerans; Dover, NH: Berg, 1985) 178–91.

[26]Félix de Ronsay, *Petite histoire de Paray-le-Monial* (Paris: Retaux, 1900) viii–ix.

(1846), Lourdes (1858), and Pontmain (1870) was another and perhaps clearer indication that the French had been chosen to deliver
warning and consoling messages to an unrepentant world. The Miraculous Medal, which was revealed to Sister Catherine Labouré just
four months after the July Revolution had shaken Paris, displayed
Mary with beams of light flowing from her extended arms to the
globe on which she stood. During the vision Sister Catherine heard the
words: "These rays are the symbol of the graces Mary obtains for all
men, and the point toward which they flow most abundantly is
France."[27] A devotional manual associated with the Miraculous Medal
circulated throughout the nineteenth century; in it, Father Aladel interpreted Mary's preference for France in the following terms:

> France, who has wrought so much evil by disseminating philo-
> sophical and revolutionary doctrines, is to repair the past by
> propagating the truth, and Mary desires to prepare her for this
> mission: Everyone knows, moreover, that the French character
> possesses a force of expansion and a power of energy that ren-
> der the French eminently qualified to maintain the interests of
> truth and justice.[28]

The predilection of Mary for France was a source of pride for
Catholics, but their devotion to her also suggests an important dimension of the French sense of mission. The model of the chosen people,
inherited from the Hebrew scriptures, presented the Jews as elected
by God, who presented himself as ruler and lawgiver. Mary was at
times a disciplinarian, as at La Salette, where she threatened the French
with famine. But her repeated appearances, and the miraculous healings
attributed to her, suggested that even though they were obstreperous
children, the French would not be abandoned. The emphasis on Mary

---

[27]René Laurentin, *Catherine Labouré et la Médaille Miraculeuse* (2 vols.;
Paris: Lethielleux, 1976) 1. 52. The Marian apparitions and their prophetic
significance are analyzed in Kselman, *Miracles and Prophecies*, 89–94; and
Eugen Weber, *My France—Politics, Culture, Myth* (Cambridge, MA: Harvard
University Press, 1991) 111–12.

[28]Jean-Marie Aladel, *The Miraculous Medal: Its Origins, History, Circulation, Results* (Baltimore, MD: Piet, 1880).

rather than God as the divine figure who addressed her people may reflect the patterns of religious life, for in nineteenth-century France women were much more likely to practice their Catholicism than were men.[29] Mary's messages were also compatible with the depoliticization of devotional life, for although royalist and prophetic literature referred to the apparitions, Mary's general calls for repentance were capable of surviving the political failure of the 1870s and the separation of church and state in 1905. The great king had not appeared, and the pope remained a prisoner in the Vatican, but by redefining their mission in more narrowly religious terms Catholics (and perhaps especially Catholic women) could still claim that the French had a universal and providential mission to convert the world.

The Republican Mission: Revolution and Liberation

Royalists and their heirs on the Right searched for a popular constituency, but the concept of "the people" was not one that they could easily introduce into their political vocabulary. While revolutionaries in the 1790s battled over "the people" and how they were to be represented, they nonetheless agreed fundamentally about popular sovereignty. For the Right, however, the crowds of the French revolutions in 1789, 1830, 1848, and 1871, and the political language of the Left that legitimized their intervention in history rendered "the people" a suspect category, one they willingly conceded to republican and socialist opponents. This gave the Left a certain advantage in defining the French mission. It could broaden the appeal of its message by including specific references to "the people" as involved in the historic destiny of France.

Jules Michelet, the most prominent French historian of the nineteenth century, provides an early and influential example of how the republican tradition linked the concepts of people and mission. In his 1846 essay *The People*, Michelet located genuine national sentiment in the peasants and the workers. "It seems that as far as national

---

[29]Ralph Gibson, *A Social History of Catholicism, 1789–1914* (New York: Routledge, 1989) 180–90; Gérard Cholvy and Yves-Marie Hilaire, *Histoire religieuse de la France contemporaine, 1800–1880* (Paris: Privat, 1985) 176–85.

sentiment is concerned. . . the higher one goes toward the upper classes, the less alive one becomes."[30] From Michelet's perspective only certain classes of people were authentically French, and these people were therefore charged with a mission to redeem the world.

> No doubt every great nation represents an idea important to the human race. But great God! how much more true is this of France! Suppose for a moment that she were eclipsed or perished; the sympathetic bond of the world would be loosened, broken, and probably destroyed. Love, which is the life of the world, would be wounded in its most vital part. The earth would enter into an age of ice which other worlds nearby have already entered.[31]

Soon after the appearance of *The People*, Michelet began publishing his *Histoire de la Revolution française*, a work which did not find a large audience until the 1880s, when popular editions led to a wide circulation.[32] For Michelet, the Revolution of 1789–1790 was a climactic moment of French history, a brief time in which people overcame their differences and demonstrated to the world the possibility of reconciling liberty, equality, and fraternity. The people of France were unable to sustain this moment, but like the God of the Hebrew scriptures, the Revolution was a constant presence calling them back to their historical and providential obligation.

The spirit of the Revolution, according to Michelet, contained the secret of all bygone times. In it alone France became conscious of herself. "When, in a moment of weakness, we may appear forgetful of our worth, it is to this point that we should recur in order to seek and recover ourselves again. Here, the inextinguishable spark, the profound mystery of life, is ever glowing within us."[33]

---

[30]Jules Michelet, *The People* (trans. John P. McKay: Champaign-Urbana: University of Illinois Press, 1973) 93–94.

[31]Ibid., 183.

[32]Gordon Wright, "Introduction," in Jules Michelet, *History of the French Revolution* (Chicago: University of Chicago Press, 1967) xiv.

[33]Michelet, *History*, 3.

Michelet's version of history assigned France a world-historical mission expressed in a language infused with religious significance. For Michelet, however, the God-given duty was assigned to a people and not to a king, and they were called to liberate themselves from both priests and kings, as well as to carry this message to an enslaved world.

The sense of French mission evoked by Michelet offered republicans a religiously informed historical perspective; this perspective could be used to challenge the Catholic vision that identified France with the Church and the monarchy. As with the Catholic prophetic tradition, however, the republican vision required constant updating in the face of current events. We have seen how the Franco-Prussian War stimulated a revival of Catholic prophecies looking forward to a great pope and a great king. Within the republican tradition, Victor Hugo can be seen as taking up the challenge posed by the French defeat and interpreting it as part of a providential design in which France played the central role in world history. Hugo was uniquely equipped for this task, for in 1870 he was the foremost poet and novelist writing in French as well as a committed republican. For the Third Republic, he was a heroic figure whose verses had become, by the 1890s, a part of the elementary education of French children.[34] His funeral in 1885 drew over a million people to the streets of Paris in what was perhaps the largest peaceful demonstration in France throughout the nineteenth century.

Hugo's theological convictions are difficult to characterize, but we can certainly state that he rejected anything like orthodox Christianity in its Catholic or Protestant forms. Nonetheless, his vision of earthly history fits into a pattern of apocalyptic writing that recalls the Book of Revelation. A battle was underway between the forces of good and evil, and Hugo had no difficulty in identifying these as republican France, on the one hand, and monarchs and the Church, on the other. In "L'Elegie des fléaux" ("In praise of plagues"), for example, which appeared in his 1877 collection *La légende des siècles*, Hugo struggled to understand the recent disasters that had fallen upon France. Floods

---

[34]Avner Ben-Amos, "Les funérailles de Victor Hugo," in Pierre Nora, ed., *Les lieux de mémoire*, vol. 1: *La Republique* (Paris: Gallimard, 1984) 474–76.

in the south were continuing the destructive work that had begun in
1870 with the invasion of the German armies in the north. France
seemed about to expire, and for Hugo the disappearance of Nineveh,
Athens, Israel, and Rome was insignificant when compared to the
"enormous eclipse" of France.

> O France! Will you die? No, because if you were to die
> Evil would live, fear would live; a window would be closed
> The first light of dawn would be extinguished;
> Death would be born, the complete death of everything.
> . . . .
> No, France, the Universe needs you to live.
> You will live. The future would die under your shroud.[35]

The struggle Hugo described is a desperate one: the forces of liberty centered in France do battle with tyrannous kings, emperors, and
popes. For a priest in Hugo's poem the troubles of France were heavenly chastisement, but the poet—a voice we can safely assume rep-
resents Hugo—rejected this interpretation as blasphemous. Despite the
evidence of defeat and devastation, France was destined to fight on
and would eventually triumph. France would not perish because it had
a unique mission in the world, a mission to challenge kings and priests
and bring liberty to all peoples. This charge was God-given, and
although a heavy responsibility, it was one that the French had accepted and would continue to carry out. The poem concludes by looking forward to a war in which people battle against princes and that
will end with French victory and the restoration of the lost territories
of Alsace and Lorraine. The defeat and devastation of France were
tragic, but nonetheless were part of a providential design that would
eventually result in triumph, not only for France, but for the world.
Like the America of the writers and ministers studied by Ernest
Tuveson, in Hugo's vision France assumes the role of Redeemer
Nation.[36]

[35]Victor Hugo, *La légende des siècles* (2 vols.; Paris: Garnier-Flammarion,
1967) 2. 284–92.
[36]Ernest Lee Tuveson, *Redeemer Nation: The Idea of America's Millennial
Role* (Chicago: University of Chicago Press, 1968).

The anticlerical dimension of the thought of Michelet and Hugo helps to explain their appeal to the republican politicians and their followers in the Third Republic; these writers clearly were hostile to the Catholic church and its clergy. They still, however, insisted on the providential nature of the French mission, and to this extent were in accord with their Catholic opponents. For many of the republicans who took power in the 1880s, this providential framework was an archaic, romantic holdover in a positivist age. Jules Ferry, for example, who headed the cabinet that pushed through the secularization of French elementary education in the 1880s, rigorously excluded all talk of God from his political language.[37] Ferry and his followers nonetheless retained a sense of mission for the French nation and her people that was unique and world-historical. This mission resembles the one preached by Hugo, but the call is no longer from a God beyond history. Instead, it comes from within history, and the meaning of this history carries an obligation that is no less burdensome or sacred for all its this-worldly origins.[38]

The work of the historian Ernest Lavisse typifies this view, which combines elements from Michelet's romantic historiography with a method and a style derived from positivism. Lavisse, like Michelet and Hugo, had an influence on French culture well beyond the circle of the educated elite. Through the manuals he wrote for the schools of the Third Republic he became, in the words of Pierre Nora, "a spokesman of the generation that worked, with Gambetta and Jules Ferry, to remake the national mood after the defeat of 1870."[39] Al-

[37]Jules Ferry, *Discours et opinions de Jules Ferry* (Paris: Colin, 1894).

[38]For an example of this shift, see Gabriel Vicaire's lyrical poem "Quatre-Vingt-Neuf," which was chosen to be the official hymn for the Universal Exposition of 1889. As with Hugo, Vicaire portrays France as carrying liberty to a world plagued by hatred, ignorance, tyranny, and despair. In Vicaire's secularized vision, however, there are no references to God or Providence. France's liberating mission comes instead from her own will as it is informed by historical memory. The text of the poem can be found in *Journal Officiel*, 12 May 1888, 1948.

[39]Pierre Nora, "Lavisse, instituteur national," in idem, *La République*, 247. See also Pierre Nora, "*L'Histoire de la France* de Lavisse," in idem, ed., *Les lieux de mémoire*, vol. 2: *La Nation* (Paris: Gallimard, 1986) 317–75.

though he came to be a defender of the Republic and the Revolution, Lavisse began his career as an aide to Victor Duruy, minister of education in the Second Empire, and as tutor to the prince imperial.[40] His republicanism was therefore imposed on a preexisting patriotism which allowed him to view the Old Regime with a sense of love and pride.[41]

Lavisse was not uniformly positive in his judgments about the French past, but he was able to find value in those who worked for the unity of France. From Lavisse's perspective, a key element in the national mission was the recovery of the territories lost in the Franco-Prussian War. This task was assigned by geography as well as by history, for France was destined to extend itself to its natural frontiers, which included the left bank of the Rhine. Earlier historians, such as Augustin Thierry, had used the idea of natural frontiers as a common ground linking monarchists and republicans. During the Third Republic, politicians quarreled over how and when this goal might be achieved and whether or not colonial expansion would distract attention from Alsace and Lorraine. The educational program introduced by the Third Republic, however, used both geography and history lessons to instruct the French that their mission included recovering the lost territories. The call to act in this case came from both geography and history, and in emphasizing the territorial aspect of French national identity, Lavisse and Vidal de la Blache, as well as other republican pedagogues, were creating the basis for a common national outlook.[42] In his emphasis on territoriality as the basis of national identity, Lavisse's work loses something of the universalist dimension present in Michelet. Lavisse's conclusion to a 1912 textbook that he wrote for elementary school students exposes this tension between a

[40]Nora, "Lavisse, instituteur national," 251.

[41]According to Nora (*"L'Histoire de la France* de Lavisse," 329), for Lavisse, "all of France's history has the right to be learned and loved, and not only the part of history that begins with the Revolution."

[42]Peter Sahlins, "Natural Frontiers Revisited: France's Boundaries since the Seventeenth Century," *AHR* 95 (1990) 1423–51, esp. 1448–50; Eugen Weber, "La formation de l'hexagone républicain," in François Furet, ed., *Jules Ferry—Fondateur de la République* (Paris: Ecole des Hautes Etudes en Sciences Sociales, 1985) 123–41; Jean-Yves Guiomor, "Le *Tableau de la géographie de la France* de Vidal de la Blache," in Nora, *La Nation*, 569–97.

mission directed at internal unity and one that includes the spread of universal ideals from their home in France.

> In defending France, we defend the land where we were born, the most beautiful and generous land in the world.
> In defending France, we behave like good sons. We fulfill a duty to our fathers, who worked so hard for so many centuries to create our fatherland.
> In defending France, we work for all men in all countries, because France, since the Revolution, has given to the world the ideas of justice and humanity.
> France is the most just, the freest, and most humane of fatherlands.[43]

In Lavisse's combination of positivist historical method and romantic nationalism, any appeal from beyond history is meaningless. Although a staunch republican, his work nonetheless resembles in this sense that of Maurice Barrès, the novelist and politician of the Right whose nationalism was based on the cult of "the land and the dead" (*la terre et les morts*). In Barrès's work, as in Lavisse's, the call to the French comes from the past and refers to universal as well as national tasks. Writing in 1902, Barrès refers to God as the force choosing France for its universal mission, but identifies God as a force within rather than outside of history.

> In truth, France has contributed so much to civilization, she has provided so many services to the highest conception of the world, to the enlargement and precision of the ideal—in other words to the idea of God—for anyone other than some small-minded corporal to suggest that God—that is to say the direction imposed on the movements of humanity—would be interested in the contraction of the nation that fought the Crusades out of a sentiment of emancipation and fraternity, and that proclaimed through the Revolution the right of peoples to decide for themselves.[44]

---

[43]Quoted in Nora, "Lavisse, instituteur national," 284.
[44]Maurice Barrès, *Scènes et doctrines du nationalisme* (1902), cited in Raoul Girardet, *Le nationalisme français, 1871–1914* (Paris: Gallimard, 1966) 191.

Barrès and Lavisse called on the French to carry on their work, which required first of all the recovery and protection of the nation. Both also referred to a more universal mission, however, and the religious language they used to express this mission cut across the political differences that divided the Right of the Action Française from the anticlerical Left.

The political battles of the Dreyfus Affair bitterly divided France in the first years of the twentieth century, and in the tense political atmosphere of the time "nationalism" was generally identified with the anti-Dreyfusard defenders of church and army, while the republicans and their allies acted on behalf of "universal" human rights. The virulence of this debate, however, veiled a shared sense of French national identity and mission that was emerging at the time and that was ultimately expressed in the *union sacrée* that linked Left and Right in 1914. In the 1870s and 1880s Catholics understood this mission as involving religious conversion and the restoration of papal territories and the Bourbon monarchy. For republicans, the French were the people chosen by God to carry liberty to the world. By the start of the twentieth century, modified versions of these ideologies were circulating, and the call to the French to carry out their unique destiny was coming from geography, history, and the dead, as well as from God. Catholics and republicans in the Third Republic differed on issues of education, family legislation, and the status of the Church in France. Both groups, however, used religiously infused language to describe a unique, sacred, and universal role for their nation, a language that shaped popular attitudes and contributed to the possibility of a *union sacrée*.

Raoul Girardet has proposed that a crucial shift in French nationalism occurred toward the end of the nineteenth century. Following the defeat by Germany, French nationalism abandoned its universalism and humanitarianism and became instead "a nationalism of retraction, strictly closed in on itself, rigid, exclusive, enclosed in several simple imperatives: a nationalism of the conquered inclined toward revenge and obsessed with the enormous humiliation from which it had developed."[45] Girardet had no trouble finding evidence to suggest

[45]Girardet, *Le nationalisme français*, 50.

that French nationalism in the last third of the nineteenth century was increasingly xenophobic and self-absorbed. Throughout this period, however, a broader, more universal understanding of French nationalism survived among all political groupings. The socialist movement, with which I have not dealt here, expressed most clearly the preeminence of universal values, and polemical exchanges between socialists such as Gustave Hervé and nationalists were common.[46] Even in the midst of these debates, however, nationalists such as Maurice Barrès and Charles Péguy retained a sense of France's universal mission, a sense derived in part from their reading of the nation's historical relationship to the Church and in part from the earlier republican and revolutionary tradition that saw France carrying liberty to the world.

During the period 1905–1914, the nationalist revival that Eugen Weber has described was driven by a series of political, social, and international crises. These led to an anxious atmosphere in which political elites sought to mobilize public opinion around the issues of French unity, power, and preparedness.[47] Weber connects the nationalist revival to "its principal cause—fear: fear of war, fear of social revolution, fear of those private opinions whose vociferousness enabled them to pass for public opinion."[48] Fear, anxiety, and desire for revenge are among the elements Weber and Girardet identified as explaining the nationalist mood in France prior to World War I. In addition to these sentiments, however, the French also continued to hear about their mission to the world. Charles Péguy, writing in 1912, placed the following words in the mouth of God:

> Our Frenchmen—They are my favorite witnesses.
>
> . . . .
>
> They have more faults than other people.

---

[46]For details on this debate as it affected school manuals, see Christian Amalvi, "Les guerres des manuels autour de l'école primaire en France (1899–1914)," *RH* 262 (1979) 359–98.

[47]Eugen Weber, *The Nationalist Revival in France, 1905–1914* (Berkeley/ Los Angeles: University of California Press, 1959) 7. A revised version of the conclusion of this study appears in Eugen Weber, *My France*, 189–204.

[48]Weber, *Nationalist Revival*, 7–8.

But with all their faults I love them still more than I do all the
others.
. . . .
They have been and always will be my best soldiers in the
crusade.
And there will always be a crusade.[49]

In this text God does not specify the cause of the crusade, but the
sense of chosenness is clear. France's special role was also clear to
Charles de Gaulle, a devout Catholic born in 1890 who developed an
enthusiasm for Péguy. The influence of Péguy can perhaps be seen in
the famous opening passage of de Gaulle's memoirs:

> All my life I have thought of France in a certain way. This is
> inspired by sentiment as much as by reason. The emotional side
> of me tends to imagine France, like the princess in the fairy
> stories or the Madonna in the frescoes, as dedicated to an ex-
> alted and exceptional destiny. Instinctively I have the feeling
> that Providence has created her either for complete successes or
> for exemplary misfortunes. If, in spite of this, mediocrity shows
> in her acts and deeds, it strikes me as an absurd anomaly, to be
> imputed to the faults of Frenchmen, not to the genius of the
> land. But the positive side of my mind also assures me that
> France is not really herself unless in the front rank; that only
> vast enterprises are capable of counterbalancing the ferments of
> dispersal which are inherent in her people; that our country, as
> it is, surrounded by the others, as they are, must aim high and
> hold itself straight, on pain of mortal danger. In short, to my
> mind, France cannot be France without greatness.[50]

De Gaulle, like Péguy, was vague about what it was Providence
had chosen the French to accomplish, although he had no doubt that

---

[49]Charles Péguy, *Basic Verities* (trans. Ann Green and Julian Green; New
York: Pantheon, 1943) 236–37.
[50]Charles de Gaulle, *War Memoirs—the Call to Honor, 1940–1942* (trans.
J. Griffon; 5 vols.; New York: Viking Press, 1955) 1. 3. For the influence of
Péguy on de Gaulle, see Jean Lacouture, *De Gaulle, The Rebel, 1890–1944*
(New York: Norton, 1990) 27.

it was something of world significance. For Péguy, de Gaulle, and the other nationalists, defending France from an external threat and recovering the lost territories were crucial. Beyond these tasks, however, a more general and universal mission survived. No longer tied specifically or exclusively to the Church or the Revolution, but based at the same time on an understanding of the past as a call to action, a sense of mission informed French nationalist attitudes in 1914 and beyond.

Response

*Caroline Ford**

In 1762, Jean-Jacques Rousseau wrote that religion could be

divided into two categories, the religion of the man and the religion of the citizen. The first, without temples, altars or rituals, and limited to inward devotion to the supreme God and the external obligations of morality, is the pure and simple religion of the Gospel. . . . The religion of the citizen is the religion established in a single country; it gives that country its gods, and its special tutelary deities; it has its dogmas, its rituals, its external forms of worship laid down by law; and to the one nation which practices this religion, everything outside is infidel, alien and barbarous.[1]

Rousseau also identified a third and "more curious kind of religion, which gives men. . . two homelands, puts them under two contradictory obligations and prevents their being at the same time both churchmen and citizens."[2] For him, this definition applied to the case of the Catholic religion: its universalistic claims were absolutely inimical to those of the sovereign nation.

Historians of France, particularly those of French nationalism, have taken Rousseau's analysis of the relationship between Catholicism and civil/political society as a self-evident truth, especially in the context of the ultramontanist nineteenth century. Thomas Kselman's paper reexamines the claim that the "religion of nationalism" replaced the religion of the churches and, more specifically, the Catholic church in

---

*Caroline Ford is Associate Professor of History and Research Associate at the Center for European Studies at Harvard University.
[1]Jean-Jacques Rousseau, *The Social Contract* (New York: Viking, 1968) 181.
[2]Ibid.

modern Europe. In a broader sense, however, he considers the question of the role of the religious language of chosenness in the political and cultural construction of French national identity. He urges us to reassess the relationship between religion and nationalism in France by exploring the ways in which the Catholic church, popular beliefs, and conceptions of chosenness worked both for and against the formation of national identity at different historical moments.

He concludes, however, that the Catholic church often came into conflict with the new postrevolutionary French nation even though nationalist discourse was at the same time steeped in religious language. Kselman's conclusion thus raises a larger question concerning the extent to which Catholicism, or religion more generally, served to shape or to impede the creation of cohesive national communities and identities. This question is complicated by apparent conflicts between elite articulations of national belonging, on the one hand, and popular conceptions on the other, and it is further compounded by longstanding conflicts regarding the rights and limits of citizenship in postrevolutionary France.

One of the most important features of the paper is Kselman's perception that definitions of the nation, which many historians imply were fixed at the time of the French Revolution, have shifted in important ways. Another is his demonstration that in the postrevolutionary period the line between nationalism of the Right and the Left became more permeable than has been thought. In making this case, Kselman focuses on the crucial period of the turn of the century. It has frequently been argued that the political birthright of nationalism was transferred from the Left to the Right during this period. In contrast, Kselman suggests that right- and left-wing conceptions of the nation converged, as evidenced in the language of France's mission in the world and the *union sacrée* of the First World War. As the nation increasingly came to be articulated in cultural, racial, and religious terms, religion and a secularized chosen people discourse cemented that union. This convergence, however, did not extend much beyond the elections of 1919 and had certainly fallen apart by 1924. It nonetheless continued to be a powerful part of the French language of nationalism. At the core of the religious language of French nationalism was the republican state's *mission civilisatrice*, which followed France's defeat in the Franco-Prussian War of 1870–1871. This mission increasingly took on religious overtones. Indeed, the republican Left both extended and repudiated the universalism of political nationalism by appealing to the nation's sacred, civilizing mission. Universal political conceptions of the nation were imbedded in the state's cultural *mission civilisatrice*, but that mission also assumed religious and Catholic forms, which were expressed in the language used by both politicians and literary elites. They found sudden popular expression in the cult of Joan of Arc during the early Third Republic. Why was this so, and why at this particular moment in France's history? We have a clear sense from Kselman as to why the Catholic hierarchy chose to associate its religious mission with the nation's redemption in the aftermath of the Franco-Prussian War, but it is more difficult to understand why the republican Left used the chosenness theme during this period. Was it a way of glossing over deep class and regional differences, particularly during the period of the *Ralliement*? How was the nation understood and imagined by the men who became citizens of the Republic and, on the other hand, by the French women who were denied this status?

At important historical moments religious discourse and metaphors shaped right- and left-wing articulations of French national identity. In contrast to the situation in nations such as Ireland or Poland, however, religion never became a central, constituent element of French national identity. The defining features of that identity have continued to be contested sharply in France. This is largely due to the legacy of the French Revolution, which spawned conflicting conceptions of who and what constituted the nation. For the republican Left, in particular, the nation was located in the sovereign people and defined in opposition to the monarchy and its political ally, the Catholic church. The claims of religion, in the words of Rousseau, created "two homelands" and put the people of France "under contradictory obligations," thus preventing them from being "both churchmen and citizens." It is true, nonetheless, that the nation was invested with a new sacrality; the language used to express its claims was steeped in religious imagery and metaphor. That which gave the language of nationalism its power was a world that is still elusive for historians: the popular beliefs and identifications of the peoples who came to comprise the imagined community of republican France.

"God Our Old Ally":
The Chosen People Theme in Late Nineteenth- and Early Twentieth-Century German Nationalism

Hartmut Lehmann[*]

W ithin nineteenth- and early twentieth-century Germany, there are several variations of the chosen people theme as well as various levels of secularization of this theme. For some devout German Catholics, for example, the persecution they suffered during the *Kulturkampf* of the early 1870s was a sign that God had chosen the Church of Rome. For orthodox Lutherans, the notion of chosenness was perhaps somewhat less strong, although they believed in the exceptional status of the church Luther had founded as much as orthodox Calvinists believed in the special role of their church. In the

[*]Hartmut Lehmann is Director of the Max Planck Institute for Historical Studies in Göttingen and Adjunct Professor of History at the University of Göttingen.

same epoch, early socialists were convinced that this-worldly salvation could be achieved by rallying behind their party and through class struggle, while liberals trusted that human reason and enlightened perfectionism would result in everlasting progress. Both socialists and liberals were deeply involved in German nationalism. For socialists, the German socialist party had a special assignment in the quest for this-worldly liberation of the workers; for the liberals, the German nation was in the vanguard of human development in the sciences and arts.[1]

For no group within German society was the notion of chosenness more important, however, than for the evangelical wing of German Protestantism.[2] For this group, the notion of chosenness provided a distinct political orientation in the field of national politics.[3] It was this group that was most influenced and inspired by the biblical example of the Old Testament covenant. In contrast to the views offered by Koppel S. Pinson in 1934 and Gerhard Kaiser in 1961,[4] I would argue that the decisive years in which Pietism influenced German nationalism—and in which religious motives must be seen as a factor in the formation of German nationalism—were not the decades from

[1]There are very important connections between socialist and Protestant views. See, for example, Lucien Hölscher, *Weltgericht oder Revolution. Protestantische und sozialistische Zukunftsvorstellungen im Deutschen Kaiserreich* (Stuttgart: Klett-Cotta, 1989).

[2]Within German Protestantism the term "evangelical" is used synonymously with "pietistic," as opposed to groups falling within traditional Lutheran orthodoxy and those groups aligned with what may be called the movement of cultural liberalism.

[3]For the context and background of my arguments see Günther Brakelmann, *Protestantische Kriegstheologie im ersten Weltkrieg: Reinhold Seeberg als Theologe des deutschen Imperialismus* (Bielefeld: Luther-Verlag, 1974); Karl Hammer, *Deutsche Kriegstheologie 1870–1918* (2d ed.; Munich: Kosel-Verlag, 1974); Arlie J. Hoover, *The Gospel of Nationalism: German Patriotic Preaching from Napoleon to Versailles* (Stuttgart: Steiner, 1986); idem, *God, Germany, and Britain in the Great War: A Study in Clerical Nationalism* (New York: Praeger, 1989).

[4]Gerhard Kaiser, *Pietismus und Patriotismus im literarischen Deutschland* (2d ed.; Frankfurt a.M.: Athenäum, 1973); Koppel S. Pinson, *Pietism as a Factor in the Rise of German Nationalism* (New York: Columbia University Press, 1934).

1789 to 1815, but rather the epoch from 1848 to 1914 with a climax in 1870–1871.[5]

A pronouncement entitled "Days of Victory, August 4 and 5," published by the Berlin-based Protestant Press Agency on 5 August 1914, may serve as a point from which to start. Key arguments and concepts in this text help us detect the role of the chosen people theme in modern German nationalism.

As the author of this pronouncement explained, at the beginning of the war it was "the old God who now talks to his own people." He "talks to them by means of the most terrible seriousness of the situation, so that their hearts open and they will listen to his consoling words: Do not be afraid, I am with you." According to this pronouncement, "in the war of the nations God our old ally with a sacred storm sweeps out everything from Germany that is not holy, not noble, or that is ungodly and un-German." It was God's intention to free the minds of the German people so that "their hearts will be ready once more to make sacrifices as in 1813, and that the free German fist will be able to deal blows as in the battles of that holy war." This readiness to devote one's life to the cause of a Christian Germany was then referred to as "the mobilization of the hearts of our people as effected by God." As the author of the article was aware, many Germans had drifted away from the Christian faith and a Christian lifestyle in the decades before 1914. He was convinced, however, that "the German people have not been forgotten by their God," and this was why he believed that in the time of crisis "the Germans rediscovered their God."[6]

As I shall explain in this essay, evangelical Germans had attempted to strengthen Christianity in their fatherland in the decades before the First World War. In their view, as in the view of the pronouncement of the Protestant Press Agency in 1914, "two enemies" in particular

[5]Hartmut Lehmann, "Pietism and Nationalism: The Relationship of Protestant Revivalism and National Renewal in Nineteenth Century Germany," *CH* 51 (1982) 39–53; idem, "The Germans as a Chosen People: Old Testament Themes in German Nationalism," *German Studies Review* 14 (1991) 261–74.

[6]All quotations in this paragraph are in "Days of Victory, August 4 and 5," (Berlin: Protestant Press Agency, 1914).

threatened the German people: the rule of parliamentary democracy and the de-Christianization and secularization of German society.

The Protestant Press Agency rejoiced, however, that at the beginning of the war both dangers had been eliminated. On 4 August, "the infighting of German parties was banned from the German parliament" so that "there are no more parties but only a united people that is resolved to stand together through all times of hardship and danger." On 5 August, moreover, "on the unforgettable day of repentance and prayer which was instituted because of the war, it was demonstrated to the world" that God stood by his German people. As the author of this pronouncement concluded, "this has been effected neither through human strength, nor through a church institution, nor even through a pious association or a new teaching, but this is God's own achievement; this is the work of God's hand."[7]

Protestant pastors expressed the same arguments in dozens of sermons from the First World War era and in dozens of similar ones from the time of the Franco-Prussian War of 1870–1871. What follows is an attempt to explore some of the motifs that throw light on the social, political, and cultural background and then to explain what may be called the rise and fall of the chosen people theme in German nationalism.[8]

"To Make Sacrifices as in 1813": The Napoleonic Wars as a Turning Point in German History

When the one-hundredth anniversary of the victory of the German and Allied armies over Napoleon at Leipzig was celebrated in 1913, a huge monument, ninety-one meters high, was unveiled. Construction of this *Völkerschlachtdenkmal* had begun in 1898 and taken fifteen years. The belief that 1813 was a very special year in German history, however, had formed much earlier. In 1863, on the occasion of the fiftieth anniversary of the battle against Napoleon near Leipzig, German Protestants proclaimed in sermons, speeches, and pamphlets that 1813 was a sacred year for Germany because God had blessed

---

[7]Gerhard Besier, *Die protestantischen Kirchen Europas im Ersten Weltkrieg: Ein Quellen- und Arbeitsbuch* (Göttingen: Vandenhoeck & Ruprecht, 1983) 35–37

[8]Lehmann, "The Germans as a Chosen People," passim.

the Germans with victory over Napoleon. Before 1848, opinions on this issue had been divided. While the ruling conservatives in both Prussia and Austria were hesitant to praise what was believed to have been at least in part a popular uprising against Napoleon in 1813, the liberals spoke of the political legacy of 1813, which in their view had been betrayed by the Congress of Vienna and Metternich. During the French-German crisis of 1840, both conservatives and liberals expressed strong anti-French sentiments. In July 1840 Nikolaus Becker, born in 1809, composed the song "Der deutsche Rhein," which soon became very popular: "Sie sollen ihn nicht haben, den freien deutschen Rhein" ("They shall never take hold of the free German river Rhine").[9] Ernst Moritz Arndt, born in 1789 and himself a writer of popular songs in 1813, responded promptly to Becker's hymn with verses of his own. In November 1840, the twenty-one-year-old Max Schneckenburger wrote the song that soon became the most popular of all and was sung in 1863 as well as in 1913 and 1914: "Die Wacht am Rhein."[10] It was through the anti-French propaganda of 1840 that 1813 became fixed in many German minds as a turning point of German history.

In 1913, the celebrations of the 1813 centenary coincided with those of the twenty-fifth anniversary of the beginning of the reign of Emperor Wilhelm II. As seen from the height of power of Wilhelmine Germany, the battles of 1813 appear to have played a pivotal role in multiple contexts. First, there is the nineteenth-century story of German-French encounters. This story begins with the devastating Prussian defeat in 1806 and continues with the victory of 1813 and with what were considered renewed French threats of 1840. It culminates with the victory in the Franco-Prussian War of 1870–1871 and German unification under Prussian leadership. This story leads from humiliation to triumph, from repentance and redemption to salvation.

[9]Nikolaus Becker, "Der deutsche Rhein," in Ernst Volkmann, ed., *Um Einheit und Freiheit, 1815–1848* (Deutsche Literatur 19.3; Leipzig: Reclam, 1936) 141–44.
[10]Max Schneckenburger, "Die Wacht am Rhein," in Volkmann, *Um Einheit und Freiheit*, 141–44. See Hasko Zimmer, *Auf dem Altar des Vaterlandes: Religion und Patriotismus in der deutschen Kriegslyrik des 19. Jahrhunderts* (Frankfurt a.M.: Thesen-Verlag, 1971).

In the minds of many Germans of the Wilhelmine era, this story was closely connected with a second one, represented by a series of "negative" dates, namely, 1789, the year of the French Revolution, and the revolutions of 1830 and 1848, which had originated in France and threatened law and order in Germany. Conservative German Protestants, as well as many German Catholics, believed that the tradition from 1789 to 1848 demonstrated the disastrous effects of the French Enlightenment. Enlightenment had led, they argued, to human arrogance, egoism, and disobedience against the order set by God. In 1913, therefore, German conservatives evoked the memory of 1813 in order to preserve and reaffirm the order that God had granted the German people in 1870.

In a broader sense, historically conscious Germans in 1913 conceived of the events of 1813 as part of an ongoing special relationship between God and the German people. This story had begun when the Germans had become Christians. In their view, it continued through the Middle Ages when German emperors defended Christianity in the Holy Land against infidels from the East and even when German emperors defended Christianity against the pope in Rome. Emperor Henry IV, who had to concede defeat to Pope Gregory VII in 1073, was a tragic hero in this narrative, as was Emperor Frederick "Barbarossa," who lost his life on the way to liberate the Holy Land. German legend related that Barbarossa sat enshrined in the Thuringian mountain Kyffhäuser, whence he would return if Germany should ever be in desperate need.[11] German Protestants of the Wilhelmine era were convinced that in 1517 God had again demonstrated German chosenness in the elevation of a simple peasant's son (in some accounts a miner's son) to lead the world against papal oppression and superstition. God had entrusted Martin Luther with the translation of the Bible and the proclamation of the eternal truths contained in the Bible.[12] Luther had not succeeded in convincing all the Germans of

[11]It is quite remarkable that in 1941 Hitler's generals called the battle plan that they had developed to attack the Soviet Union the "Barbarossa Plan." For details see Arno J. Mayer, *Why Did The Heavens Not Darken? The "Final Solution" In History* (New York: Pantheon, 1988) 200–233.

[12]Hartmut Lehmann, "Martin Luther as a National Hero in the 19th Century," in J. C. Eade, ed., *Romantic Nationalism in Europe* (Canberra: Hu-

the superiority of Protestantism, this story continued, but the pious kings of Prussia had led the German people out of the misery of the Thirty Years War. In 1681, Louis XIV captured Strasbourg, one of the medieval jewels among German cities and a leading city of the Reformation. There were other bitter defeats, but Frederick the Great withstood all attacks by the Catholic French and Austrian anti-Prussian coalition, and here the story merged with the one that started with the Prussian defeat of 1806. After 1806, Napoleon, who had beaten the Prussian army in the battles of Jena and Auerstädt in that year, symbolized all those French, Roman Catholic, and enlightened values against which German Protestants directed their efforts of renewal and regeneration.

In 1914, the sentence "to make sacrifices as in 1813" contained two lessons or messages for conservative German Protestants. The first of these lessons was the belief that there were formative periods in the life of the German people in which decisions of far-reaching importance were taken. "To make sacrifices as in 1813" asked all Germans to sacrifice their lives for the cause of Germany's future salvation. The other message was what can be called the myth within the myth, namely, the belief that God had intervened in German history time and again, especially in 1813 and 1870. By making "sacrifices as in 1813" the Germans implored—if not provoked—God to intervene on their side once again. In 1914, for example, German soldiers carried a belt with the slogan "Gott mit uns" ("God with us"). This phrase has to be understood to mean that God could be expected to take the German side and that German soldiers would do everything necessary to secure God's intervening grace.

"The Mobilization of the Hearts of Our People": The Struggle for National, Social, and Religious Renewal

In a sermon preached on 5 August 1914, a pastor from Kiel explained to his congregation that whenever the Germans had been divided, and whenever Germans had stood against one another, foreign powers had oppressed them. "Waren wir aber einig," he contin-

---

manities Research Center, 1983) 181–201; Hartmut Lehmann, "Martin Luther als deutscher Nationalheld im 19. Jahrhundert," *Luther: Zeitschrift der Luther-Gesellschaft* 55 (1984) 53–65.

ued, "dann war Gott immer mit uns" ("But when we were united, God was always with us").[13] Within the German context, several steps in the development of this notion need to be distinguished. In the decades before 1848, pious German Protestants hoped for the revival of small Christian congregational group meetings in addition to official church services and for the awakening, or reawakening, of God's loyal children in Germany. Revived Christian belief and reawakened Christian loyalty were perceived primarily as matters of individual piety, not as matters of the church or Christian society at large. Of course, the pious were expected to make sacrifices for foreign missions, to be active in promoting the printing and distribution of Bibles, and to help the poor as well as orphans and the handicapped. Besides strict obedience to the laws of the political powers instituted by God, however, not much was expected from them in the political arena. Some pietists emigrated shortly after 1815, and others emigrated in the 1830s and early 1840s. As I mentioned above, they generally disliked the teachings of the Enlightenment, which they associated with French influence and culture.

During the 1848 revolution, Johann Hinrich Wichern of Hamburg developed the new concept of *Innere Mission* ("domestic mission").[14] This concept possessed three essential components combined in one strategic plan: religious renewal, national unification, and social regeneration. Wichern's master plan explained that none of these aims could be achieved if pursued by itself and that the one and only way of solving these problems was to treat them in relation to each other. National unification of Germany would and should be accompanied by the return of the Germans to the Christian faith, and both objectives would and should in turn be accompanied by a succcessful struggle for social justice. By mastering these aims, Wichern stressed, Germans would be spared the sad experience of another revolution.

Since the national question could not be solved (or at least so it seemed in 1848–1849 and in the 1850s), Wichern and his fellow

---

[13]Cited in Hammer, *Deutsche Kriegstheologie*, 215.

[14]Johann Hinrich Wichern, *Die innere Mission der deutschen evanglischen Kirche* (1848; new ed. by Martin Gerhardt; Hamburg: Agentur des Rauhen Hauses, 1948).

members on the board of the executive committee of *Innere Mission* worked hard to improve social relations. They also attempted to bring the biblical message to some of those who had drifted away from Christian faith and Christian congregations. It is hard to measure the success they may have had. They certainly did receive a fair amount of support from conservative Protestant circles. In the 1850s, Sixt Karl Kapff of the Württemberg Lutheran Church openly sided with those who hoped that the king of Prussia would unite the German states; in doing so, he risked alienating himself from the king of his native Württemberg.[15] In the 1860s, Friedrich von Bodelschwingh started a new branch of the domestic mission at Bethel, and many others also tried to give life and meaning to Wichern's program of inner renewal.

When the German army defeated the French in 1870 and the Prussian leadership used the occasion to bring about German unification, Wichern, Kapff, Bodelschwingh, and their friends were overwhelmed with joy. Since they had labored hard in the area of domestic mission for many years, they did not expect that the execution of Wichern's master plan would be triggered by the solution of the national question. At the same time, they could not but understand national unification as a gift from God who thus legitimized the endeavors they had pursued since 1848. They no longer believed that God was using the French to punish the sinful Germans or a revolution to demonstrate to the Germans the sad state of their spiritual condition; rather, God had now used the Germans to humiliate the French and given victory and triumph to his Germans.

In 1870–1871, Bodelschwingh recognized more than anyone else the need for pious Germans—and indeed for all Germans—to live up to God's expectations and to prove worthy of the blessings that they had received. It was necessary, he argued, to complement national unification with religious revival and social regeneration. Otherwise the Germans would not be able to retain God's favor and the blessings God had bestowed upon them. This explains why Bodelschwingh made the suggestion to institute the day of victory over Napoleon III

[15]Hartmut Lehmann, *Pietismus und weltliche Ordnung in Württemberg vom 17. bis zum 20. Jahrhundert* (Stuttgart: Kohlhammer, 1969) 226–34.

at Sedan on 2 September as a national day of repentance and thanks-giving.[16] As Bodelschwingh was soon to discover, however, his idea was corrupted within only a few years. *Sedantag* became a popular holiday, a day of patriotic speeches and the planting of oaks all over Germany, but also a day of much drinking and boasting; thus, in Bodelschwingh's eyes, it became a day of shame. By the late 1870s, he was completely disillusioned and feared God's punishment. In the mid-1890s he tried to reform *Sedantag* by organizing a union of Christian veterans. Again he failed, as the new veterans organization founded in 1900, the *Kyffhäuserbund* ("Kyffhäuser Veterans Alliance"), was not able to challenge the example set by the *Deutsche Kriegerbund* ("German War Veterans League"), founded in 1873, which dominated all *Sedantag* celebrations.

Although the initiation of a national holiday with religious impli-cations on *Sedantag* did not produce the results Friedrich von Bodelschwingh had desired, *Sedantag* indicated that pious German Protestants were committed to occupying public time and public space. Just as *Sedantag* was intended to be a yearly reminder of God's bless-ings, the German people were also involved in setting up local re-minders that were intended to mark the German fatherland as sacred soil. Starting in the 1870s, in all German towns and in many German villages, memorials were dedicated to German soldiers who had lost their lives in the Franco-Prussian War. Some of the larger of these *Kriegerdenkmäler* recounted all the battles; all of them were supposed to convey the belief that those whose names were listed had given their lives for a holy national cause.[17] Furthermore, in special loca-tions certain "icons" were set up to mark special sacred spaces. The

---

[16]Hartmut Lehmann, "Friedrich von Bodelschwingh und das Sedanfest," *Historische Zeitschrift* 202 (1966) 542–73. In his *Der Militarismus der "Kleinen Leute": Die Kriegervereine im Deutschen Kaiserreich 1871–1914* (Munich: Oldenbourg, 1990), Thomas Rohkrämer forgets to mention Bodelschwingh's most significant role.

[17]In the 1920s, in most German cities and villages, these *Kriegerdenkmäler* were expanded so that they also included a commemoration of the losses of World War I. It is only after World War II that new memorials were created that conveyed a new sense of mourning and not the glorification of death for the fatherland.

Völkerschlachtdenkmal near Leipzig, the memorial commemorating the victory over Napoleon in 1813, is one example; the *Kaiser-Wilhelm-Denkmal* erected on the Kyffhäuser mountain in 1890–1896 (with a monumental heroic statue of a sitting Barbarossa waiting for his return) is another example, as are the *Kaiser-Wilhelm-Denkmal* at the *Deutsche Eck* in Koblenz, built between 1894 and 1897, and the *Kaiser-Wilhelm-Denkmal* set up in the city of Halle between 1898 and 1901.[18]

It is interesting to note that all of these monuments were designed by Bruno Schmitz, whose work is considered by art historians to be an embodiment of Wilhelmine architecture.[19] In addition, many smaller monuments were created in the same epoch not only devoted to Kaiser Wilhelm but also elevating *Germania* and commemorating Otto von Bismarck as a national hero. As a result, between 1890 and 1914 public spaces in the German Reich were filled with "icons" signaling the outstanding importance of the victories of 1870–1871. They also reminded the next generation of Germans of the heroes who had led the Germans to victory: the patriarch-monarch Wilhelm, the redeemer and savior Bismark, and the spirit of Germanness, *Germania*. In the minds of many Germans, these monuments may have appeared as a national personification of Father, Son, and Holy Ghost.

Perhaps the most ambitious plan to give expression to the belief that the Germans were the people of a new covenant was developed in the 1890s by circles close to Emperor Wilhelm II. They planned to build no less than a dozen churches at strategic locations in the city

[18]George L. Mosse, *The Nationalization of the Masses: Political Symbolism and Mass Movements in Germany from the Napoleonic Wars through the Third Reich* (New York: Meridan, 1975) 42–72; Thomas Nipperdey, "Nationalidee und Nationaldenkmal in Deutschland im 19. Jahrhundert," *HZ* 206 (1968) 529–85; reprinted in idem, *Gesellschaft, Kultur, Theorie: Gesammelte Aufsätze zur neueren Geschichte* (Göttingen: Vandenhoeck & Ruprecht, 1976) 133–76.

[19]Siegmar Holsten, *Allegorische Darstellungen des Krieges 1870–1918: Ikonologische und ideologiekritische Studien* (Munich: Prestel, 1976) 25–33; Julius Posener, *Berlin auf dem Weg zu einer neuen Architektur: Das Zeitalter Wilhelms II* (Munich: Prestel, 1976) 81–105; Wulf Wülfing, Karin Bruns, and Rolf Parr, *Historische Mythologie der Deutschen 1798–1918* (Munich: Fink, 1991) on Bismarck, see 154–209.

of Berlin, thus intending to demonstrate that the capital of the German nation was the foremost Christian city of the world. The first and best-known of these churches was the *Kaiser-Wilhelm-Gedächtniskirche* ("Emperor Wilhelm I Memorial Church"). Wilhelm II's trip to the Holy Land in 1898 was another way of demonstrating that the Hohenzollern were the foremost Christian dynasty and that the land they ruled, the German Empire, was the foremost Christian nation of the world.

Friedrich von Bodelschwingh did not like such demonstrations of Christian-German power. Since the 1890s he had labored to develop an aid program for rural homeless people (*Wanderarme*). In this way, he continued to show his commitment to the task of re-Christianizing the German people. Although he died in 1910, had he lived in 1914 he too would probably have hoped for a "mobilization of the hearts of our people." He too would have believed that through the demanding means of war God had given his Germans another chance to return to Christian values and a Christian way of life. He also would have recalled Wichern's plan of national unity, religious renewal, and social regeneration.

More than any other group within German society, pious German Protestants supported the war effort of 1914. In 1917, many of them rejoiced. Now, they thought, God could no longer deny victory. Hindenburg, as leader of the German army, was considered in pious German Protestant circles an active man of prayer. Walter Michaelis, the *Reichskanzler* who succeeded Bethmann-Hollweg in 1917, had a pietistic background, and his brother Wilhelm Michaelis was the leader of the *Gnadauer Gemeinschaftsverband* (the alliance of evangelical organizations formed at Gnadau in 1888), the most influential fundamentalist pressure group. Finally, the four-hundredth anniversary of Luther's courageous act of nailing the theses to the church door in Wittenberg, observed on 31 October 1917, seemed to provide an excellent opportunity to redirect and lift the German people's spirits. When the war ended in defeat a year later, German Protestants were shaken more than any other group. Why had their prayers not been answered? Why had God not given credit to their efforts?

During the First World War, my grandfather, Heinrich Fausel— born in 1864, the same year as Max Weber—was the pious headmaster of a middle school in southern Germany. He was a follower of the Christian Socialist reformer Friedrich Naumann. On 1 August 1914, he started to note political events, using the section of the family Bible where he normally noted the births of children, the deaths of family members, and other important family matters. That he should consider political events as important as family matters is remarkable in itself. It is even more remarkable to see what he considered so important that it should be incorporated into the Bible. His remarks may be typical of the way pious German Protestants understood the First World War.

On the first of August 1914, he noted,

> outbreak of the terrible world war / 1915: Continuation of the murderous struggle / 1916: The same / January 1, 1917: Third New Year in wartime. Serious but not without hope / January 1, 1918: Fourth new year in wartime. No end yet, but hope for peace / August 1, 1918: Beginning of fifth year of war. Terribly serious, but we do not despair. God is our protector / November 9, 1918: Outbreak of the mischief causing German revolution. Sudden end of emperor and empire. Rule of most wicked socialism. Deepest upset of people and fatherland in their very foundations. Resignation of emperor and king [of Württemberg] / November 11, 1918: Conclusion of armistice with conditions that are regretfully nothing short of shameful and humiliating for Germany. Slow return of the German army / December 1918: Serious passage from the old year to the new. But our old God is still alive / June 28, 1919: Signing of the so-called treaty of Versailles, of the shameful treaty which, by blackmailing the Germans to admit their guilt for the outbreak of the war, has condemned the subjugated German fatherland to long years of slave labor for our triumphant enemies seething with hatred. Are they still Christians?[20]

For those who, like my grandfather, had grown up believing that the Germans were a chosen people, it was hard to accept and to admit that many may be chosen.

[20]This implies that in his view, after formulating the clauses of the Versailles treaty, the Entente powers no longer had any right to call themselves Christians.

"The Germans Rediscovered Their God": The Coalition of God's Children in Late Nineteenth- and Early Twentieth-Century Germany

There is no comprehensive study of the social composition of those nineteenth- and early twentieth-century Germans who considered themselves not liberals, but loyal, fervent children of God. Nor are there local or regional studies on this topic or studies about certain time periods. Despite this quite unsatisfactory state of research, some observations on the background and the professions of the members of this group are possible. They came from different professions and different social groups. This is why I label their common efforts in building God's kingdom in Germany those of a coalition.

In the period from 1815 until 1848, it seems that groups of German Protestants who can be called "fundamentalist" in lifestyle and thinking could be found mainly among the middle and lower middle strata of society. Their strongholds were small towns and villages in the countryside. Before 1848, Germany suffered from a lack of industrialization and the impoverishment of those who did not find well-paying jobs. In these hard years, when thousands upon thousands decided to emigrate, dozens of pastors in small towns and villages preached of God's everlasting grace and salvation for those who were ready to follow their lead. In pietistic circles and conventicles, primary school teachers (*Volksschullehrer*—who had little training at that time) assembled with artisans, merchants, and local office holders along with their family members and servants, if they had any. In Prussia, pietists could also be found among some of the noble families. For the most part, revivals and the awareness of the revival of others were local and at best regional.

One of the great achievements of Johann Hinrich Wichern's *Centralausschuss für Innere Mission* ("Central Committee for Domestic Missions") was its creation of a national organization of the pious and a national network of communication. Although not all local conventicles joined Wichern's *Centralausschuss* as members, Wichern's activities were supported by people from all parts of Germany. In the 1850s and 1860s, several groups in particular were active in the field of *Innere Mission*: the directors of institutions and hostels serving orphans, the handicapped, and other poor people (*Rettungsanstalten*), as well as some members of the higher state bureaucracy, notably some officials serving in Prussian ministries. In this period of economic transition, at what W. W. Rostow calls the take-off period of the industrial revolution in Germany, these groups believed that *Innere Mission* was the most effective way of solving what was now called "the social question" (*die soziale Frage*). For these groups, the events of 1870–1871 appeared as most important steps in the right direction. They hoped that under Prussian leadership and in a united Germany they would be able to stem the rising tide of secularization and curb the activities of the socialist party.

In 1878, a socialist attempted to assassinate Emperor Wilhelm I. For many pious German Protestants this was a clear sign that social and moral conditions had not improved since Germany had been united. It was quite to the contrary, they thought: conditions had deteriorated. They applauded Bismarck's *Sozialistengesetz* ("Law against Socialist Activities"), which made activities of the socialist party illegal. In the late 1870s and early 1880s, moreover, members of a younger generation of pietists were looking for new ways of gaining influence beyond what the *Innere Mission* was able to achieve.

From 22 to 24 May 1888, one hundred and forty-two people assembled at the Moravian settlement Gnadau for the first of a series of *Gnadauer Pfingstkonferenzen* (Pentecost conferences of Evangelical organizations to be held at Gnadau). After years of preparation, the sixty-eight theologians and seventy-four lay persons who met at Gnadau were eager to explore new modes of Christian activity. In particular, they hoped to strengthen voluntary elements such as the role of conventicles and evangelization campaigns. Furthermore, they wanted to give one another spiritual support and new hope in their work for the kingdom of God in their time.[21] All of those assembled at Gnadau in 1888 agreed that Germany should play a more prominent role in

[21]Jörg Ohlemacher, *Das Reich Gottes in Deutschland bauen: Ein Beitrag zur Vorgeschichte und Theologie der deutschen Gemeinschaftsbewegung* (Göttingen: Vandenhoeck & Ruprecht, 1986); idem, "Die Anfänge der Gemeinschaftsbewegung," *Pietismus und Neuzeit* 15 (1989) 59–83; Hartmut Lehmann, "Neupietismus und Säkularisierung: Beobachtungen zum sozialen Umfeld und politischen Hintergrund von Erweckungsbewegung und Gemeinschaftsbewegung," *Pietismus und Neuzeit* 15 (1989) 40–58.

salvation history. They considered themselves to be *entschiedene Christen*—professed, reborn Christians. It is in this capacity that they were ready to give a new meaning to the German quest to be God's chosen.

Among those in attendance, many were involved in *Rettungsanstalten* as well as other activities or organizations of the *Innere Mission*. This was true, for example, of Baron Jasper von Oertzen, owner of an estate and chairman of the board of *Innere Mission* in Schleswig-Holstein. These disciples of Wichern were joined by people like Elias Schrenk of Marburg, the first German missionary to make a career as a revivalist preacher independent of a state church; Eduard Graf Pückler, a Berlin lawyer in the service of the Prussian state; Theodor Christlieb, professor of theology at the University of Bonn; Theodor Jellinghaus, former missionary to India and in 1888 head of a school for biblical studies in Berlin; Jacob Gustav Siebel, the owner of a factory east of Bonn; Christian Dietrich, headmaster of a primary school in Württemberg and chairman of the society of Württemberg pietists; and Friedrich Fabri, a director of the missionary society in Wuppertal. As these names indicate, the *Gnadauer Gemeinschaftsbewegung* (the evangelical movement initiated at Gnadau in 1888), which was the center for the reawakening of German pietism in the late nineteenth century (*Neupietismus*), consisted of a coalition of people from different regions and different professions.

On the morning of 23 May 1888, Pastor Ernst J. Dammann of Essen led the service for those in attendence at Gnadau. He used the occasion to elaborate on the theme of the conference, explaining that

> our congregations have to be assembled for prayer meetings and Bible lessons. . . . There is so much to do. Time is running out. Many souls feel that Jesus is on his way. We do not know the time or the hour. But we should wake up and be prepared, impelled by the love of Christ and filled with the Holy Spirit to welcome the bridegroom.[22]

---

[22]Ohlemacher, "Die Anfänge der Gemeinschaftsbewegung," 65.

Dammann's sermon indicates what may be called the "halfway" position of *Neupietismus* in Germany. On the one hand, these reborn Protestants stressed eschatology more than their pietistic forerunners had. They were convinced of the coming of Christ in the near future and of the need for extra work in order to build the kingdom of God in Germany. They were distressed to see the progress of secularization in general and socialism in particular, and they devoted their lives to re-Christianizing the Germans. On the other hand, they did not leave the state church, although they were well aware that state churches had failed. They also remained loyal citizens of the state, although they knew only too well that the state had failed to protect Christian values. In a curious way, therefore, they were outsiders and insiders at the same time. They were outsiders to Wilhelmine German society insofar as they were devout Christians in a time of progressing secularization, but they remained insiders in that they did not establish organizations independent of the state churches. What they wanted was to supplement church activities. Moreover, whenever possible, they used official contacts, which meant that they remained close to those in power.

In a recent study, Martin Riesebrodt has analyzed the social-moral milieu of fundamentalism in the United States. Leaders of the fundamentalist movement sharply criticized public morals; they deplored foreign influence; and, like conspirators, they were above all convinced that they were the ones to whom God had entrusted his work. According to Riesebrodt, fundamentalism prospered in the rapidly growing cities. On the basis of the separation of state and church, and making full use of the free exercise clause in the First Amendment, the leaders of fundamentalism vigorously resisted the effects of industrialization and urbanization; in this sense it was the very social-moral milieu of industrialized, urbanized America that energized fundamentalism and helped produce its influence.[23] By contrast, German *Neupietismus* and the *Gnadauer Gemeinschaftsbewegung* avoided any

[23]Martin Riesebrodt, *Fundamentalismus als patriarchalische Protestbewegung: Amerikanische Protestanten (1910–28) und iranische Schiiten (1961–79) im Vergleich* (Tübingen: Mohr/Siebeck, 1990) 75–80.

wholehearted entry into the social-moral milieu of German cities. While they deplored the social and moral effects of industrialization and urbanization, only part of their activities was city-based. It was out-side of the cities that they best expressed and applied their conviction that things had taken a negative turn in cities like Berlin. In the 1880s, Adolf Stoecker had initiated his *Stadtmission* in Berlin. He had never, however, been able to challenge the activities of the So-cialist Party, which had not ceased to operate after it had been out-lawed in 1878. The same was true for other German cities such as Hamburg or Stuttgart. By the turn of the century in the German cities, groups such as the Adventists, the Methodists, the Baptists, the Sal-vation Army, and also the Mormons were more active and more suc-cessful in winning new members than German *Neupietismus*. In 1905, moreover, the *Gnadauer Gemeinschaftsbewegung* faced a challenge from within. This challenge took the form of the *Pfingstbewegung*, a spiritual movement whose members were strongly influenced by re-cent revivals in Wales.

The sentence, "The Germans rediscovered their God," as proclaimed by the Protestant Press Agency in 1914 carried, it seems, a double message. There are many reports that church services were very well attended in late July and early August 1914. In times of crisis, one could argue, many Germans sought to rediscover something that had been lost long ago. This is only one aspect, however, and it describes what was a temporary, passing behavior typical of people in times of much insecurity. The other aspect is the impression that the *Gnadauer Gemeinschaftsbewegung* seems to have been quite successful at in-stilling in some of the leading political circles the belief that God had in fact chosen the Germans as his people. The *Deutsch-Christliche Studentenvereinigung* ("Union of German Christian Students") and the *Deutsche Komitee für evangelische Gemeinschaftspflege und Evangelis-ation* ("German Committee for Promoting Evangelical Communities and Evangelization"), both founded in the 1890s, and journals such as *Philadelphia*, along with many other activities of *Neupietismus*, gen-erated, it seems, the effect of a self-fulfilling prophecy: those who spread the message—and their friends—believed in the message. It is in this sense that the *Gnadauer Gemeinschafts-bewegung*, despite all setbacks, successfully created the belief that German Christians possessed a special mission.

"Two Enemies of the German People": The Continued Progress of Secularization and De-Christianization, 1870–1914

The role attributed to the "two enemies of the German people" in the proclamation of the Protestant Press Agency in the early days of the First World War—that is, the role attributed to parliamentary democracy, on the one hand, and to the effects of de-Christianization and secularization, on the other—helps to explain Protestant views of German politics at that time. Furthermore, in retrospect these "two enemies" appear as formidable forces that weakened the Protestant belief that God had chosen the Germans as his people.[24] Just as pious German Protestants abhorred the legacy of 1789 and detested the spirit of 1848, they refused to accept the principles of democratic government. That government should be based on the rights of the people, that individual citizens should have specific, unalienable rights, that there should be a division of powers as well as checks and balances: none of these essential elements of democratic procedure was fully accepted. The rule of law was the one element that German Protestants were able to combine with trust in the reign of the monarch as the authority installed by God. If the proclamation of 1914 praised as a victory the fact that the infighting of German parties had been overcome, this should be interpreted as praise of a victory over the drive for more democracy. The proclamation of the Protestant Press Agency of 1914, therefore, foretells in a revealing way that pious German Protestants would never accustom themselves to Weimar democracy, and it indicates why many of them readily approved of Adolf Hitler's seizure of power and the abolition of political parties in 1933.

The influence of the other "enemy" mentioned in the 1914 proclamation, the antichurch movement of the decades before 1914, can

[24]For background, see Thomas Nipperdey, *Deutsche Geschichte 1866–1918*, vol. 1: *Arbeitswelt und Bürgergeist* (Munich: Beck, 1990) 468–507; Lehmann, "Neupietismus und Säkularisierung," passim.

only be understood properly if we put it in the right historical context, which means that we have to point out the connections with other "enemies" of Christian faith and Christian churches, such as nationalism, socialism, and Darwinism. Since the 1890s there had been an organized movement in both the Reich and Austria-Hungary to convince people to leave the church. The motives of those working against the Christian churches were neither hatred of the clergy, nor necessarily disapproval of church services, nor necessarily disgust with Christian doctrine or articles of faith. Instead, the members of these groups were inspired by ideas derived from materialism (as the core belief of socialism), from chauvinism (as an extreme form of nationalism), and from racism (as a radical variety of Darwinism). In order to understand the impact of these three motives, it is necessary to distinguish their roots.

During and after the Franco-Prussian war, many German Protestants came to believe not only that God had granted them a victory over their archenemy, but also that by doing so God had significantly elevated them. In the years that followed, the notion of a new covenant between God and the German people was modified—from a theological perspective one may also say that it was corrupted—in two ways: it was filled with considerations of power politics, and it was closely linked to considerations rooted in Darwinism. After the 1880s, therefore, even among Protestants the belief in a new covenant gradually gave way to ideas of German uniqueness and German superiority based on power and race. In the same measure, as German power continued to expand in the center of Europe in the Wilhelmine period, the belief in the redemptive force of power politics developed a logic and a momentum of its own. By contrast, Darwinism took somewhat longer to take hold in the minds of Germans.

By 1914, however, substantial portions of the educated and well-to-do middle class, the *Bildungsbürgertum*, found belief in the superiority of Teutons convincing and easily compatible with politics based on power and military might. The idol of German *Bildungsbürgertum* was Bismarck. He was considered the hero who had excluded the Austrians from German affairs in 1866 and who had masterminded the victory over France in 1870–1871. He was stylized in many articles and books as the prototype of a strong-willed, power-oriented

Germanic politician. In order to analyze de-Christianization in Germany before 1914, we must interpret the shifting values and the changing convictions of German *Bildungsbürgertum* in this period and not look simply at a small pressure group of determined atheists who organized an antichurch movement.

In the process of de-Christianization, socialists played yet another role. On the one hand, socialist thought had incorporated much of Christian eschatology, although in a transformed, transmuted way.[25] Socialists believed in a coming realm of peace and justice; they trusted in the steady progress towards this-worldly salvation, moving forward in dialectical leaps through revolutions; they preached to their followers that they should participate in this struggle. Of course, there were very few Protestants who were aware of this congeniality, this *Wahlverwandtschaft*, and those who joined forces with socialists, like the Württemberg pietist Johann Christoph Blumhardt, were ostracized by their fellow Protestants. On the other hand, ever since socialist thought had been formulated and put in print by the young Karl Marx and groups had formed that accepted Marxist theories as their guiding principles, Protestant pastors fought vehemently against what they perceived as a new kind of atheism.

Thus, almost all Protestant plans to solve the "social question" were developed in order to defeat socialism, and the leaders of the socialist party retaliated with an equal measure of hostility. Since the revolution of 1848 there had never been any common ground between the two ideologies. While socialists gained influence step by step among German workers, the Protestant clergy remained closely connected to German *Bildungsbürgertum* and German *Obrigkeit* (the traditional secular authority, that is, the rule of monarchs only in part controlled by parliamentary bodies). As a result, in the decades before the Franco-Prussian war, Protestant pastors lost control over an ever-growing part of their flocks. No wonder they considered this war an excellent opportunity to launch a missionary campaign, hoping to win back to Christianity those who had estranged themselves from the congregations. This is also the reason why Protestants embraced war

[25]This is discussed by Hölscher in *Weltgericht oder Revolution*.

in 1914 as if they were about to begin a campaign for the re-Christianization of the German people.[26]

For pious German Protestants, the First World War was a "holy war." It seems that for many other Germans it was a kind of "secularized holy war," with nationalism and power having attained the importance of transcendent values. The stakes were especially high, however, for German Protestants who prayed and implored God for victory. The renewed quest for German exceptionalism carried the potential for a deep fall and bitter disappointment. This is exactly what happened in 1918. Once the German army had been defeated and the German leadership had signed an armistice, German Protestants were in a state of shock. Very few of them explained the new situation in a theological manner and blamed themselves and their leaders for causing defeat through having sinned. The majority of German Protestants were not ready to accept that God had punished the Germans because of their arrogance or other kinds of un-Christian behavior. Rather, the stab-in-the-back legend appealed to them; this postulated that the German army had not been defeated and had only been forced to sign an armistice because the socialists had caused disruption and revolution on the home front. Instead of pointing to their own mistakes, they used theories of conspiracy and treason as an explanation for German defeat. Starting in 1918–1919, therefore, many German Protestants began to dream of and prepare for revenge.

Even some of the Protestants who demanded repentance in 1918 were reluctant to distance themselves from the forces that had caused the defeat. On 29 November 1918, for example, the leading Protestant weekly explained that "no people had ever understood the biblical message as well as the German people, and no people had given expression to the biblical message as well as they had, including the Scandinavians whom they had influenced." The writer of this article

---

[26]This article cannot discuss in detail how well the Wilhelmine political system was suited to stop the progress of secularization and de-Christianization. Since the monarch was head of the state as well as of the state church, Protestant preachers were tempted to invoke the example of the kings of the Old Testament. One can also argue, however, that in an age of growing pluralism, this approach may have prevented those who wanted to re-Christianize German workers from achieving real success.

concluded that this "godly mission should be preserved through repentance."[27] German Protestants, it seems, considered themselves God's chosen people in times of victory, as in 1870–1871, just as they did in defeat, as in 1918–1919. Victory demanded gratitude. This had been Bodelschwingh's message when he proposed the inauguration of *Sedantag*. Defeat demanded repentance. This is what the Protestant weekly pointed out; because of the way the argument was stated, however, it almost seems as if the call for repentance was not genuine, but was used as a tactical move in a last-ditch effort to keep God on the German side.

Within the scope of this volume, there is no need to detail what followed these events. As we know, in 1933 the German quest for chosenness was renewed, with fatal consequences; another German defeat came in 1945, reinforced by a principle of unconditional surrender that allowed no renaissance of the stab-in-the-back legend. Late in 1945, all German Protestant church leaders signed the *Stuttgarter Schuldbekenntnis* ("Stuttgart Confession of Guilt"), an unequivocal and unconditional public confession of having sinned. This document has to be seen both as an end and as a new beginning. Those who signed the *Stuttgarter Schuldbekenntnis* put to rest the belief in a special relationship between God and the German people. After the Holocaust, even the most fervent Protestants had to concede that this notion had been an illusion. In 1945, therefore, the story that began in 1813 and that had come to a climax in the decades from 1870 until 1914 was brought to a conclusion. How German Protestants came to terms with the problem of de-Christianization after 1945 is yet another story, one that began in the 1950s with the *Wirtschaftswunder* and all the moral ambiguities that economic recovery implied.[28]

---

[27]*Allgemeine Evangelische Lutherische Kirchenzeitung* 48 (29 November 1918) 1040. I am grateful to Ulrich Gäbler for pointing out this passage to me.

[28]Jochen-Christoph Kaiser and Anselm Doering-Manteuffel, eds., *Christentum und politische Verantwortung: Kirchen im Nachkriegsdeutschland* (Stuttgart: Kohlhammer, 1990).

Response

*Conrad Cherry**

Hartmut Lehmann's analysis of the concept of chosenness in modern German nationalism impresses the student of American religion with numerous parallels that can be drawn between two nations on either side of the Atlantic. For every German example—the apotheosis of national heroes, the joining of biblical themes with the national experience, the role of the clergy in the articulation of national exceptionalism, the anxious efforts of a people to establish national unity in times of crisis, the squabbles over ownership of religious symbols and myths, the coalescing of sacred time and space in material culture—a counterpart can be produced in the American situation. The glaring instances of chauvinism, xenophobia, and racism, along with the delusions of national grandeur to which Lehmann alludes, evoke a definite nod of self-recognition on the part of the American.

Parallels between national perspectives can be pushed too far, to the neglect of the distinctions between national situations. The parallels do, however, point to a commonality of mythic framework among modern nations that have adopted the notion of chosenness, and there are thus advantages in interpreting as a national myth the story that Lehmann tells, a myth complete with its own motivating circumstances and narrative embellishments. Lehmann's essay documents a general mythic structure that has defined the goals and aspirations of modern nations. It also demonstrates that changes rung on mythic themes spring from specific, dramatically altered social conditions within a national experience. Lehmann's essay instructs us in our need to attend to both culture and society—to the value systems that constitute

*Conrad Cherry is Distinguished Professor of Religious Studies, Adjunct Professor of American Studies, and Director of the Center for the Study of Religion and American Culture at Indiana University-Purdue University at Indianapolis.

world views and to the transitions in the social order that induce changes in these world views.

It is perhaps obvious after so many years of the comparative study of "civil religions" that the motif of chosen people has not functioned as an abstract philosophical idea but has served, instead, as a socially and politically empowering interpretation of national history. To point to the obviously mythic character of the motif, however, is also to propose what may not be so obvious: myths have their own "logic." Persuasive myth, like effective propaganda and unlike convincing rational discourse, is governed by the power of broad, inspiring explanation rather than the principle of rational consistency. This point is tellingly illustrated throughout Lehmann's article. Pious Germans could take military defeat as an occasion for optimism or despair, and antisocialist clergy along with their socialist opponents could appropriate Christian eschatology for their own particular interpretations of the course of German history. The logic of an empowering myth is one that, rather than scrupulously avoiding contradiction, ranges across the experiences of a people, scoops up dominant images, and blends them into a compelling world view.

The mythological framework of the chosen people theme also makes us mindful of the kind of primary literature that the historian must take most seriously in the analysis of the theme. We are most likely to mine the mythic national world view from hortatory literature that is addressed to a wide segment of a populace. In these sources resides the blending of religious vision and national ideals devised for popular consumption, constructed for the purpose of calling citizens to action, and bent toward the justification of national causes. Lehmann properly looks to the popular literature of the pulpit, the platform, and the tract for his primary data.

To approach the theme of chosen people in terms of its mythic structure, however, is also to challenge too neat a division between the religious and the secular. My only reservation regarding Lehmann's interpretation of the story that he tells so well concerns his occasional dependence upon a general theory of secularization. It is one thing to observe the unhitching of the chosen people theme from its biblical moorings and its subsequent tethering to Darwinism and biological racism, to probe the alienation of German clergy and other Christians from the movement of democratic liberalism, or to demonstrate the theological liabilities entailed in the baptism of the idea of German uniqueness in the font of Christian doctrine—all of which Lehmann does convincingly. It is quite another matter to conclude that these occurrences denote a pattern of secularization. They more clearly point to declericalization, de-Protestantization, and perhaps even de-Christ-ianization. The power of religious/national myth endures, even if torn from its biblical and churchly contexts, and appeals to secularization underestimate this myth's continuing potency. The hold that the dog-mas of racism and progress have exerted on the minds of Western nations, including Germany, depends in no small part upon the reli-gious, mythic force of the dogmas. It stems, in other words, from their ability to create a sacred world view. The development of the theme of chosen people in both Germany and the United States be-tween 1880 and 1920 illustrates the protean character of the myth of religious nationalism. It has proven itself able to assume the identity of multiple biblical and nonbiblical images without loss of its mythic power. Moreover, judging by the appearance in the early 1990s of neo-Nazism among socially disenfranchised youth in the United States and Germany, the myth is still capable of showing its ugliest face.

The great strength of Lehmann's analysis of the chosen people theme in German nationalism resides in the careful attention he de-votes to the social sources of the changing intentions of the myth. His examination of transitions in the German social order as sources of changes in the national myth of exceptionalism avoids the ahistoricism that sometimes plagues comparative mythology in the "history of religions." Limiting the analysis of the chosen people theme to the mythological structure would yield little insight into the social appeal of the theme. It would also ignore the concrete social experiences of the German people that have prompted their appropriation of different versions of the myth. A strictly structural analysis, moreover, would move too quickly to parallels between the functions of the myth in the careers of modern nations, a parallelism uninformed by social history.

To be sure, there are some striking social parallels between Germany and the United States, and thus similar interpretations of the myth of chosenness have arisen in both countries. What Lehmann calls the "stab-in-the-back" legend invoked by German Protestants to explain defeat in the First World War bears a noticeable resemblance to the "Great Alibi" theory that some American Southerners adopted following the Civil War.[1] Both conjured up conspiracies to explain military and economic loss. The transformation of *Sedantag* from holy day to holiday finds its American counterpart in the mutations of Thanksgiving and the Fourth of July. The ambiguous mixture of repentance and pride in the rhetoric of German Protestants and the language of the American political jeremiad suggests similar social experiences that have bred guilt and self-righteousness simultaneously.

Still, the German story departs in significant ways from the American. Lehmann observes that late nineteenth- and early twentieth-century German Protestant leaders never accustomed themselves to the principles of democracy emerging in their nation and that they continued to adhere to the notion that monarchy was divinely ordained. With few exceptions, American clergy were their nation's most avid defenders of democratic rights and the severest critics of monarchy. The distinctive experiences of democratic revolutions, and the differing meaning attached to them, resulted in critical differences between American and German religious leaders as they assigned a divine meaning to their national histories. Furthermore, despite the privatization of American religiosity resulting from the principle of the separation of church and state, the absence of a state church in the United States quickly motivated American clergy of diverse denominations to define themselves as the moral guardians of their new social order. The slow process of redefining the "domestic mission" of pious Protestantism to include large social goals, so typical of the German clergy, characterized only a minority of the American clergy in the nineteenth century. The ordeals of losing or winning the Second World War also affected future interpretations of the myth of chosenness. Although American religious leaders insisted on the need for a victo-

---

[1]See Robert Penn Warren, *The Legacy of the Civil War: Meditations on the Centennial* (New York: Vintage, 1964) 54–59.

rious nation to stand under the judgment of a forgiving God,[2] such admonitions scarcely carried the same weight as the *Stuttgarter Schuldbekenntnis*, which Lehmann describes as "an unequivocal and unconditional public confession of having sinned."

Lehmann claims that 1945 marked the concluding chapter in the German Protestant belief that a special relationship obtains between God and the German people. Both the postwar story in Germany and the distinctive history of German Protestantism leading up to the war would suggest the accuracy of Lehmann's claim. He remarks further that postwar Germans had to come to terms with the problem of "de-Christianization." I find the language of "de-Christianization" a much more apt description of this final chapter than "secularization." This language, however, also intimates for me that the chapter could conceivably be reopened. It implies that if Christian and clerical proclivities toward the chosen people theme have waned in Germany and other nations, the religious impulse itself has not necessarily diminished. The myth of national chosenness is a deep, enduring legacy in the West. It requires only massive structural changes and national crises—decided traits of modern life—for its revivification, its appeal to a national citizenry, and its vainglorious attempt to reconcile national particularities with universal claims.

---

[2]See, example, Reinhold Niebuhr, "Justice for the Enemy," *Christianity and Society* 9 (1944) 6.

The Construction of
Afrikaner Chosenness

André du Toit[*]

During the closing decades of the nineteenth century, notions of chosenness and of mission, directly or indirectly derived from religious sources, began to figure in a variety of political and public discourses in the South African context. It was only much later, after the National Party had gained power in 1948 with the ideology and policy of apartheid, that the idea of the Afrikaners as a chosen people became quite pronounced and was also most vigorously contested. The roots of this particular fusion of religion and nationalism, however, can be traced to the turn of the century. It is significant that at that time such ideas of national and ethnic chosenness were by no means unique to emergent Afrikaner nationalism: in the context of the

[*]André du Toit is Professor of Political Studies at the University of Cape Town.

South African War, for example, religious interpretations of the imperial and British mission figured even more prominently.

I shall outline some historical and critical perspectives on the emergence of elements of an Afrikaner chosen people discourse between 1880 and 1920. I shall be as much concerned, however, to stress the complications, paradoxes, and tensions in the story as to construct a smooth narrative. If we find an infusion of religious notions into secular political discourse, then this is by no means merely a one-way process: the key notions of chosenness and mission were available in secularized versions, while this period also saw a marked increase in religiosity. In a time of rapid and radical social, economic, and political change, both religion and nationalism tended to be Janus-faced: "invented traditions" possessed a marked backward-looking aspect even when serving definite modernizing functions.[1] In short, chosen people expressions, when we do begin to find them, derived from a range of sources, both secular and nonsecular, so that the religious connotations and political manipulations in this nationalist discourse can hardly be disentangled.

Getting the Context Right: Empire and Mission

From the vantage point of the late twentieth century, it is understandable that a historical investigation of ideas of chosenness and mission in South Africa a hundred years earlier will tend to focus unduly on the rise of Afrikaner nationalism in that era. After all, it was Afrikaner nationalists who, in the 1940s and after, imposed the ideology of apartheid and sought to justify it in religious terms. To read the situation of the mid-twentieth century back into the earlier period is, however, anachronistic. It leads, in particular, to two sorts of error. First, a too narrow emphasis on specifically Afrikaner elements will almost inevitably fall prey to the extraordinary hold of what may be termed the Calvinist paradigm of Afrikaner history and politics. This Calvinist paradigm is the historical myth of a deeply

---

[1]See Eric Hobsbawm and Terence Ranger, eds., *The Invention of Tradition* (Cambridge: Cambridge University Press, 1984); Anthony Smith, "The Modern Janus," in Tom Nair, ed., *The Break-up of Britain: Crisis and Neonationalism* (London: NLB and Verso, 1981) 329–64.

rooted strain of Afrikaner notions of chosenness, supposedly derived from the seventeenth-century Calvinist founding fathers. The Calvinist paradigm has proved persuasive to popular and academic historians alike, as well as to many social scientists.[2] It is a myth, however, and recent scholarship, including my own work, has come to question much of the historical evidence and theoretical basis of the Calvinist paradigm, at least as it may be applicable before the modern period and the reception of neo-Calvinist ideas from abroad.[3] At the same time, alternative explanations have arisen for the rise of modern Afrikaner nationalism and its associated ideology of apartheid.[4]

Second, there were certainly powerful and pervasive discourses of chosenness and mission prevailing on the public domain of South Africa around the turn of the century, but these were primarily the ideologies of empire and of (Christian) mission in a colonial context. By comparison, the first stirrings of Afrikaner notions of ethnic chosenness were—viewed in the context of their own times—both peripheral and derivative. Thus we must briefly deal with both these errors to clear the ground and to get the context right.

To begin, I shall briefly recapitulate the controversy regarding the paradigm of Afrikaner "primitive Calvinism" and its critique. In outline,[5] the main propositions of the Calvinist paradigm of Afrikaner history are that, from their countries of origin, the Afrikaner founding fathers brought with them to the new settlement at the Cape the basic

[2]See the "Bibliographical Comment," in André du Toit, "Puritans in Africa? Afrikaner 'Calvinism' and Kuyperian Neo-Calvinism in Late Nineteenth Century South Africa," *Comparative Studies in Society and History* 27 (1985) 239–40.

[3]André du Toit, "No Chosen People: The Myth of the Calvinist Origins of Afrikaner Nationalism and Racial Ideology," *AHR* 88 (1983) 20–52; idem, "Captive to the Nationalist Paradigm: Prof. F. A. van Jaarsveld and the Historical Evidence for the Afrikaner's Ideas on his Calling and Mission," *South African Historical Journal* 16 (1984) 48–79.

[4]See, for example, Martin Legassick, "The Frontier Tradition in South African Historiography," in Shula Marks and Anthony Atmore, eds., *Economy and Society in Pre-Industrial South Africa* (London: Longman, 1980) 44–79; Dan O'Meara, *Volkskapitalisme: Class, Capital and Ideology in the Development of Afrikaner Nationalism* (Cambridge: Cambridge University Press, 1983).

[5]The following is based on du Toit, "No Chosen People."

tenets of seventeenth-century Calvinist thought, and that in the isolated frontier conditions of *trekboer* society this mode of thought became fixated and survived for generations in the form of "primitive Calvinism." This "primitive Calvinism" then emerged like Rip van Winkle in the early nineteenth century, providing much of the motivation for—as well as the self-understanding of—the central event in Afrikaner history, the Great Trek. Accordingly, it was thought that the Voortrekkers and the Republican Afrikaners conceived of themselves as a chosen and covenanted people, like Israel in the Old Testament. It was also believed that early Afrikaners in this way presumed a divine mandate to smite the heathen peoples and reduce them to their preordained position as perpetual hewers of wood and drawers of water. Supposedly all of this gave rise to, and was used to justify, the unequal and repressive racial orders characteristic of latter-day Afrikaner-dominated societies.

Very little of this purported historical explanation will stand up to rigorous critical scrutiny. The key historical propositions are supported neither by specific historical evidence nor by more general considerations. Critical investigations show that the contemporary evidence simply does not provide any clear and unambiguous support for the presence among early Afrikaners of a set of popular beliefs that may be recognized as "primitive Calvinism," or of any ideology of a chosen people with a national mission. Nothing of the kind appears in the contemporary accounts of travelers or other well-placed observers before the 1850s, nor are such views articulated at all by Afrikaners themselves before the last decades of the nineteenth century. The origins of the Calvinist paradigm can in fact be traced to the writings and intellectual framework of David Livingstone in the 1850s and to the specific configuration of his polemical concerns at the time rather than to any firsthand knowledge of early Afrikaner thinking. Livingstone's account profoundly influenced the subsequent nineteenth-century literature, which in turn provided much of the direct and indirect source material utilized in support of this myth in more recent South African historiography, in both the liberal and the Afrikaner nationalist traditions.

Thus the earliest stirrings of Afrikaner notions of chosenness must be situated in the closing decades of the nineteenth century and in the context of the prevailing discourses of chosenness and mission at that time. In the colonial condition of South Africa these were, above all, the ideologies of empire and of (Christian) mission. It is important to note that one of these prevailing discourses was distinctly secular (although with key categories of residual religious provenance), while the other was still closely linked with organized religion. Let us, however briefly, consider each in turn.

The end of the nineteenth century was marked worldwide by a variety of imperialist discourses, often informed by secular mutations of chosen people traditions. In the United States, for example, the year 1898 marked the crisis of "American Imperialism," with a resurgence of notions of Manifest Destiny rooted in a long-standing tradition of American redemptive and messianic mission.[6] The closing decades of the nineteenth century also saw the apogee of the British Empire, marked by confident expressions of imperial supremacy and mission. The expansionist drive of Victorian imperialism had been rooted, in Ronald Robinson and John Gallagher's words, in a pervasive world view "suffused with a vivid sense of superiority and self-righteousness, if with every good intention."[7] Typically, however, this imperial idea of a noble and special mission of Great Britain[8] no longer took the form of an overt chosen people discourse in any recognizable religious sense, although the heritage of England as God's elect champion, or the new Israel, which dated to the sixteenth cen-

[6]Charles L. Sanford, ed., *Manifest Destiny and the Imperialism Question* (New York: Wiley, 1974); Ernest Lee Tuveson, *Redeemer Nation: The Idea of America's Millennial Role* (Chicago: University of Chicago Press, 1968) chap. 5; Albert K. Weinberg, *Manifest Destiny* (Baltimore: Johns Hopkins University Press, 1935) chap. 10; Theodore P. Greene, ed., *American Imperialism in 1898* (Boston: Heath, 1955); Norman A. Graebner, ed., *Manifest Destiny* (Indianapolis: n.p., 1968); Edward M. Burns, *The American Idea of Mission: Concepts of National Purpose and Destiny* (New Brunswick, NJ: Rutgers University Press, 1957).

[7]Ronald Robinson and John Gallagher, *Africa and the Victorians: The Official Mind of Imperialism* (London: Macmillan, 1961) 2.

[8]C. C. Eldridge, *England's Mission: The Imperial Idea in the Age of Gladstone and Disraeli, 1868–1880* (London: Macmillan, 1973) 238–44; A. P. Thornton, *The Imperial Idea and its Enemies: A Study in British Power* (London: Macmillan and New York: St. Martin's Press, 1959) 38.

tury and John Foxe's *Book of Martyrs* remained somewhere in the background.[9] Instead, we find secularized notions of a "civilizing mission," paternalistic notions of trusteeship and the "white man's burden," and even elements of social Darwinism.[10] This imperialist ethos, pervading the work of Rudyard Kipling, Charles Kingsley, and John Buchan, was represented in the South African arena by such figures as Cecil Rhodes and Lord Milner.[11]

When the imperial idea was unexpectedly and unaccountably challenged at its zenith during the Boer War of 1899–1902, this challenge provoked unabashed popular assertions of jingoist supremacy both in metropolitan Britain and in colonial South Africa.[12] The dominant imperialist ethos provided the political and intellectual context and counterfoil for the emergent "colonial nationalisms" which self-consciously located their assertions of nationality and independence within a wider context of empire.[13] Local colonial traditions, including the emergent Afrikaner nationalist movement, had to define their own

[9]William Haller, *The Elect Nation. The Meaning and Significance of Foxe's Book of Martyrs* (New York: Harper & Row, 1963).

[10]L. H. Gann and Peter Duignan, *Burden of Empire: An Appraisal of Western Colonialism in Africa South of the Sahara* (New York: Praeger, 1967) chaps. 3–4; D. M. Schreuder, "The Cultural Factor in Victorian Imperialism: A Case Study of the British 'Civilising Mission,'" *Journal of Imperial and Commonwealth History* 4 (1976) 283–317; Gertrude Himmelfarb, *Victorian Minds* (London: Knopf, 1968) 314–22; A. P. Thornton, *Doctrines of Imperialism* (New York: Wiley, 1965) chap. 4.

[11]Richard Koebner and Helmut D. Schmidt, *Imperialism: The Story and Significance of a Political Word, 1840–1960* (Cambridge: Cambridge University Press, 1964) chaps. 7–8; Richard Faber, *The Vision and the Need: Late Victorian Imperialist Aims* (London: Faber, 1966); and Robin W. Winks, ed., *British Imperialism: Gold, God, Glory* (New York: Holt, Rinehart and Winston, 1963). For examples of "the rhetoric of imperialism," with extracts from W. E. H. Lecky, Benjamin Kidd, and Joseph Chamberlain, see esp. Ibid., 77–81.

[12]See Thornton, *The Imperial Idea*, chaps. 2–3; Eldridge, *England's Mission*, 251–55; J. A. Hobson, *The Psychology of Jingoism* (London: Richards, 1901) chap. 3.

[13]John Eddy and Deryck Schreuder, eds., *The Rise of Colonial Nationalism: Australia, New Zealand, Canada and South Africa First Assert Their Nationalities, 1880–1914* (Sydney/Boston: Allen & Unwin, 1988).

ideas, values, and aims very much within the ambit of this hegemonic imperialist discourse even (and perhaps especially) where they deliberately set themselves against it. The notions of national mission invoked by Afrikaner nationalists at this time thus need not necessarily have been the product of a specifically religious tradition; they could also indicate a transference of secularized categories of mission from the prevailing imperialist discourses.

Discourses involving notions of chosenness and mission that were linked more closely to organized religion were by no means absent in the colonial context of nineteenth-century South Africa, which had become a major field of missionary activity. The dual projects of empire and mission entered a new phase of even closer interaction in the context of the imperialist "scramble for Africa" following the Berlin Conference of 1884.[14] Missionary ideologies exhibited an uneasy and ambiguous alliance between the overriding religious aim of evangelization and the more general cultural tasks of spreading "civilization."[15] Apart from the sometimes overtly political interventions by missionaries in the colonial context, the functions of missionary ideologies were complex and involved a number of different processes in relation to the spread of imperialism.[16] Jean and John Comaroff have rightly stressed that mission work as such had subtle but pervasive cultural implications and was based on distinctive assumptions.[17] Inherent in the very project of evangelization and in its

[14]See John Philip, *Researches in South Africa* (London: Duncan, 1828) i–xvii; D. J. Bosch, "Afrika word lig," in F. Denkema, M. A. Kruger, and J. A. Van Rooy, eds., *Evangeliseer!* (Pretoria: Kerk, 1990) 17–20.

[15]Torben Christensen and William R. Hutchison, eds., *Missionary Ideologies in the Imperialist Era: 1880–1920* (Aarhus: Aros, 1982).

[16]Norman Etherington, "South African Missionary Ideologies 1880–1920: Retrospect and Prospect," in Christensen and Hutchison, *Missionary Ideologies*, 192. For more polemical and apologetic discussions of the missionary involvement in imperialism and colonization, see, for example, Noshipo Majeke, *The Role of the Missionaries in Conquest* (Johannesburg: Society of Young Africa, 1953); and the address that Monica Wilson gave at the opening of the S. A. Missionary Museum: "Missionaries: Conquerors or Servants of God?" (Lovedale: South Africa Missionary Museum, 1976).

[17]Jean Comaroff and John Comaroff, "Christianity and Colonialism in South Africa," *American Ethnologist* 1986 (13) 2, also 11–18; see idem, *Of Revela-*

implicit challenge to indigenous cultures and society were notions of a special divine calling. At the same time the biblical message also made available a new "charter for liberation: the message of the chosen suffering in exile, whose historical destiny was to regain their promised land."[18] These biblical notions of chosenness, together with more general ideas of (religious) calling, were internalized by the converted and in due course applied to the cultural and political aims of their societies. Mission had introduced a novel world view in the colonial context, but could not deliver the full social promise it entailed, leaving as legacy a new discourse of chosenness.

Early Afrikaners already belonged to a church, the Dutch Reformed church, and relations with missionaries were often strained. Some, like Dr. John Philip, director of the London Missionary Society, were vigorous critics of colonial dispossession and exploitation of the indigenous peoples. For its part the early Dutch Reformed church had only limited missionary activities of its own, and the very idea of missionary work met with considerable resistance from many of its members. During the second half of the nineteenth century, however, attitudes toward evangelization, including mission work, began to change, and the Dutch Reformed church itself mounted an increasingly systematic and vigorous missionary project both in South Africa and in Southern and Central Africa.[19] By the late 1880s, the "mission wing" of the Dutch Reformed church began to make a distinctive contribution to public discourse. In Cape Town, for instance, a number of locally trained Dutch Reformed church ministers including the Reverend C. F. J. Muller, published a newspaper, *De Volksbode*, with a definite mission-oriented perspective. They set out to challenge the prevailing colonialist rationales for conquest and expansion, opening up all sorts of questions about ethnic and cultural assumptions of

---

tion and Revolution (Chicago: University of Chicago Press, 1991). See also Arthur Schlesinger, "The Missionary Enterprise and Theories of Imperialism," in John K. Fairbank, ed., *The Missionary Enterprise in China and America* (Cambridge, MA: Harvard University Press, 1974) 360–65.

   [18]Comaroff and Comaroff, "Christianity and Colonialism," 16. See also Michael Walzer, *Exodus and Revolution* (New York: Basic Books, 1985).

   [19]Johannes du Plessis, *The Evangelisation of Pagan Africa* (Cape Town: Juta, 1929).

superiority. White supremacist notions, they warned, were in principle similar to claims of a British imperial mission, claims that could be turned against Afrikaners themselves.[20] While thus opposing colonialist assertions of white supremacy, *De Volksbode* attempted to articulate the "different principles" of Christian evangelization and mission as a basis for colonial race policies.[21] This attempt to link the religious notion of Christian mission with the communal position of Afrikaners ("I am the son of an Afrikaner boer. . . but yet I am first a Christian and then an Afrikaner")[22] was fraught with problems in the colonial context. It would acquire additional significance as the Dutch Reformed church moved toward becoming a *volkskerk* ("people's church") and as Afrikaner nationalism became a more potent force.

By the opening decades of the twentieth century, we find Cornelis Spoelstra, a Dutch Reformed church functionary with strong missionary connections, offering a historical interpretation of Afrikaner religious life since the Great Trek; its central theme was that of a special ethnic calling to evangelize Africa. The Trekkers, Spoelstra now maintained, had not been "emigrants" from the Colony (as they had designated themselves at the time) but had a divine mission; in fact, the Dutch-Afrikaans race had a "providential missionary task" to open up Africa for the gospel.[23] Spoelstra's views were by no means widely shared; this particular accent on an actual missionary task for the Afrikaner nation was probably limited to mission-oriented circles in the Dutch Reformed church. Still, it must be of some significance that a seminal text of the new Afrikaner nationalist consciousness, Tobie Muller's "Die Geloofsbelydenis van 'n Nasionalis" ("The Confession of Faith of a Nationalist"),[24] was written in 1913 by a Dutch Reformed church minister and, moreover, a son of the same Reverend C. F. J. Muller who had been one of the editors of *De Volksbode*.

[20]Letter from Kolonist, *De Volksbode* (Cape Town) 14 March 1889.

[21]Ibid., 21 March 1889.

[22]Ibid., 14 March 1889.

[23]Cornelis Spoelstra, *Het Kerkelijk en Godsdienstig Leven der Boeren na den Grooten Trek* (Kampen: Kok, 1915) 7–8.

[24]Tobie Muller, "Die Geloofsbelydenis van 'n Nasionalis," in B. B. Keet and Gordon Tomlinson, eds., *Tobie Muller: 'n Inspirasie vir Jong Suid-Afrika* (Cape Town: Nasionale Pers, 1925) 126–53.

Tobie Muller eschewed any explicitly religious notions of chosenness or mission for the Afrikaner people, but his strong emphasis on the moral basis and the idealist nature of Afrikaner national consciousness may well be seen as the secular equivalent of the missionary discourse prevailing in the Dutch Reformed church context from which he came. There is a vast difference between Tobie Muller's idealist Afrikaner nationalist discourse in 1913 and the aggressive Afrikaner nationalism that would some decades later be associated with the policy and ideology of apartheid; however, the origins of these later Afrikaner notions of chosenness may be located in the historical context of the turn of the century with respect to the discourses of (Christian) mission and empire that were paramount at that time.

Transplanting Neo-Calvinism in Colonial Conditions

The extent to which the prevailing discourses of empire and (Christian) mission provided the ideological context and counterfoil for emergent Afrikaner nationalism offers an example of a more general condition of intellectual life in colonial society. The social and intellectual history of colonial discourses cannot be studied solely in their own terms. Not only did colonial settlements transplant fragments of cultures and traditions rooted in the parent societies,[25] but also colonial traditions did not develop autonomously in some relatively self-contained social and political universe. Culturally and ideologically the imperial power and metropolitan center continued to be of primary significance to colonial developments, even to the local nationalist movements that challenged imperial control. The intellectual history of nationalism in the colonial context is characterized by the kind of combined and uneven development in which transplanted ideologies and intellectual vocabularies are often already available before the local social and cultural developments that could sustain them. Notions of chosenness derived from the discourses of empire and mission offer a case in point.

The peculiar nature of the colonial context affected the intellectual articulation and development of local religious and political traditions

---

[25]Louis Hartz, *The Founding of New Societies* (New York: Harcourt, Brace & World, 1964).

in a second and more specific way, namely, through the special role of "foreigners" as key cultural interlocutors and entrepreneurs. Typically for a colonial settlement (and contrary to their later nationalist historical self-conception), early Afrikaners had never constituted a total community, that is, a self-contained Afrikaner society that articulated autochthonous intellectual traditions through public debates of its internal affairs. As a segment of an evolving plural and colonial society, one that had long lacked a native intellectual class, early Afrikaner political thinking had often been articulated by relative outsiders.[26] Even in the Boer republics of the Transvaal and the Orange Free State, it was immigrants—especially from the Netherlands— who tended to function as ministers of religion, teachers, journalists, lawyers, and senior officials.[27]

These "Hollanders" and other recent immigrants often played a crucial role in articulating the Republican or Afrikaner cause or in fashioning the emergent religious and theological traditions of the local Afrikaner churches. Inevitably their contributions were filtered through political vocabularies and intellectual frameworks derived from their own European education and cultural background. More specifically, this phenomenon was linked, as the Dutch historian G. J. Schutte has carefully documented, to the upsurge of Dutch nationalism at the end of the nineteenth century.[28] This nationalism was a modern phenomenon, but it also had its own deep historical roots in Dutch versions of a chosen people civil religion that dated to the eighteenth century and earlier.[29] These themes of national election informed the

---

[26]André du Toit and Hermann Giliomee, *Afrikaner Political Thought: Analysis and Documents*, vol. 1: *1780–1850* (Berkeley: University of California Press, 1983) xxv.

[27]In the 1890s more than a third of all teachers in the South African Republic, more than fifteen percent of all officials, and many prominent ministers of religion were Hollanders (G. J. Schutte, *Nederland en de Afrikaners: Adhesie en Aversie* {Franeker: Wever, 1986] 50, 52, 181; see also idem, *De Hollanders in Krugers Republiek 1884–1899* [Pretoria: UNISA Communications C63, 1968]).

[28]Schutte, *Nederland en de Afrikaners*, chaps. 2, 7.

[29]Ibid., 200; see also Cornelis Huisman, *Neerlands Israel: Het Natiebesef der Traditioneel Gereformeerden in de Achtiende Eeuw* (Dordrecht: Van den Tol, 1983).

religious and political thinking of Isaac Da Costa, Guillaume Groen van Prinsterer, and Abraham Kuyper, who spearheaded the nineteenth-century revival of neo-Calvinism with its self-conception as the historical core of the Dutch nation. The new Dutch nationalism typically took the form of a kind of cultural imperialism, the ideal of a "Greater Netherlands" sphere of culture and influence in which the emergent Transvaal was destined to play a major part. The contributions of Dutch immigrants in the Republics to the articulation of the local Afrikaner cause fitted into these wider political and intellectual contexts. The Kuyperians among them explicitly set out to transfer to the South African context both the neo-Calvinist philosophy of "sovereignty in its own sphere," and a strategy of "strength through isolation" derived from Dutch confessional politics. In various ways, this contributed to the peculiar fusion of religion and nationalism that would come to characterize the so-called Christian Nationalism.

The earliest concerted attempts to graft the Kuyperian program onto a local nationalist movement had been made in the 1880s by the Reverend S. J. du Toit, the leading figure in the Cape Afrikaans language movement. Du Toit failed, however, in his attempts to get the newly founded Afrikaner Bond, the first Afrikaner political organization, to adopt his version of Kuyper's neo-Calvinist program of principles. The Cape Afrikaner Bond still preferred the more secular and pragmatic colonial nationalism espoused by Jan Hendrik Hofmeyr.[30] Following the Anglo-Boer War of 1899–1902, however, a distinctive subtradition of neo-Calvinism and Christian Nationalism did become entrenched, centered in the small university town of Potchefstroom in the Western Transvaal and the *Gereformeerde* or *Dopper* church, the smallest of the three Afrikaans churches. In this context S. J. du Toit's son, the theologian and poet Totius, had a seminal importance for the civil religion of the emergent Afrikaner nationalism.[31] The transplanted Kuyperian neo-Calvinism of the Potchefstroom school thus amounted to an invented tradition appro-

---

[30]For a fuller discussion, see André du Toit, "Puritans in Africa?" 230–32.
[31]Irving Hexham, *The Irony of Apartheid: The Struggle for National Independence of Afrikaner Calvinism against British Imperialism* (New York: Mellen, 1981); idem, "Dutch Calvinism and the Development of Afrikaner Nationalism," *African Affairs* 79 (1980) 195–208.

priated in local conditions, and so it contributed to the fusion of religion and nationalism that would become known as Christian Nationalism.

Transitional Processes: The Changing Roles of Religion and the Church

The colonial context did not remain unchanged. On the contrary, especially after 1880, the discovery of diamonds and gold launched colonial and rural South Africa into the modern, urban, and industrial age. We may distinguish at least four underlying processes that transformed South African society: (1) the rapid economic development brought by closer incorporation into the world economic system and the infusion of aggressive capitalist enterprise; (2) the social changes and dislocations, as well as the different labor practices and class relations, attendant on the onset of primary industrialization and rapid urbanization;[32] (3) the growth of civil society through the spread of a range of social institutions, organized education, news media, voluntary associations, and cultural organizations at local and regional levels; and (4) the basic processes of state formation, both prior to the Anglo-Boer War and leading up to Union.[33] For our purposes, the transitional processes bearing on the relation between religion and nationalism are of special relevance: the transformation of institutionalized religious life and the changing role of the Dutch Reformed churches, on the one hand, and the creation of the conditions for the rise of the Afrikaner nationalist movement, on the other hand. Of these, the latter has been the object of close study and analysis,[34] while the former topic has been relatively neglected.

[32]Stanley Trapido, "South Africa in a Comparative Study of Industrialization," *Journal of Development Studies* 7 (1971) 309–19.

[33]Shula Marks and Stanley Trapido, "Lord Milner and the South African State," in Philip Bonner, ed., *Working Papers in Southern African Studies* (3 vols.; Johannesburg: African Studies Institute, University of Witwatesrand, 1977–81) 2. 52–81.

[34]O'Meara, *Volkskapitalisme*; Hermann Giliomee, "The Beginnings of Afrikaner Nationalism, 1870–1915," *South African Historical Journal* 19 (1987) 115–42; Isabel Hofmeyr, "Building a Nation with Words: Afrikaans Language, Literature and 'Ethnic Identity,' 1902–1924," in Shula Marks and Stanley

It can be argued that the 1850s and 1860s constituted a major watershed in the history of the Dutch Reformed church, especially in the Cape Colony. This was directly related to more general social changes. The economic incorporation of the region into the modern world economy, the establishment of organized secondary education, the increasing effectiveness of central and local governments and the closing of the frontiers, the coming of the railways, and the increasing circulation of local and regional newspapers—all of these contributed to the growth of towns and a more "regular" civil society in the Colony. (In many ways the process was repeated in accelerated fashion during the 1880s and 1890s in the Free State and Transvaal.) The Dutch Reformed church itself played a direct part in these processes, with the establishment of new congregations often intimately linked to the founding of new towns and the spread of commercial enterprise.[35]

The process also meant the institutionalization and thereby transformation of religious life itself. The Dutch Reformed church experienced substantial institutional growth: the number of functioning congregations sharply increased, the local Dutch Reformed church synod became an increasingly influential institution in public life, a local theological seminary was established at Stellenbosch, and the first generations of Afrikaner ministers of religion began to take key positions in the Dutch Reformed church next to Dutch and Scotch churchmen. In this context, the great "liberalism struggle" that wracked the Dutch Reformed church during the 1860s, with conservative churchmen locked into battle with proponents of the liberal tendency in a number of different contexts, constituted nothing less than a battle for its soul. The outcome, although a defeat for the liberal tendency, should not be regarded simply as a victory for the conservative forces in the Dutch Reformed church; in effect a return to the premodern religious sensibilities was no longer possible. Instead, as I have argued elsewhere, the "conservatives" were also in their own way mod-

---

Trapido, eds., *The Politics of Race, Class and Nationalism in Twentieth Century South Africa* (London/New York: Longman, 1987) 95–123.

[35]Jean du Plessis, "Colonial Progress and Countryside Conservatism: An Essay on the Legacy of Van der Lingen of Paarl" (M.A. diss., Stellenbosch University, 1988).

ernizers and effectively contributed to the transformation of the earlier religious sensibility.

The great evangelical revivals starting from 1860 enabled the conservative modernizers—the Hofmeyrs, Neethlings, and Murrays, who gained control of the emergent institutional structure of the Cape Dutch Reformed church—to fashion the particular blend of pragmatic evangelical piety that would henceforth characterize the Dutch Reformed church tradition.[36] In the Transvaal the growing institutionalization of religious life took the form of a plurality of churches, with the Dutch Reformed church in competion with the *Gereformeerde* (*Dopper*) and *Hervormde* churches, each with its own synodical organization, theological seminaries, and church press. The surface rivalry mattered less, however, than the growth of a similarly institutionalized Afrikaner religiosity, linked as this was to a steady increase in the density of commercialization and its attendant social changes. Robert Ross has argued persuasively that this significantly contributed to the conditions for the reception of Kuyperian neo-Calvinism by the turn of the century. Without the steady increase in the level of Afrikaner religiosity during the second half of the nineteenth century, "Christian nationalist ideology would not have gained the hold it did, and such nationalism as there might have been would have taken a very different form."[37]

To fill out this picture, another and parallel set of developments in the Dutch Reformed church tradition must be traced: the process through which the Dutch Reformed church increasingly developed into a *volkskerk* the social identity of which was intimately tied up

[36]André du Toit, "The Cape Afrikaners' Failed Liberal Moment 1850–1870," in Jeffrey Butler, Richard Elphick, and David Welsh, eds., *Democratic Liberalism in South Africa: Its History and Prospect* (Middletown: Wesleyan University Press, 1987) 35–63. On the impact of evangelical pietism as a formative factor on Afrikaner civil religion, see D. J. Bosch, "The Roots and Fruits of Afrikaner Civil Religion," in J. W. Hofmeyr and W. S. Vorster, eds., *New Faces of Africa: Essays in Honour of Ben Marais* (Pretoria: University of South Africa, 1984) 25–26.

[37]Robert Ross, "The Fundamentalisation of Afrikaner Calvinism," in Herman Diederiks and Chris Quispel, eds., *Onderscheid en Minderheid: Sociaal-historische Opstellen over Discriminatie en Vooroordeel aangeboden aan Professor Dik van Arkel* (Hilversum: Verloren, 1987) 209.

with the needs and concerns of the Afrikaner community. Historically, the Dutch Reformed church had been an established church, and even under the British administration, from the beginning of the nineteenth century Dutch Reformed church ministers continued to receive state stipends. Socially and politically, this tended to reinforce the cultural distance of Dutch- or Scotch-born and trained Dutch Reformed church ministers as state functionaries in relation to local congregations. Characteristically the leadership tended to align itself with the policies and interests of the colonial state rather than with the views and initiatives of local communities: the Dutch Reformed church opposed the Great Trek and vigorously resisted the Afrikaans language movement, for example. When the "Voluntary Principle," that is, the separation of church and state, was first proposed in the Cape Parliament by Saul Solomon in the 1850s, it was strongly resisted by the Dutch Reformed church hierarchy. The Dutch Reformed church continued to fight for almost two decades, but in retrospect the eventual defeat suffered in the 1870s can be seen as a crucial step in cutting the links with the colonial state and in tying local ministers of religion, who were henceforth directly dependent on voluntary contributions, much more closely to their congregations. In these changed circumstances, the Dutch Reformed church was now among the first to take up the plight of Afrikaner "poor whites" in the 1890s, while a series of political traumas, from the Jameson Raid of 1895 to the Anglo-Boer War of 1899–1902, forged ever closer links between the Dutch Reformed church and an emergent Afrikaner nationalism. The transition of the Dutch Reformed church into a *volkskerk* was most clearly consolidated in the course of a series of searching synodical and public debates defining the church's relation to the Afrikaner Rebellion of 1914.[38]

It is in this context of a Dutch Reformed church well on its way to becoming a *volkskerk* that the revival and institutionalization of the Covenant should be situated, and it should be located more particularly in the Orange Free State from the 1890s. The original Covenant

---

[38]C. F. A. Borchardt, "Die Afrikaanse Kerke en die Rebellie 1914–15," in J. H. Eybers and A. König, eds., *Teologie en Vernuwing* (Pretoria: UNISA, 1975) 85–116.

had been made by the military force under the Trekker leader Andries Pretorius on 16 December 1838, prior to the Battle of Blood River, which secured the Afrikaner presence in Natal when the Trek itself was threatened by the powerful Zulu forces under Dingane. The Covenant, taken as a special historical bond of the Afrikaner nation with God, would become one of the central institutions in the civil religion of modern Afrikaner nationalism, reaching its apogee in the 1930s.[39] The political, historical, and religious significance with which the celebration of the Day of the Covenant on the sixteenth of December came to be charged in this later context should not be confused, however, with its original meaning in the minds of the participants themselves. What constituted that meaning is in fact an elusive problem of historical reconstruction precisely because the Trekker Covenant did *not* occur in the context of a well-established tradition. The fact of the matter is that early Afrikaners knew neither the Puritan practices of regular days of fasting and of thanksgiving nor the New England institution of election days, both of which fused political occasions and public religious reflection. The liturgy of the Dutch Reformed church also did not include anything similar to the Wesleyan "Renewal of the Covenant" services.[40] Moreover, whatever the origins of the Trekker Covenant may have been,[41] it almost im-

---

[39]See, for example, F. A. van Jaarsveld, "A Historical Mirror of Blood River," in A. König and H. Keane, eds., *The Meaning of History* (Pretoria: University of South Africa, 1980) 8–59; Leonard Monteath Thompson, *The Political Mythology of Apartheid* (New Haven: Yale University Press, 1985) chap. 5.

[40]David Tripp, *The Renewal of the Covenant in the Wesleyan Tradition* (London: Epworth, 1969).

[41]Thompson, *The Political Mythology of Apartheid*, 156–65. It is possible that some clues to the contemporary meaning of the Trekker Covenant may be found in the significance attached to oaths and sworn allegiances by *trekboers* on the open frontier. There are indications that frontiersmen regarded the oaths sworn by *heemraden* and *veldkornets* on taking office to be of special significance, and on a number of occasions the significance of political enterprises was marked by some form of collective vow. Thus in 1795 the Graaf-Reinet rebels recorded their grievances against *landdrost* (magistrate) Maynier in the form of an elaborate *Tesaamenstemming* (petition), vowing to stand by each other to the last drop of blood (J. S. Marais, *Maynier and the First Boer*

mediately fell into disuse except for a few who commemorated it privately as a family affair.[42] Even Andries Pretorius, the Trekker leader who had proposed the Covenant in the first place, did not subsequently give any indication of attaching particular significance to it. In total contrast to the dominant significance it would gain in the modern period, the Trekker Covenant was thus an isolated and almost forgotten episode in prenationalist Afrikaner history.

The commemoration of the Covenant was first revived in 1864 by two Dutch ministers of the Dutch Reformed church in Natal, the Reverends Frans Lion Cachet and Pierre Dammes Huet. This seems to have been a local and passing episode and, although the Transvaal Volksraad in 1865 declared the sixteenth of December a public holiday and day of thanksgiving, it was only after the "renewal" of the Covenant at Paardekraal at the outset of the Transvaal War of Independence of 1881 that the Covenant reentered public discourse at a national level.[43] Following the war, a series of public meetings were held at Paardekraal in mid-December of each year to celebrate the restoration of Republican independence, which was thus implicitly linked with the commemoration of the Trekker vow. Invocations of a covenant figured prominently in the Paardekraal addresses by President Paul Kruger, although the specific historical meaning of these

---

Republic [Cape Town: Maskew Miller, 1944] 78–79). In 1815 the Slagtersnek rebels swore in a solemn oath to remain true to each other (see J. A. Heese, *Slagtersnek en sy Mense* [Cape Town: Tafelberg, 1973] 24; Thompson, *The Political Mythology of Apartheid*, 162–63). Furthermore, when Piet Retief was installed as "Governor" of the Trekkers in June 1837, he was required to take a number of elaborate oaths, while a number of resolutions setting out the allegiances of members of the Trekker community were also adopted (see P. S. de Jongh, *Die Lewe van Erasmus Smit*, [Cape Town: HAUM, 1977] 134–38). If these cases do in some respects provide precedents for collective vows, the *religious* connotation of the Trekker Covenant remains unique in early Afrikaner history, and its precise meaning within its historical context must remain largely a matter of speculation.

[42]Marius Swart, *Geloftedag* (Cape Town: HAUM, 1961) 10–35; D. W. Kruger, *Die Viering van Dingaansdag: 1838–1910* (Cape Town: Nationale Pers, n.d. [1910?]) 8–19; Thompson, *The Political Mythology of Apartheid*, 154–65.

[43]Van Jaarsveld, "A Historical Mirror of Blood River," 11.

invocations is a matter of interpretation and controversy.[44] Kruger was by no means an Afrikaner nationalist in the modern sense, and although he personally constituted a direct link with the Trekker past, the Paardekraal commemorations were not focused specifically on the Trekker Covenant of 1838. They were rather a continuation of the series of popular *volksbyeenkomste* ("national gatherings") which had done so much to forge a political identity among Transvaal Afrikaners during the events leading to the War of Independence in 1881. After 1883 the official Paardekraal commemorations were held only every five years (effectively only in 1886 and 1891) and lost much of their original political-religious Republican thrust.[45] Instead some local Afrikaner communities began to celebrate the sixteenth of December, with 1888 as the fiftieth anniversary of the vow and the Battle of Blood River. It was only in the 1890s, however, and then especially in the Orange Free State, that the celebration of the Trekker Covenant became a regular institution on the sixteenth of December, which was popularly known as *Dingaansdag* ("Dingane's day").[46]

By the 1890s the growth of a settled Afrikaner farming community with organized secondary education, functioning Dutch Reformed church congregations, and an active local press provided some of the institutions of civil society and the basis for a more active public life in the Free State. Among other manifestations, this took the form of a rapidly growing number of local "debating societies" as forums for intellectual and political discussion and social intercourse, especially for the younger generation.[47] In 1893 a militant young men's organization took the initiative in reviving the celebration of the Trekker Covenant on the sixteenth of December, and in 1894 this was instituted as a public holiday. Sermons on biblical texts by Dutch Re-

---

[44]T. Dunbar Moodie, *The Rise of Afrikanerdom: Power, Apartheid, and the Afrikaner Civil Religion* (Berkeley: University of California Press, 1975) chaps. 1–2; see du Toit, "Puritans in Africa?" 221–27.

[45]Daniel Wilhelmus Kruger, *Paul Kruger* (2 vols.; Johannesburg: Dagbreek, 1961–63) 1. 263–64.

[46]W. A. Stals, "Die gelofte: Die Instelling en Viering van Geloftedag," *Handhaaf* 9 (1971) 9–12.

[47]Bun Booyens, *"Ek Heb Geseg!": Die Verhaal van ons Jongeliede en Debatsverenigings* (Cape Town: Human & Rousseau, 1983) 61–63.

formed church ministers played a central part in the proceedings, and
sometimes the full text was reproduced in the press. Thus in 1895 the
Bloemfontein newspaper *De Express* published the full text of a
Dingaansdag sermon with Num 14:24 and the covenant with Caleb as
text: like Israel of old, the Trekkers had been called to a special
mission in Africa, the land of darkness, and what was needed was a
revival of true patriotism and trust in God.[48] The following year the
Reverend W. Robertson of Petrusburg took Ruth's plea, "Your people
are my people, and your God is my God" (Ruth 1:16b), as text for
a sermon linking the Trekker Covenant to the need for national feeling and unity.[49] We have here the beginnings of an institutionalized
linkage between religion and nationalism, focused on the renewal of
the Trekker Covenant on the sixteenth of December with Dutch Reformed church ministers providing a biblical discourse for emergent
Afrikaner nationalist concerns. In December 1895, Dutch Reformed
church ministers also took a prominent part in the ceremonial reburial
of the victims of the 1838 massacre by Dingane's Zulus in Weenen in
Natal. More generally, there was at this time increasing public interest in the memoirs of the surviving members of the Trekker military
force involved in the original Covenant.[50] This growing consolidation
of the links between the Dutch Reformed church and the Afrikaner
volk would be severely disrupted—but in other ways also reinforced—
by the trauma of the Anglo-Boer War.

The Impact of the War

The Anglo-Boer War of 1899–1902 profoundly affected both religious and political sensibilities. In the short term, the crisis and drama
of the war inflamed passions and heightened public rhetoric, even
taking on eschatological connotations. In the long term, the war prepared the ground for the rise of an Afrikaner nationalist movement
with a potent sense of political martyrdom and mission.

The war posed special problems and complications to the church.
With Christians involved on both sides of the war, churches could not

[48]A Minister of the Dutch Reformed Church in the Free State, *De Express*
(Bloemfontein) 27 December 1895.
[49]The Reverend W. Robertson, *De Express* (Bloemfontein) 18 December 1896.
[50]Thompson, *The Political Mythology of Apartheid*, 172–76.

readily take an unqualified partisan stand, while the Cape Dutch Reformed church, whose sympathies were strongly drawn to the Republican cause, had to operate in colonial territory ruled by imperial forces. During the course of the war, however, churches soon became increasingly polarized; the Dutch Reformed church and the Anglican Church, which prior to the war had maintained close and cordial relations that at one point had led almost to church unity, drifted irrevocably apart as each identified with one of the two parties in the war.[51] Thus in November 1899 the official mouthpiece of the Anglican Church could still counsel moderation with regard to the "terrible and internecine war."[52] After only a few months of conflict, however, the same *Cape Church Monthly* editorialized about a "holy war" in which "one of the judgements of God is upon us."[53] Similarly, *De Fakkel*, official organ of the Dutch Reformed church in the Free State, wrote of the war as a "war of faith" in which "God has fought on our side. . . . Our battlefields testify to the powerful miracles which God has wrought."[54] While the Cape Dutch Reformed church officially maintained some pretence of neutrality, in the Republics a number of ministers joined the commandos and participated actively in the fighting; some even described an intense religious commitment to the war as an act of faith.[55]

It is not possible here to go into the complex interactions of political and religious notions in the context of the Anglo-Boer conflict. Sermons in the Dutch Reformed churches provide an especially rich source for investigation, ranging from an intense pietistic spiritualizing of the traumas of battle[56] to ritualized affirmations that God had his divine purposes with the Afrikaner people. One minister stated

[51]See Bosch, "The Roots and Fruits of Afrikaner Civil Religion," 23.

[52]Pastoral letter of the Archbishop, *Cape Church Monthly and Parish Record*, November 1899, p. 119; see also Editorial, *Church News for South Africa*, November 1899, p. 9.

[53]Editorial, *Cape Church Monthly and Parish Record*, January 1900, p. 6.

[54]Editorial "Aan Ons Volk," *De Fakkel*, December 1899, pp. 126–28.

[55]See, for example, the report filed from "near Ladysmith," *De Fakkel*, December 1899, pp. 137–41.

[56]See, for example, the sermon "In War Time: Praying in Gethsemane," *De Kerkbode*, December 1899, pp. 805–7.

that "God led us into war; it is to chastise us, but He has His sacred goal. . . . He will not let us perish, but will confirm us through this baptism of fire. The Lord Himself planted us in South Africa and let us flourish. . . . [Like Israel] we are going through the Red Sea, but it will make us into a separate people."[57] Very suggestive material is also to be found in such sources as the war diary of the Afrikaans poet Jan F. E. Celliers. Celliers came from a secular and intellectual background in Pretoria, giving a different edge to his perceptive comments on the ways in which the experience of war deepened the merely formal adherence to religion as a social institution. Of considerable interest is the evidence of a tendency toward eschatological beliefs which Celliers recorded during the closing stages of the war,[58] a stage when President Paul Kruger himself tended towards an eschatological discourse in his official communiques to his officers and burghers.[59]

Of particular interest in this connection were the debates prior to the Peace Treaty of Vereeniging in 1902, when the political and military leaders of the Boer forces met to decide whether the British terms for surrender should be accepted. The thorough and searching discussions of these "bitter-enders" covered a wide range, including military, strategic, diplomatic, and political considerations, but throughout the debates a crucial set of arguments linked the issue of national survival with religious faith. Those who were determined to continue the war at all costs also insisted most strongly that the war had always been and must remain an act of faith in God. In the words of General Christiaan de Wet: "The war is a matter of faith. If I had not been able to do so in faith, I would never have taken up arms. Let us again renew our covenant with God. . . . The entire war is a matter of faith. I have to do with a fact only when I remove it."[60] As against this, others stressed the importance of coming to terms rationally with

[57]Pastoral letter "To our beloved Brethren, the Burghers on Commando," *De Fakkel*, February 1900.

[58]A. G. Oberholster, ed., *Oorlogsdagboek van Jan F. E. Celliers, 1899– 1902* (Pretoria: Raad vir Geesteswetenskaplike Navorsing, 1978).

[59]"De Staatspresident aan alle Officieren en Burgers," Preller Collection A 787, vol. 158, pp. 313–14, State Archives, Pretoria.

[60]J. D. Kestell and D. E. van der Velden, *The Peace Negotiations between the Governments of the South African Republic and the Orange Free State, and*

the facts, but significantly they too invoked religious arguments, although to opposite effect. Most memorably General Johannes de la Rey declared

> With reference to our cause, I do not wish to shut my ears and eyes to the facts. If there is deliverance for the Afrikaner people, then I am with them, and if a grave must be dug for that people then I go into it with them. . . . You speak of faith. What is faith? Faith is 'Lord, *Thy* will be done—not *my* will to be the victor.' . . . That is what I understand by the faith in which God's children must live.[61]

Some religious arguments insisted on the moral responsibility to ensure the survival of the Afrikaner people, even at the price of military and political defeat. The proponents of these arguments proved stronger than those to whom the righteousness of their cause meant that pragmatic considerations could be discounted. A noteworthy feature of these debates was the extent to which such a religious discourse was assumed as a shared vocabulary for dealing with national and political issues. In this respect there were only two exceptions among the delegates at Vereeniging, and interestingly these were to become the two major political leaders of postwar South Africa. General J. B. M. Hertzog objected to bringing religion into politics: "It grieves me that on every public meeting the question of religion is touched upon. It is continually said that this or that is God's finger. Now, although I have my belief, I say that neither you nor I know in the least what is the finger of God!"[62] General Jan Christiaan Smuts also declined simply to reiterate the religious discourse. Instead, he put it to carefully calculated political uses; having decided that the time for the "bitter end" had come, he argued this position in the religious terms familiar to those who wanted to pursue the war:

> We must bow to God's will. The future is dark, but we shall not relinquish courage and our hope and our faith in God. No one

---

the Representatives of the British Government which terminated in the Peace concluded at Vereeeniging on the 31st May, 1902 (London: Clay, 1912) 154.
[61]Ibid., 156.
[62]Ibid., 175.

will ever convince me that the unparalleled sacrifices laid on the altar of freedom by the Afrikaner people will be in vain and futile. . . . Perhaps it is His will to lead the people of South Africa through defeat and humiliation, yea, even through the valley of the shadow of death, to a better future and a brighter day.[63]

These words indicate the arrival in South African politics of an astute and wily politician who would help to direct and shape political events for decades to come. They also indicate the availability of a religious discourse that might readily be put to a variety of political uses. These uses became evident in the context of an emergent Afrikaner nationalist movement of which the agnostic Hertzog—rather than Smuts—would be the main political leader.

Conclusion

The decades following the Anglo-Boer War were dominated by processes of state-formation leading up to, and following from, Union in 1910.[64] In the new political context, earlier regional and local identities were subsumed and transformed as national structures and organizations were launched. The South African Party, built on the alliance of "maize and gold" and headed by the former Boer generals Louis Botha and Jan Smuts, took power in 1910, but the scene had been set for the emergence of nationalist movements. In 1912, the African National Congress was formed, followed in 1914 by the founding of the (Afrikaner) National Party headed by Hertzog. Arguably, twentieth-century South African politics have been dominated by the complex struggles between these rival African and Afrikaner nationalisms, a conflict skewed by the formal exclusion of the former from the parliamentary arena, which enabled the latter to impose apartheid after coming to power in 1948.

The political discourse of modern Afrikaner nationalism was not lacking in implicit and explicit notions of ethnic and national chosenness; sometimes these notions contained an evident religious connotation, but more often they were secular and of indeterminate provenance. Consider the statement by Dr. Daniel F. Malan, a former

---

[63]Ibid.
[64]Marks and Trapido, "Lord Milner and the South African State," 52–81.

Dutch Reformed church minister who later became the National Party prime minister in 1948; it is often cited as a classic example of Afrikaner nationalist notions of ethnic chosenness. Around 1914, in an address on language and nationality, Malan asserted as his considered view that

> we are Afrikaners and ever ought to remain that, for every nationality, which God has created according to history and national circumstances, has an inherent right to exist. . . . God wills the difference of nationality and nationality. And this is His will, since God has a distinctive destination and a distinct calling for each people, as He has for each individual. If I read the history of my own people, a history showing me the birth and growth of a people despite itself, a people that has become one without its own doing—one might almost say, against its own will—then I cannot escape the impression that God has willed our national existence. And He has willed that because He has a distinct calling for our people with its own national character.[65]

The religious provenance of Malan's notion of ethnic mission is evident, but it clearly does not carry any exclusivist implications. It is not incompatible with neo-Calvinist doctrines, but neither does it indicate a specifically neo-Calvinist orientation as distinct from general evangelical notions of mission. It is considerably removed from the highly charged political-religious discourse of the wartime debates, but it assumes this historical experience. In short, it would be very difficult to come to any determinate interpretation of the meaning, assumptions, and implications of Malan's articulation of a notion of ethnic chosenness precisely because it issues out of such a wide and diverse range of relevant sources. This indeterminacy continued to be characteristic of Afrikaner nationalist notions of chosenness and mission during the early decades of this century. Thus the task ahead for South African scholars is a challenging one: to investigate the formation of the more pronounced and determinate Afrikaner chosen people discourse articulated by mid-century.

---

[65]Daniel F. Malan, "Taal en Nationaliteit," in *Wij Zullen Handhaven* (Proceedings of the Stellenbosch Studente Taalkonferentie, 1914) 38.

Response

*Conor Cruise O'Brien**

A ll of us who are interested in the interplay between religion and nationalism in various cultures are indebted to André du Toit's thorough and sustained critique of the historical bases of a particular equation between religion and nationalism: that of the ideologues of apartheid. Du Toit's warnings against facile generalizations and ideologically skewed retrospects need to be taken into account by all of us who are interested in this general subject matter, even outside du Toit's immediate South African context.

In earlier articles, du Toit put his central thesis in a somewhat polemical manner, as appears from the title of his leading contribution on the subject: "No Chosen People: The Myth of the Calvinist Origins of Afrikaner Nationalism and Racial Ideology."[1] Du Toit's fierce commitment to this particular thesis is also evident in the article he cites in his third footnote: "Captive to the Nationalist Paradigm: Professor F. A. van Jaarsfeld and the Historical Evidence for the Afrikaner's Ideas on his Calling and Mission."[2] To an outsider it seems strange that Flors van Jaarsfeld should have been singled out as "captive to the nationalist paradigm," since nobody had done more, or paid an uglier price, precisely for calling in question "the Afrikaner's Ideas on his Calling and Mission." On 28 March 1979, van Jaarsfeld was tarred and feathered in front of a theological conference at the University of South Africa in Pretoria. The subject on which Profes-

*Conor Cruise O'Brien is Senior Research Fellow at the National Center for the Humanities, Research Triangle Park, North Carolina.
[1]André du Toit, "No Chosen People: The Myth of the Calvinist Origins of Afrikaner Nationalism and Racial Ideology," *AHR* 88 (1983) 920–52.
[2]André du Toit, "Captive to the Nationalist Paradigm: Professor F. A. van Jaarsfeld and the Historical Evidence for the Afrikaner's Ideas on his Calling and Mission," *South African Historical Journal* 16 (1984) 49–82.

sor van Jaarsfeld had attempted to address the conference was the historical reassessment of the Day of the Covenant, the central element in the cult of sacral nationalism which both du Toit and van Jaarsfeld, with different emphases, have challenged. The dispute between them must have given satisfaction to their common enemy: the fanatics of apartheid.

The title of du Toit's present paper, "The Construction of Afrikaner Chosenness," seems preferable to the peremptory "No Chosen People" of his earlier article. The whole subject of the interrelations between religion and nationalism is so complex and murky that writings about it should be more studded with question marks than they usually are. In my own writings, of a different general tendency from du Toit's particular ones, I plead guilty to having sometimes had too light a hand with the question mark.

One great problem in relation to this whole field is that we are dealing with the feelings of large numbers of people, most of whom have left no record of what they felt about these matters. All that we know about them is that, in certain circumstances, they responded in large numbers to appeals coming from leaders and the molders of opinion. Did the feelings evident in their responses long antedate those responses? Or did the feelings spring up, as a result of recent stimuli, around the time that the appeals were formulated? The general trend of du Toit's writings, including the present article, is to favor a negative response to the first question and a positive one to the second. Yet in the past—in "Captive to the Nationalist Paradigm"— he has implicitly acknowledged a certain basis for a positive answer to the first question. In that article, he conceded that in the 1830s the direct influence of the Hebrew scriptures on Voortrekker rhetoric "can hardly be disputed." He agreed, moreover, that on the frontier in that period the "use of biblical terminology, allusions to and analogies with events and figures in the Old Testament, and an easy recourse to providential language" were ubiquitous.[3] In such passages, du Toit seems to be conceding a greater continuity to Afrikaner ideology than the bulk of his writings, including the one in this volume, implies to be credible. In the present article du Toit writes that

[3]Ibid., 69.

critical investigations show that the contemporary evidence simply does not provide any clear and unambiguous support for the
presence among early Afrikaners of a set of popular beliefs that
may be recognized as "primitive Calvinism" nor of any ideology
of a chosen people with a national mission. Nothing of the kind
appears in the contemporary accounts of travelers or other well-
placed observers before the 1850s, nor are such views articulated at all by Afrikaners themselves before the last decades of
the nineteenth century.

If we know anything of the Afrikaners, we know that the Bible
was their most treasured possession and that the Old Testament (as
Christians call the Hebrew Bible) was especially dear to them. The
Old Testament is itself the carrier of an "ideology of a chosen people
with a national mission." It has conveyed that ideology, with the
required community variations, to the French, the English, the Germans, the Russians, the Poles, the Americans (both white and black),
and to the Irish (both Catholic and Protestant). Du Toit agrees that a
Covenant was "made by the military force under the Trekker leader
Andries Pretorius on 16 December 1838, prior to the battle of Blood
River." If Pretorius and Sarel Cilliers proposed the Covenant to their
followers in those desperate days, we must suppose that the analogy
with the people of Israel was already present to the minds of their
Voortrekker following and strengthened their morale.

Du Toit makes much—and I think rather too much—of the fact
that the Covenant did not figure prominently in Afrikaner discourse
in the years following Blood River and did not come to the forefront
until the late nineteenth century. This does not seem to me surprising.
For the various peoples who have at different periods identified themselves as chosen peoples, the idea—probably always knocking around
at the back of their minds—tended to become explicit and urgent only
at times of national crisis. An early example is the English occupation
of France in the fifteenth century, to which Joan of Arc's holy war for
the holy kingdom was the response. For the Voortrekkers, the victory
at Blood River ended the Zulu danger. The Covenant had done its
work, and no need was felt to go on about it in more relaxed times.
Only as new dangers defined themselves, later in the century, did the
themes of the chosen people and the Covenant come to be seen as

relevant again: helpful for morale against the British, as once against the Zulus, and then again, by the mid-twentieth century, against the blacks of South Africa in general, and against a hostile world. But the fact that these ideas have left little or no explicit record in times of relatively little pressure does not demonstrate that they did not remain around in the folk mind, available to be called upon in times of trouble. Du Toit is surely right in holding that "Calvinism," "neo-Calvinism," or any other formal theology has much less relevance than has often been suggested. The Bible was always there, however, and Christians and Jews have always turned to the Bible, looking for messages relevant to their situation, especially in times of stress and danger.

In a distant but similar culture, that of the Ulster Protestants, there has been the same kind of intermittence in the expression of the chosen people theme. The victory of the Protestant William III over the Catholic James II at the Battle of the Boyne in 1690 was always remembered by the Protestants as a God-given deliverance. For nearly a hundred years after the deliverance in question, however, Protestant Ulster did not celebrate it with any great enthusiasm. It was only in July 1886, after Gladstone's First Home Rule Bill, that Ulster Protestants, *feeling again under threat,* began a series of solemn annual celebrations of the Battle of the Boyne. (These continue into our own time under the theme, "The Bible the Secret of England's Greatness"— Ulster Protestants being felt to be the cutting edge of English Protestantism.) It would be a mistake, however, to conclude that, because this pattern of feelings found little overt expression, for example, in the first half of the nineteenth century, it had ceased to be around during that period. It was only dormant, and the renewed threat awakened it a little more than a hundred years ago. It is still awake.[4]

---

[4]A recent work that I recommend warmly examines themes related to chosenness with a remarkable combination of expertise and sensitivity. This is Donald Harman Akenson's *Covenant and Land in South Africa, Israel and Ulster* (Ithaca, NY: Cornell University Press, 1992).

The American Israel:
Protestant Tribalism and Universal Mission

James H. Moorhead*

It is a scholarly commonplace that Americans have believed themselves to be providentially chosen for a special mission. The Puritan settlers in the 1600s embarked on a divinely appointed errand in
the wilderness. Subsequent generations pushed the boundaries of the
nation relentlessly westward under the banner of Manifest Destiny
and endowed their wars with apocalyptic meaning. Presidents have
invoked the rhetoric of special mission. Abraham Lincoln described
the Union as "the last best hope of earth"; John F. Kennedy asserted
that "we in this country. . . are by destiny, rather than choice, the
watchmen on the walls of world freedom"; Ronald Reagan envisioned

*James H. Moorhead is Mary McIntosh Bridge Professor of American
Church History at Princeton Theological Seminary, Princeton, New Jersey.

America as a shining, exemplary city. Two biblical motifs formed the historic taproot of this sense of destiny: Americans' identification with ancient Israel and their conviction that they had a major role to play in preparing the way for the kingdom of God. These images were subsequently jumbled together, however, with other ideas such as America's democratic, civilizing mission and the superiority of the Anglo-Saxon peoples. Given the protean character of American exceptionalism, one should not construe it as a logically consistent "abstract philosophic idea," in Conrad Cherry's words. Instead, as Cherry has cautioned, American exceptionalism has functioned as "an empowering national myth. . . that, rather than scrupulously avoiding contradictions, ranges widely across the experience of a people, scoops up some dominant images, and blends them into a compelling worldview."[1]

Chief among these contradictions has been the ascription of universal significance to the inherently limited experience of a single nation. Perhaps, as several other essays in this volume imply, the difficulty is endemic to any mythology of a chosen people. Unless the myth places that people at the center of a sacred cosmos, it loses its power to inspire or to bind. Unfortunately, such mythology also cloaks parochialism under a false universality and thus contributes to the incalculable mischief done by religiously motivated nationalisms in the modern era.

[1]Lincoln is quoted in Winthrop S. Hudson, *Nationalism and Religion in America: Concepts of American Identity and Mission* (New York: Harper & Row, 1970) 85; Kennedy in John F. Kennedy, *The Burden and the Glory* (ed. Allan Nevins: New York: Harper & Row, 1964); and Ronald Reagan in idem, *Speaking My Mind: Selected Speeches* (New York: Simon & Schuster, 1989) 214. The citation from Cherry is excerpted from a perceptive critique (unpublished) of the "conference" draft of this essay. On the American sense of special destiny, see Sacvan Bercovitch, *The American Jeremiad* (Madison: University of Wisconsin Press, 1978); Winthrop S. Hudson, ed., *Nationalism and Religion in America: Concepts of American Identity and Mission* (New York: Harper & Row, 1970); and James H. Moorhead, "Theological Interpretations and Critiques of American Society and Culture," in *Encyclopedia of the American Religious Experience: Studies of Traditions and Movements* (3 vols.; ed. Charles H. Lippy and Peter W. Williams; New York: Scribner, 1988) 1. 101–5.

These contradictions and dilemmas were apparent in mainstream Protestant discussions of America during the years between 1880 and 1920. A short article in *The Methodist Review* in 1890 provides a case in point. The author, O. B. Super, who taught modern languages at Dickinson College, asserted that God had elected a modern chosen people analogous to ancient Israel. Jews had "forfeited their high privilege by their rejection of the Christ"; to the Anglo-Saxon "has passed the privilege as well as the responsibility of civilizing as well as Christianizing the world." Several facts testified to the providential role of the Anglo-Saxon. Of all tongues, English seemed best suited to become the universal language, and of all peoples the Anglo-Saxon seemed best adapted to thrive in various environments. Indeed, the "enduring vigor" of the Anglo-Saxon would probably cause the race to supplant weaker races such as the American Indians, the aboriginal Australians, and perhaps even blacks in Africa. What identified the modern chosen people most, however, was the message they had to bear. "In politics and morals the Anglo-Saxon, especially the American, seems destined to be the teacher of the world." Republican principles and a pure spiritual Christianity would provide the example others would emulate. Super predicted that other peoples would "adopt his [the Anglo-Saxon's] language, his civilization, and his religion." Concluding his ruminations, Super declared in a paraphrase of the poet:

> May we not, with due reverence and humility, claim to be God's chief instruments in bringing about the time of which Tennyson sings, when "The war drums throb no longer, and the battle-flags are furled / In the parliament of nations, the federation of the world," as well as that more glorious time when "the kingdoms of this world are become the kingdoms of our Lord and of his Christ, and he shall reign for ever and ever?"[2]

Super managed to compress into fourteen pages most of the disparate—sometimes mutually reinforcing, sometimes contradictory—strands

[2]All quotations in this paragraph are taken from O. B. Super, "The Mission of the Anglo-Saxon," *Methodist Review* 72 (1890) 853–67. Super's citation of Tennyson is a misquotation.

that made up the myth of America as a chosen nation. His vision of America was at once biblical and secular, parochial and universal, pacific and menacing. The United States was a new Israel and a harbinger of the millennium. Yet this biblical imagery became fused with prevailing racial notions of the superiority of the Anglo-Saxon stock, and the gospel became virtually identical with democratic institutions. The American mission was one of peaceful example, but it also might entail the displacement of Rudyard Kipling's lesser breeds. The Americans played a unique role, yet they shared it with other English-speaking peoples; both together fulfilled a cosmopolitan destiny on behalf of all peoples.

While such antinomies had long existed within the mythology about America, they were especially pronounced between 1880 and 1920. One need not look far to discover plausible explanations. A social and cultural transformation of great magnitude was underway. Major cities groaned under the dislocations imposed by industrialization and the lack of urban planning. The rapid influx of new immigrants, mostly Catholic or Jewish from eastern and southern Europe, called into question the ability of old-line Protestantism to determine the national ethos. Agrarian protest and labor strikes threatened to become a social revolution. America inched toward a more aggressive involvement on the international stage. Given the disordered reality they faced, it is little wonder that mainstream white Protestants thrashed about, sometimes inconsistently and perhaps frantically, to comprehend what it meant for Americans to be, in Super's words, "God's chief instruments."[3]

Since the notion of a chosen people was rooted in the Bible, inquiry properly begins with the question: Did Protestants find nationalist exceptionalism explicitly written in scripture? A few did. Presbyterian S. C. Alexander, for example, argued in 1885 that the United States was the final world kingdom foretold in Daniel 2, and

[3]Ibid., 867. Among the many treatments of this era, see, for example, Alan Dawley, *Struggles for Justice: Social Responsibility and the Liberal State* (Cambridge, MA/London: Belknap, 1991); Nell Irvin Painter, *Standing at Armageddon: The United States, 1877–1919* (New York/London: Norton, 1987); Robert H. Wiebe, *The Search for Order, 1877–1920* (New York: Hill & Wang, 1967).

he rejoiced that "the destiny of the world is placed in our hands, according to the divine programme."[4] Other persons, enamored of the theory proposed by the English navy lieutenant Richard Brothers during the Napoleonic wars, contended that the Anglo-Saxon people were the direct descendants of the lost tribes of Israel. By the 1890s, this idea found expression in the Society of the Ten Tribes in the United States, headquartered in Denver, Colorado. One of the proponents of the movement explained its significance: "The Saxon people, England and America, stand in a new light to the world by the teachings of the Bible. Being Israel or the Ten Lost Tribes, they become the chosen agents of God for the glorious purpose of evangelizing the whole world, and finally, by reducing the whole world to the place of universal liberty and peace."[5]

Such views won only a handful of adherents. Despite the prevailing belief in America's special world mission, many impediments prevented acceptance of the idea that the nation was explicitly foretold in the Bible or that Americans were lineal descendents of the Israelites. Modern scholarship made such uncritical use of the Bible appear ludicrous. Even when they suggested that modern America occupied a place analogous to ancient Israel, Protestants proceeded cautiously. For most postmillennialists, it was an article of faith that God's promises to Israel had been fulfilled in and superseded by Christianity. In God's plan, the chosen nation Israel had found its end—a kind of Hegelian *Aufhebung*—in a universal spiritual religion. Thus no particular nation, group, or clan could claim to be a precise counterpart to the ancient Hebrews. Individual nations might, by providential circumstances, play a unique role in the advancement of God's purposes, and the Israel of the Old Testament might function as a paradigm for the righteous nation in covenant with God. In this sense, analogies between America and Israel were deemed legitimate and were frequently made; the comparison, however, could never be exact. The rising cohort of premillennialists, especially those of the

---

[4]Quoted in John Edwin Smylie, "Protestant Clergymen and America's World Role, 1865–1900: A Study of Christianity, Nationality, and International Relations" (Th.D. diss., Princeton Theological Seminary, 1959) 143.

[5]Quoted in ibid., 147.

dispensationalist persuasion, had their own reasons for avoiding the identification of America as a new chosen people; they believed that God had never revoked his election of the Jewish people and that biblical prophecies about their restoration would yet be literally ful-filled. Dispensationalists looked to the first stirrings of Zionism, not to America, when they wished to identify the elect nation. Moreover, dispensationalists flailed the supposed Christian societies of the West for their spiritual decadence and predicted a further slide into apos-tasy before the end. Their scenario did not offer many likely candi-dates for election among then existing nations.[6]

The meaning of America was interpreted, instead, through the domi-nant religious motif of the kingdom of God. As understood by most Protestants outside the premillennial camp, the kingdom of God was an order already in process of realization. The kingdom appeared wher-ever men and women submitted to the rule of Christian ideals and principles; in due course, this kingdom was destined to become uni-versal. As Washington Gladden declared before the State Association of Congregational Churches of Ohio in 1894: "Every department of human life—the families, the schools, amusements, art, business, na-tional politics, international relations—will be governed by the Chris-tian law and governed by Christian principles." Then "the day shall come for which the whole creation waits, and He whose right it is shall reign over all the earth."[7]

History moved toward that day by many means. The conversion of persons to Christianity—or alternately, in more liberal schemes, the nurturing of Christian values—provided the chief vehicle for the ad-

[6]For further information on postmillennialism, see James H. Moorhead, "The Erosion of Postmillennialism in American Religious Thought, 1865–1925," *CH* 53 (1984) 61–77; and idem, "Between Progress and Apocalypse: A Reassessment of Millennialism in American Religious Thought, 1800–1880," *Journal of American History* 71 (1984) 524–42. On premillennialism, consult Timothy P. Weber, *Living in the Shadow of the Second Coming* (enlarged ed.; Chicago/London: University of Chicago Press, 1987); and Ernest R. Sandeen, *The Roots of Fundamentalism: British and American Millenarianism, 1800–1930* (Chicago/London: University of Chicago Press, 1970).

[7]Washington Gladden, *The Church and the Kingdom* (New York: Revell, 1894) 8, 40.

vancement of the kingdom. Yet Christianity did not advance in a cultural vacuum. With it went democracy, material progress, education, the improvement of the status of women, and social reform. Several years after the close of the Civil War, Presbyterian Albert Barnes uttered words that could have served as the motto for many Protestants in the late nineteenth century. The forces of secular progress have, he wrote, "an essential connection with Christianity. They become incorporated with it. They carry Christianity with themselves wherever they go."[8] While some disputed whether American Christians could safely promote these "civilizing" trends as a way of creating a wedge for the entrance of Christianity, few doubted Barnes's central point: secular improvements would indeed advance side by side with the faith. Together they were harbingers of the coming kingdom of God.[9]

Providential circumstances dictated that the United States and England should exercise a pivotal influence in this historical process. At the 1893 Parliament of Religions at the Columbian Exposition in Chicago, a missionary summarized the argument succinctly. Because of their geographically strategic locations, sturdy racial traits, far-flung commerce, wealth, and political systems, England and the United States enjoyed an unprecedented opportunity to mold the future of the entire planet. All of these powers would work together for good because of "the moral and religious character" of the English-speaking peoples. "These great nations," he explained, "are permeated with the principles of the Bible. . . . Such principles as these are destined to mold and control all mankind."[10]

Assertions of Anglo-Saxon mission occurred, of course, amid a widespread outpouring of racist actions and policies. The years between 1880 and 1920 produced the legal apparatus of Jim Crow,

[8]Albert Barnes, *Life at Threescore and Ten* (New York: American Tract Society, 1871) 130–31.

[9]On the subject of the relationship of civilization and Christianity, see William R. Hutchison, *Errand to the World: American Protestant Thought and Foreign Missions* (Chicago/London: University of Chicago Press, 1987).

[10]Henry H. Jessup, "The Religious Mission of the English Speaking Nations," in J. W. Hanson, ed., *The World's Congress of Religions* (Chicago/Philadelphia: International, 1895) 794.

epidemic lynching of African-Americans, the reemergence of the Ku Klux Klan, and efforts to limit immigration of those who were not northern European. Sometimes even genteel versions of Anglo-Saxonism stepped over into full-blown racism when, for example, the idea was amalgamated with eugenics or when in 1916 Madison Grant wrote *The Passing of the Great Race.* Yet most proponents of the idea mitigated its overt racism. Anglo-Saxons allegedly embodied universal ideals capable of adoption by others. Moreover, many understood Anglo-Saxonism as elastic. It could, even while influencing other peoples, simultaneously absorb the best they had to offer. The others might become, as it were, honorary "Anglos" and in the process contribute to a broadening and strengthening of the identity of the English-speaking peoples. As John Higham has admirably summarized, the prevailing Anglo-Saxonism "kept parochial and cosmopolitan ideas revolving in a single orbit."[11]

The Congregational clergyman Josiah Strong provided one of the best examples of this ambiguous conjunction of themes. His book *Our Country*, published in 1886 on behalf of the home mission movement, contained one of the most often quoted passages from an American minister. After extolling the Anglo-Saxon or English-speaking peoples as "the die with which to stamp the peoples of the earth" and noting that the "principal seat" of this power would reside in the United States, Strong moved to a stirring conclusion:

> It seems to me that God with infinite wisdom and skill is training the Anglo-Saxon race for an hour sure to come in the world's future. . . the *final competition of races, for which the Anglo-Saxon is being schooled.* . . . Then this race of unequaled energy, with all the majesty of numbers and the might of wealth behind it—the representative, let us hope, of the largest liberty, the purest Christianity, the highest civilization—having developed peculiarly aggressive traits calculated to impress its institutions upon mankind will spread itself over the earth. . . . Can anyone doubt that the result of this competition of races will be the "survival of the fittest." . . . Is there any reasonable doubt

---

[11]John Higham, *Strangers in the Land: Patterns of American Nativism, 1860–1925* (2d ed.; New York: Atheneum, 1971) 33.

that this race. . . is destined to dispossess many weaker races, assimilate others, and mold the remainder, until, in a very real sense, it has Anglo-Saxonized mankind?[12]

This extraordinary passage appears to be the very epitome of Anglo-Saxon superiority and conquest, premised upon pseudo-Darwinian notions of natural selection. Yet the chauvinistic language hinted at cosmopolitan ideals—"the largest liberty, the purest Christianity, the highest civilization." Read in context, *Our Country* was designed to promote a vision of world-wide progress, and Strong subsequently shifted his emphasis to more universal themes. He opposed the exploitation of Chinese and Africans by Western powers, asserted that immigrants who were not Anglo-Saxon had strengthened the American racial stock, affirmed that no race should literally displace others, and called for a heightened awareness of global interdependence. In the movement toward what he called a "new era," the English-speaking peoples indeed occupied a place of providential significance. They did so, however, not as Anglo-Saxon tribalists, but as representatives of all humankind. Moreover, Strong, along with Washington Gladden and other advocates of the social gospel, often used the idea of American election as a basis for calling the nation to repentance and summoning it to the reform of abuses in its economic system. Much in the manner of the Puritan preachers of the jeremiad, Strong and others argued that the United States must purge itself of its defects before it could move forward revitalized in fulfillment of its world errand.[13]

Even those thumping nativist drums generally sounded some universal notes. For example, the Reverend James King, General Secretary of the National League for the Protection of American Institutions, warned in 1899 that foreign-born Roman Catholics threatened Ameri-

[12]Josiah Strong, *Our Country: Its Possible Future and Its Present Crisis* (ed. Jurgen Herbst; Cambridge, MA: Belknap, 1963) 205, 206, 213–14, 216–17.

[13]Dorothea R. Muller, "Josiah Strong and American Nationalism: A Reevaluation," *Journal of American History* 53 (1966) 487–503; Ronald C. White, Jr., *Liberty and Justice for All: Racial Reform and the Social Gospel* (New York: Harper & Row, 1990) 18–20.

can society, and he called for restrictions upon both immigration and the ballot. The rationale for these proposals, however, was allegedly not parochial. America needed to protect itself so that its people might realize their global mission. He described this mission in millennial terms: "Anglo-Saxon Christian civilization in its perfect work would put an end to war by bringing in the reign of universal peace, curb selfish competition by charity, banish poverty with plenty, prevent crime by the prevalence of justice and righteousness, destroy pestilence with purity and prolong life by obedience to natural and moral law."[14]

The war with Spain further disclosed the ambivalent mind of the American chosen people. Initially divided as to whether the nation should intervene in Cuba on behalf of the rebels fighting their Spanish overlords, most Americans—and their churches—closed ranks after the declaration of war in April 1898. The nation went to war simultaneously convinced of its own uniqueness and the universality of its cause. Preaching from his Brooklyn pulpit on the last Sunday in April, the Reverend David Gregg gave utterance to both sides of that common conviction. Gregg opened his sermon with a comparison of America to the ancient Hebrews and suggested that the United States was offering the world what it needed: "a nation with the truth of God, a nation in covenant with God. . . . When a nation is such, then like Israel of old it blesses the whole circuit of the earth." American war aims thus transcended merely parochial interests:

> My fellow-citizens, our motto must be "America for the world," for God, in Jesus Christ, has given us, who are Americans, principles which are not local, but universal. The principles which He has given us for our national life are cosmopolitan. Our national ideals lace and interlace into the interests of broad humanity. . . . It [the American cause] is out-and-out altruistic. There is no revenge in it. It is not mercenary in the least atom. It is principle from Alpha to Omega. If there were no Christ and

[14]James M. King, *Facing the Twentieth Century; Our Country: Its Power and Peril* (New York: American Union League Society, 1899) 593.

Christianity[,] it could never be. It partakes of the brotherhood
of man.[15]

With even more expansive rhetoric, a Methodist minister said of the
conflict: "This war is the *Kingdom of God coming!* Coming to poor
Cuba—the sunrise of a better day for the Philippines!" His nineteen-
year-old son had enlisted in the army, and the minister compared him
to another agent of the kingdom: "With Christ in his heart, the New
Testament in his pocket, 'Look Up and Lift Up' [the badge of the
Methodist youth league] on his shirt, and forty rounds of ammunition
in his belt, we have sent out the first missionary in the family!"[16]

American victories in the Philippines and Cuba ended the war with
decisive speed and opened major debate on national policy. Should
the United States keep as colonies the territories it had wrested from
Spain? Supporters of annexation often framed their case in the language of America's providential mission to lead the world to a better
day. To a group of church leaders, President William McKinley explained in words frequently cited by historians "that there was nothing left for us to do but to take them all, and to educate the Filipinos,
and uplift and civilize and Christianize them, and by God's grace to
do the very best we could by them as our fellowmen for whom Christ
died."[17] To Senator Albert Beveridge, one of McKinley's supporters
and chief among the jingoists, the acquisition of empire represented
the fulfillment of America's grand destiny. Since the days of the Pilgrims, events had conspired to make America "the master Nation of
the world," and thus it was futile to resist "the eternal movement of
the American people toward the mastery of the world."[18]

[15]David Gregg, "The National Crisis, or God's Purposes Worked Out Through
International Relations" (Brooklyn: Brooklyn Citizen Job Print, 1898) 2, 5,
13.

[16]Quoted in Kenneth M. MacKenzie, *The Robe and the Sword: The Methodist Church and the Rise of American Imperialism* (Washington, DC: Public
Affairs Press, 1961) 72–73.

[17]Quoted in Hudson, *Nationalism and Religion,* 115.

[18]Quoted in Conrad Cherry, *God's New Israel: Religious Interpretations
of American Destiny* (Englewood Cliffs, NJ: Prentice-Hall, 1972) 152–53.

Many Protestant leaders echoed these rationales for empire. The Reverend H. K. Carroll of Plainfield, New Jersey, declared that the United States was "possessed of an idea capable of infinite expansion. This idea is that of individual liberty combined with universal cooperation." Closely linked to this political ideal was a religious one. As the nation planted its institutions along with its flag, American Protestants must preach the gospel in those places. For Carroll, the central issue was easily stated: "We must take up the 'white man's burden.' It is laid upon us because we are strong and able to bear it. It is laid upon us because our backs are fitted to it. . . . Our Gospel was meant for expansion. . . . We have a Gospel for the world; the world needs it, and it is our duty to give it to the world."[19] Wallace Radcliffe, the moderator of the General Assembly of the Northern Presbyterian Church, read a similar message in the events of the war. "Imperialism is in the air," he explained; but unlike former scrambles for empire, "it has new definitions and better intentions. It is republicanism 'writ large.' It is imperialism, not for subjugation, but for development; not for absolutism, but for self-government. American imperialism is enthusiastic, optimistic, and beneficial republicanism." Like Carroll, Radcliffe linked America's political expansion to the expansion of its religious ideals. In one of the baldest equations of political and religious mission ever penned, he wrote, "I believe in imperialism because I believe in foreign missions. . . . If the nation multiplies its sails, we must write on every one of them glad tidings of great joy. We have come into the kingdom for such a time as this. The imperialism of the Gospel is the emancipation of humanity."[20]

Since the American mission meant "the emancipation of humanity," the peoples subjected to its beneficence had little ground on which to register a dissent. Persons whose cultures were backward or barbaric were by definition not competent to determine their own best interest; that judgment lay with the heralds of civilization and Christianity. For example, Swift Holbrook in October 1899 dismissed as

---

[19]H. K. Carroll, "Expansion a Political and Moral Opportunity," *Methodist Review* 82 (1900) 9–20.

[20]Wallace Radcliffe, "Presbyterian Imperialism," *The Assembly Herald* 1 (1899) 6.

irrelevant the Philippine independence movement led by Emilio Aguinaldo. Even if the rebel leader commanded the support of a majority of his people—a possibility that the author denied—Aguinaldo had no valid reason for contesting American control. Because Filipinos were an unfree people subject to disease, sloth, and ignorance, one might fairly ask, "To what extent, then, must they obey the dictates of the more enlightened members of the human family?" To the author, the answer appeared self-evident. As Washington Gladden asserted of the Filipinos: "We have the right to civilize them. To leave them to themselves and permit them to cover and curse vast regions of the earth is not a rational proposition."[21] The practical meaning of this policy was bluntly stated by James C. Fernald in a book appropriately entitled *The Imperial Republic*. Writing of the need for the American troops occupying Cuba to provide better sanitation for the inhabitants, Fernald suggested, "Military authority, absolute and imperious, can simply do what needs to be done, without waiting for a vote. The gratitude of humanity will be the subsequent ratification of the accomplished fact."[22]

The imperial version of American election did not go unchallenged. The treaty ratifying the acquisition of the Philippines barely achieved the two-thirds vote of the Senate necessary for ratification. Among the prominent leaders of the anti-imperialist movement was William Jennings Bryan, the once and future electoral opponent of McKinley. A number of well-known ministers also lent their names to the cause. Yet even as they attacked the quest for empire, opponents indicated that they, too, shared visions of America as a special or chosen people. Bryan, for example, argued that America would renovate the world through its example. "The growth of the principle of self-government, planted on American soil," Bryan argued, "has been the overshadowing political fact of the nineteenth century. It has made this Nation conspicuous among the nations, and given it a place in history such as no other nation has ever enjoyed." To "cast aside the omnipotent

[21]Quoted in Smylie, "Protestant Clergymen and America's World Role," 510, 520.
[22]James C. Fernald, *The Imperial Republic* (New York: Funk & Wagnalls, 1898) 188.

weapon of truth"—the mission of peaceful example—and "seize again the weapon of physical warfare" was to betray America's mission. Bryan's opposition to imperialism also rested on a measure of ethnocentrism: "Are we to bring into the body politic eight or ten million Asiatics, so different from us in race and history that amalgamation is impossible? Are they to share with us in making the laws of the Republic?"[23] The Reverend Henry Van Dyke, preaching from his New York pulpit on Thanksgiving Day 1898, contended that the acquisition of colonies represented a decision "to sell the American birthright for a mess of pottage in the Philippines." This surrender of America's divine election threatened to propel the nation into future wars and augured an antimillennium for which "we must prepare to beat our ploughshares into swords and our pruning hooks into spears." Van Dyke's attack on imperial expansion rested in part on an idealistic "faith in freedom" for all peoples, but it also took for granted that there were "inferior races" and that the imperialism of the United States was impolitic because Americans, unlike the English, had no "natural genius for governing" such peoples. Van Dyke assumed, moreover, that the United States was indeed a special nation, "the one country on earth whose goal is not to subjugate the world but to enlighten it"; he envisioned the American flag floating at "the mountain-peak of nations, lonely, if need be, till others have risen to her lofty standard."[24] To note the assumptions that anti-imperialists shared with their opponents is not to erase the significant differences between them. It is to underscore that even as critics attacked the imperial venture, they often endorsed the notions of cultural or racial superiority that undergirded American expansion.[25]

Sixteen years after the war with Spain, Europe plunged into the struggle that soon bled it white in the trenches of France. President Woodrow Wilson proclaimed a lofty neutrality above the sordid *Realpolitik* animating the Central Powers and the Allies. America's

---

[23]Ray Ginger, ed., *William Jennings Bryan: Selections* (Indianapolis: Bobbs-Merrill, 1967) 64, 66.

[24]Henry Van Dyke, "The American Birthright and the Philippine Pottage" (New York: Scribner's, 1898) 4, 11, 14, 16.

[25]For more on anti-imperialism, see Robert L. Beisner, *Twelve Against Empire: The Anti-Imperialists, 1898–1900* (New York: McGraw-Hill, 1968).

mission was to embody the ideal of a just international order—an order in which peace without victory might be achieved. In time, Wilson hoped, the warring parties would repair to this platform. Despite the fact that some warmongers clamored for American intervention, most Americans appeared to embrace their president's goals. Shortly before the nation abandoned neutrality, the *Homiletic Review* canvassed the opinions of a number of leading clergymen and educators. They, too, looked for a universal vantage point above the conflict. William H. P. Faunce, the Baptist president of Brown University, called upon American churches to drive out racial hatred, cultivate an international mindset, and work for a world organization which would promote peace. A New York minister urged the American church to "demand arbitration instead of force. . . . Then alone will she rise to her duty, and command the world's respect and love." E. Y. Mullins, a moderate Southern Baptist leader, called for lifting "the whole question of diplomacy to a higher level. . . . If the nations of the world will adopt Christian principles in dealing with one another, it goes without saying that another war such as that which is at present raging in Europe will be impossible." Newman Smyth, a liberal patriarch of New England Congregationalism, demanded an attack upon all parochial allegiances, including ecclesiastical ones, as a means of addressing the causes of the war. He envisioned a new John the Baptist, proclaiming that "even now the ax is being laid at the root of. . . denominational trees. . . . Now is the time for each church to repent of its part in the common sin of continuance in a state of schism. Confessing our sin we are to take up all together the work of preparing the way of the Lord."[26] A common assumption lay beneath these prescriptions. The nation and its churches would realize their unique vocation by remaining unentangled in the struggles of Europe, and by example the United States would lead a warring world to a new cosmopolitan order of justice.

On Good Friday, 1917, freedom from entanglement ended when President Wilson appeared before Congress to recommend war against the Central Powers; but the hope for a new international order lived

[26]"The Clear and Urgent Duty of the Church in the Present World Crisis," *Homiletic Review* 73 (1917) 20–25

on. His message and subsequent pronouncements justified war on the basis not of parochial American interests but of universal ideals: making the world safe for democracy and ending all wars.[27] Many Protestant leaders echoed these themes. They were reluctant to speak directly of America as a chosen nation, for this notion smacked of the pretensions of Kaiser Wilhelm's Germany. America's role was to take its part in the community of nations. America's destiny lay in helping to make a true concord of all peoples, heretofore an ideal, a reality. Such a community would not rest on narrow national loyalties, carefully balanced against one another, but upon moral law guaranteeing freedom to all people. This vision of American destiny drew chiefly upon two biblical motifs: the Hebrew prophets' belief in a God who judged all nations according to the impartial standards of righteousness, and the kingdom of God as both immanent in human affairs and capable of further actualization.[28]

Analyzing the meaning of the World War, Daniel Dorchester concluded that the peoples of the world were "travailing in pain" for "spiritual guidance and control." Their agony derived from a loss of the "ideal of a Divine Kingdom transcending Church and State, and immanent in both." Consequently, the state had been "degraded into a purely secular institution" recognizing "no higher law than its own necessity and no power other than military force." Thus Christians were called by the war to set forth the transcendent ideal of the kingdom of God that alone could bind all peoples into an harmonious unity.[29]

President Wilson, that son of the Presbyterian manse who epitomized the religious commitments of many fellow Protestants, pro-

[27]See, for example, John Milton Cooper, Jr., *The Warrior and the Priest: Woodrow Wilson and Theodore Roosevelt* (Cambridge, MA: Belknap, 1983) 288–323.

[28]John F. Piper (*The American Churches in World War I* [Athens: Ohio University Press, 1985] 8–31) has made a strong case for the presence of an international vision among Protestant leaders and thus corrects the one-sided portrayal of narrow chauvinism offered by Ray H. Abrams, *Preachers Present Arms* (New York: Round Table, 1933) 51–75.

[29]All quotations in the paragraph are from Daniel Dorchester, "The Imponderables and a Better World Order," *Methodist Review* 102 (1919) 350–56.

vided the classic embodiment of this new internationalism: a proposed League of Nations. In presenting to the Senate the treaty containing provision for the League, Wilson explained that it would "establish a new order which would rest upon the free choice of peoples." As the president understood the matter, American entrance into the League did not repudiate the nation's special mission but fulfilled it. He declared that

> the stage is set, the destiny disclosed. It has come about by no plan of our conceiving, but by the hand of God who led us in this way. We cannot turn back. We can only go forward, with lifted eyes and freshened spirit, to follow the vision. It was of this that we dreamed at our birth. America shall in truth show the way. The light streams upon the path ahead, and nowhere else.[30]

Wilsonian rhetoric about America's role as a light to the nations—perhaps an echo of Isa 60:3: "nations shall come to your light"—serves as a reminder that even the new internationalism retained a special or chosen place for the American people. In November 1917, the *Homiletic Review* printed a Thanksgiving sermon the text of which, applied by the preacher to the United States, came from Psalm 147: "He hath not dealt so with any nation."[31] Americans had little doubt that the Allies, especially the United States, best embodied universal values, nor did they question that the Central Powers symbolized the antithesis of these ideals. Thus the *Homiletic Review*, in another sermon published shortly before the Armistice, observed, "God is on the side, not of America against Germany, but on the side of humanity against inhumanity, on the side of justice against injustice. We shall win, not because by our selfish prayers or servile worship we shall be able to bribe God to favor our cause, but because we have allied ourselves with the cause of humanity, which is God's own cause."[32]

---

[30]Quoted in Cherry, *God's New Israel*, 288.
[31]Charles Edward Locke, "The American Nation a Child of Providence," *Homiletic Review* 74 (1917) 409.
[32]William E. Barton, "The Moral Meanings of the World War," *Homiletic Review* 79 (1918) 242.

Negatively, preachers made the point by abundant comments on the savagery of the Hun, the "devils of the Potsdam gang," or the "unspeakable depth of depravity. . . [of] Prussianism."[33] Chosenness remained significant and was perhaps less susceptible to critique because it was cloaked in the universal language of the kingdom of God and the prophetic moral vision.

Sometimes the cloak was pulled aside, however, revealing an ugly parochialism. Robert E. Speer, for example, encountered fierce opposition after he declared in a speech at Columbia University in 1918 that the war aims of the United States needed to rise above "pure national individualism" to embrace "universal ideals and the universal spirit."[34] Critics accused him of "weakening patriotism" and of displaying "Teutonic susceptibilities."[35] Attacks against Speer fit into a larger pattern of a resurgent Anglo-Saxon tribalism. Even before the United States entered the war, the Ku Klux Klan had revived in 1915; within a decade it became a nationwide organization. To its old antiblack platform it added new nativist planks opposing Catholic and Jewish immigrants. In the first stages of the war, fear of alien influence rested upon German Americans; by the end of the conflict this worry had a new object. The success of the revolution in Russia prompted many to fear a supposed disloyal fifth column of Bolsheviks in the United States, particularly among the foreign-born. This anxiety fueled the notorious Red Scare and the arrest of aliens begun by Attorney General A. Mitchell Palmer. This fear of contamination by foreign influence also contributed to the Senate's rejection of American entrance into the League of Nations and prepared the way for the passage of immigration restriction legislation in 1924. In the debate over this legislation, a representative from Maine spelled out bluntly the logic of Anglo-Saxonism.[36] The nation, he said, was "God-

---

[33]Charles E. Locke, "The New Day," *Methodist Review* 101 (1918) 583, 584.

[34]Quoted in Piper, *American Churches*, 45.

[35]Quoted in ibid., 52, 53.

[36]Higham, *Strangers in the Land*, 194–330; David H. Bennett, *The Party of Fear: From Nativist Movements to the New Right in American History* (Chapel Hill: University of North Carolina Press, 1988) 183–237. Opposition

intended to be the home of a great people. English speaking—a white race with great ideals, the Christian religion, one race, one country, one destiny."[37]

Even as many Americans succumbed to the blandishments of "one-hundred percent Americanism," however, the cosmopolitan ideal reappeared under tribal auspices. For example, Senator Charles Thomas of Colorado approved the attacks on subversive aliens but also provided a sop to universalism. Protecting national purity was important because "the ark of Democracy's covenant was committed to Anglo-Saxon keeping long ago."[38] The evangelist Billy Sunday, second to none in his blasts against foreign subverters of American institutions, made a similar appeal: "It so happens that America is placed in a position where the fate of the world depends largely on our conduct. If we lose our heads down goes Civilization."[39]

Sunday's comment on America's world role merits comment, for he was one of the rising number of premillennialists. At first glance this form of eschatology, with its emphasis upon the inevitable slide of all nations toward moral doom, would appear to have offered little grounds for a special American destiny. What premillennialists excluded at the front door, however, they readmitted surreptitiously through a back door. The United States might play a providential role in setting the stage for the fulfillment of biblical prophecies. When President Wilson endorsed the Balfour Declaration calling for the establishment of a Jewish homeland in Palestine, premillenarians saw this as a sign of the end time and rejoiced in their nation's contribution to it. The capture of Palestine by General Allenby's British army during the war prompted some to observe that God was using "the Anglo-Saxon forces to restore Jerusalem."[40] Furthermore, premillennialists had long be-

---

to the League is treated in Ralph Stone, *The Irreconcilables: The Fight against the League of Nations* (Lexington: University Press of Kentucky, 1970).

[37]Quoted in Martin E. Marty, *Modern American Religion*, vol. 2: *The Noise of Conflict, 1919–1941* (Chicago/London: University of Chicago Press, 1991) 60.

[38]Quoted in ibid., 72.

[39]Quoted in ibid., 74.

[40]Quoted in Dwight Wilson, *Armageddon Now! The Premillenarian Response to Russia and Israel Since 1917* (Grand Rapids: Baker, 1977) 45.

lieved that Russia would play a major role as the villain in the drama of the end times; in the wake of the Bolshevik Revolution, this conviction made many of them more than willing to participate in the Red Scare. Similarly, the long-held belief that an evil international confederacy would arise in the last days made them suspicious of the League of Nations and eager to stand for the right by fighting such godless incursions upon American sovereignty.[41] At times the cause of God seemed so fully to overlap that of "one-hundred percent Americanism" that premillennialists, occasionally forgetting that no nation except Israel could be elect, gave full-throated voice to American exceptionalism. Thus John Roach Straton declared, "Can anyone doubt that God has lodged with us in this free land the ark of the covenant of humanity's hopes? So surely as God led forth ancient Israel for a unique and glorious mission, so does he seem to have raised up Christian America for such an hour as this."[42]

Rather like a warped glass in a fun house, premillennialism mirrored in distorted—although still recognizable—form the larger culture's ambiguities about the meaning of America. From one perspective, the millenarian vision was cosmopolitan. All nations, the United States included, shared in the declension of the later days, and redemption would come only when God supernaturally established the millennial age. At another level, however, America could, by standing against the tide of rising wickedness and aiding in the accomplishment of prophetic events, acquire an extraordinary place in God's plan for the last times. Moreover, premillennial fundamentalists, although ostensibly apolitical, often identified the ideal social order with a supposed nineteenth-century evangelical dominance of America. Thus, despite an eschatology that seemingly predicted inevitable doom for all nations, they could, when aroused, readily fall in with crusades to reestablish America's unique place in the world.[43] American exceptionalism would not be downed easily.

[41]Ibid., 42–58.

[42]Quoted in George M. Marsden, *Fundamentalism and American Culture: The Shaping of Twentieth Century Evangelicalism, 1870–1925* (New York: Oxford University Press, 1980) 163.

[43]On the political views of fundamentalists, see Marsden, *Fundamentalism*, 85–93.

Amid the immense varieties in the notion of Americans as a chosen people, one encounters a recurrent theme, best expressed as an oxymoron: American chosenness assumed a cosmopolitan tribalism. Perhaps the roots of this paradox lay in the biblical passages that affirmed Israel's election. According to the Hebrew scriptures, God conferred singular benefits upon Israel unlike those given to any other nation. Yet the favored people were, according to other texts, blessed in order that they might be a blessing and serve as a light to the nations. This universalism was subsequently reinforced by the New Testament's vision of Christianity as a religion for all people. The same ambivalence may be read in the numerous statements that located American exceptionalism in the nation's Protestant culture, republican institutions, and material progress. These attributes, although they found their preeminent embodiment in the Great Republic, were also designed for export to all the nations. Similarly, the common Anglo-Saxonism, so often blatantly racist and ethnocentric, was tempered (at least theoretically) by the belief that the English-speaking peoples performed a universal civilizing and uplifting mission.

At bottom, the idea of national chosenness rested upon the assumption that the particularities of the American experience embodied universal values. What Wallace Radcliffe in 1899 offered as the rationale for his denomination's missionary enterprise could also stand as a rubric for the prevailing idea of national mission. "If Presbyterianism has a right for any existence, or any place," asserted the moderator, "it has a right for every existence and for every place. If it is suitable for any condition or any age, it is suitable for all conditions and all ages."[44] If one changed "Presbyterianism" to "American values and institutions," this remarkable passage could serve equally well as a description of many citizens' understanding of their national vocation.

The equation of American particularity with the universal provided a mixed legacy. On occasion, it prompted self-criticism and reform of abuses within the United States; in some instances it may also have encouraged a measure of genuine altruism in the nation's relations

[44]Radcliffe, "Presbyterian Imperialism," 6.

with other peoples. Most Protestants unquestionably aspired to such a vocation and would have gladly echoed the Methodist minister who wrote in 1889, "It is only as we aid in molding for good the destiny of humanity, as we exert our mighty energies in ameliorating the condition of mankind, in redeeming the world from ignorance and sin and renewing it in knowledge and in holiness, that we can conceive or realize a mission worthy of the great American Republic."[45] The grandiosity of this self-understanding was also the undoing of America. It left the United States prone to illusions of universality, masking parochialism, self-interest, and a national will to power.

[45]Alexander Martin, "The Mission of the Republic," *Methodist Review* 71 (1889) 686–87.

Response

*Knud Krakau**

Although the given time frame of 1880–1920 helps to sharpen and focus our analysis, it may also blind us; a longer historical view is indispensable in perceiving specifics and differences. Other nations have also produced missionary ideologies as they developed their power and brought it to bear on the international arena. If the American sense of mission is different or unique, this is partly because America was *born* with this ideology and has continued to live by it ever since: from John Winthrop's *Arbella* sermon, through the American Revolution and the period under review here, to George Bush's rationalization of the Gulf War. "Like Israel of old," as one recent self-analysis put it, "we were a messianic nation from our birth."[1]

If these views have evolved into a "scholarly commonplace," however, they are, as such, often the hardest sort of ideas to explain. It may not be too difficult (after much path-breaking work by Perry Miller and later historians) to unravel the Puritans' basic interpretive (biblical) patterns in their attempts to make sense of their New World experience by viewing it as providential history in America and linking it to the history of ancient Israel. But we cannot be simply satisfied to note that "these images were subsequently jumbled together, however, with other ideas such as America's democratic, civilizing mission and the superiority of the Anglo-Saxon peoples." Surely they were. America's unique facility to blend or fuse the religious with the secular, the rational, the political, and the social has often been noted. But how did this really happen? The long and critically important process of secularization of those biblical-religious images and inter-

*Knud Krakau is Professor of History at the John F. Kennedy Institute for North Amrican Studies, Free University, Berlin.

[1]Reinhold Niebuhr and Alan Heimert, *A Nation So Conceived: Reflections on the History of America from its Early Visions to its Present Power* (1963; reprinted Westport, CT: Greenwood, 1983) 123.

pretations, their marriage to sociopolitical Enlightenment concepts, and finally their transplantation to a more mundane, political, ideological level that is part of a larger, worldwide (at least Atlantic world) process of secularization—this transformation certainly needs much more intensive study, even after Alan Heimert's or Nathan O. Hatch's recent interpretations, which in different ways link the Great Awakening to the Revolutionary period.

Precisely because this "jumbling" has taken place—however it developed—it may not help much to insist on such theological distinctions as those between pre- and postmillennialism, or between premillennialists and dispensationalists. How can we be sure that these theological categories are appropriate tools for dealing with texts from the period we are analyzing? Should we not evolve new "jumbled" categories, that is, synthetic concepts that are new but at the same time preserve and combine the religious and the secular dimensions of these developments (which remain *aufgehoben*, in the Hegelian sense)? It is probably here that the "civil (or political or secular) religion" approach exerts its attractions, whatever its other problems.

The observation that the Chosen People or mission *topoi* are powerful arguments in American public discourse in and beyond the period under review remains uncontroverted. Yet it is decidedly unclear, in terms of dogmatic or systematic theological reasoning, whether these *topoi* emanate from traditional religious sources or from politicians and publicists. Where the source is religious, the particular denomination does not matter. Kenneth Mackenzie's *The Robe and the Sword*, published in 1961, richly documented Methodist views on America's chosenness, mission, and imperialism. A book on any of the other Protestant denominations would come to much the same conclusions. In 1885 Josiah Strong, the nineteenth-century Congregationalist, demonstrated the point in *Our Country*. What is important here is not the exercise in theological semantics but the political, psychological, and broadly cultural consequences of the chosen people/ mission topos. Its impact upon American political discourse and America's collective psyche leaves the country with a sense of collective identity and national purpose in the world. This, of course, is an important anthropological understanding of the meaning of myth. The pressures from a democratically organized marketplace of ideas reinforce this tendency to blur theological distinctions. At the same time, a culture as broadly religious as America implicitly understands biblical imagery and rhetoric, analogy and typology, explanation and justification, as means employed for ascribing religious meaning to political events.

Psychologically speaking, the chosenness/mission theme would appear to be among the classical mechanisms for reducing internal insecurity and tension by projecting one's own values abroad. A case probably could be made for the importance of such a mechanism in those phases of American history that are especially characterized by internal collective anxieties, beginning with the early Puritans. Our designated period certainly is such a phase, marked by deep cultural, social, and economic change following immigration, urbanization, industrialization, and alleged overproduction. These problems appeared real and intractable at the time and created serious doubts as to the viability and future stability of American society and democracy. Josiah Strong expressed these anxieties as a contemporary, and Robert Dallek has recently analyzed American foreign policies of the period using this analytical approach.[2]

Viewing chosenness/mission as part of American mythology has the advantage of making contradictory attitudes and objectives appear reconcilable. The influence that Alexander Hamilton in the first Federalist paper identified as deriving from America's mere "conduct and example"—from the perfecting of values and institutions at home—becomes compatible, within this mythology, with that which is pursued by way of active overseas intervention; both appear as modes of realizing the same basic missionary responsibility. Similarly, chosenness-as-myth was able to reconcile and give equal weight, in 1900, to both imperialism and anti-imperialism, and then to inform not only Woodrow Wilson's early stance of neutrality in the First World War, but also his later intervention.

[2]Robert Dallek, *The American Style of Foreign Policy: Cultural Politics and Foreign Affairs* (New York: Knopf, 1983) chap. 1 and passim.

A mythological interpretation cannot, however, explain the shifts from one "contradictory" stance to another. If we are interested in this sort of change, we have to consider the alternations between expanding/extrovert and contracting/introvert moods and phases in American public thought. We would need, moreover, to examine each of these moods in relation to changing international political configurations and the broader cultural and political parameters of American society.

In the view of the missionaries, of course, the values to be transported abroad by the American mission were eminently universal. Critical examination of this assumption has usually been confined to unmasking the sometimes outrageously facile identification of national, political, and economic self-interest with these universals. Senator Albert J. Beveridge was famous (or infamous) for providing striking examples of this sort of procedure. Further critical examination, however, should question whether these values were "universal" in the first place. They may turn out to be products of Western or North Atlantic culture, widely shared yet limited, and not nearly so universal as is all too easily assumed.

Speaking as the "scholarly commonplace" does about *the* American mission and American chosenness presupposes a homogeneity in American society and culture that we know does not exist with respect to religious beliefs, class distinctions, and ethnic-cultural orientation. This *topos* has been produced traditionally by members of the middle classes: the clergy of colonial and later periods, writers, intellectuals, and politicians. Whom did they reach, however? The more millennialist churches in the late eighteenth century counted perhaps roughly half the population among their adherents, including "virtually all the largest economic groups in the white social hierarchy."[3] It remains, however, to ask about the other nonmillennialist denominations at that time. Even the Roman Catholic Church, the traditional millennialist Antichrist that would soon grow into the largest single church in the nation, adapted to chosenness/mission concepts without sharing the specific theological assumptions on which they rested. We

[3]Ruth H. Bloch, *Visionary Republic: Millennial Themes in American Thought, 1756–1800* (Cambridge: Cambridge University Press, 1985) xv.

should also consider social strata or classes that were not even reached by the original propagators of the chosenness/mission theme, but were later addressed by its more modern secularized successors, the publicists or politicians in the public realm. I have in mind the lower-class masses of industrial America, the ethnically and culturally heterogeneous groups of immigrants. How did they respond to our theme? What meaning (social, political, or psychological) can we assign to their response or lack of it? The available evidence points to no single conclusive answer. On the one hand, we can plausibly argue that given these centrifugal forces in American society, the *topos* is in the process of degenerating into increasingly empty and irrelevant rhetoric. On the other hand, in view of precisely these same conditions, it can also be viewed functionally as a nationalizing, socially integrating myth, or it can be interpreted in categories of civic-political-secular religion. Given the often notable intensity of belief in and recurrence of the chosen people theme in American public discourse (political, religious, cultural), it would seem that through the efforts of scholars and other interested parties at any specific time the myth has been made to appear all-pervasive, transcending time and class and ethnic-cultural orientation. It has probably served, and also been consciously manipulated to serve, as a powerful agent for social integration. Sometimes, as has been argued, this has entailed outright suppression of dissent among the less privileged classes that may not share its assumptions.[4]

Because of the externally directed racist elements in the chosenness/mission theme that James H. Moorhead has rightly noted, it may be appropriate here to refer to the response of African Americans as one of the oldest such underprivileged groups within American society. African Americans have developed, as Albert J. Raboteau argues, an independent chosenness/mission myth that stands in opposition to

[4]For the social integration argument, see Daniel Bell, "The End of American Exceptionalism," *Public Interest* 41 (1975), reprinted in Nathan Glazer and Irving Kristol, eds., *The American Commonwealth—1976* (New York: Basic Books, 1976) 223; for the latter argument, see Aristide R. Zolberg, "Troubled Hegemon: The Impact of Global Engagement on American Democracy" (unpublished paper prepared for the Conference Group on Political Economy at the ASPA meeting in Atlanta, GA, August 1989) esp. p. 27.

American culture and society, even though in the last analysis it seems to gain recognition within that culture and society. At the same time, there are also moving examples of unqualified adoption of and support for the dominant white model of the outwardly directed chosenness/mission myth.[5] Clearly, African Americans have strong reasons for rejecting the myth of the dominant culture. Where they have nonetheless subscribed to that myth, the motive would appear to be a desire or demand for acceptance, the insistence on a form of participation historically denied to black Americans.

One last comment concerns the heavily self-centered orientation of the entire chosenness and mission discourse. It is conducted only in terms of motivation (*Gesinnungsethik*, to use Max Weber's term) and hardly ever takes into account the impact on third parties of actions based on these motives. Considering this impact and practicing an ethic of accountability (*Verantwortungsethik*) could serve as a corrective to the more extreme, and basically parochial, formulations of the chosenness/mission myth that Beveridge and others promulgated in the early twentieth century.

[5]Vincent Harding, "Is America in Any Sense Chosen? A Black View," in Walter Nicgorski and Ronald Webers, eds., *An Almost Chosen People: The Moral Aspirations of Americans* (Notre Dame/London: University of Notre Dame Press, 1976) 119–30.

Part Two

············

COUNTERPOINT:

SUFFERING SERVANTS AND

UNCHOSEN PEOPLE

Exodus, Ethiopia, and Racial Messianism:
Texts and Contexts of African American Chosenness

Albert J. Raboteau*

The particular history that people of African descent have endured in this nation, a history burdened by slavery and oppression, has given rise to a sense of specialness that black Americans have expressed in a variety of ways. The oldest and most enduring images of African American chosenness have clustered around three biblical texts, one from the Book of Exodus, one from the Psalms, and the third from Second Isaiah. Applying these texts to explicate their people's history, generations of black preachers, writers, and leaders have defined a distinct identity and a providential destiny for African Americans in terms that have contradicted racist doctrines of black

*Albert J. Raboteau is Henry W. Putnam Professor of Religion at Princeton University.

inferiority and called into question the national myth of American chosenness.

Exodus

In British North America, enslaved Africans and their descendants encountered European Christianity in its Protestant form; by the end of the eighteenth century, they were increasingly adopting the language, symbols, and world view of this religion, especially as the rising evangelical movement of Baptists and Methodists permitted blacks to exercise spiritual leadership as exhorters and preachers. During the 1770s and 1780s, African Americans began to form their own congregations, led by pastors of their own race. Nurturing Christian communities among slaves and free blacks, these early black ministers interpreted Christianity to fit the day-to-day lives of their people, in effect developing an independent black Christianity. In the North, the abolition of slavery after the Revolution and the disestablishment of religion made it possible for black religious autonomy to take institutional form. In the South, laws restricting the separate assembly of blacks for any purpose hindered black religious independence, but slaves nonetheless developed their own "invisible institution" of extra-ecclesial religious life in which they made Christianity their own.[1]

At the center of the African American interpretation of Christianity was the God pictured in the Bible not just as the creator and ruler of the cosmos, but as the lord of history, a God who lifted up the lowly and cast down the mighty, a God whose sovereign will was directing all things toward an ultimate end, drawing good out of evil. One story in particular caught the attention of black Christians and fascinated them with its implications for their own situation—the story of the Exodus, God's liberation of the children of Israel from bondage in Egypt. In the nineteenth century, the Exodus story took on the dimensions of an archetypal myth for African Americans. Just as God had delivered Israel from slavery in Egypt, so would he deliver them from

---

[1]See Albert J. Raboteau, *Slave Religion: The Invisible Institution in the Antebellum South* (New York: Oxford University Press, 1979) 96–150, 212–19.

slavery in America. Black Christians appropriated the story of the Exodus as the paradigm of their own experience. The Exodus symbolized their common history of oppression and their common destiny as a chosen people, like Israel of old, eventually to be free.

The story of the Exodus contradicted the claim of white Christians that God intended Africans to be slaves. The Exodus proved that their enslavement was against God's will and that inevitably he would free them, even though time and manner of this liberation were hidden in his will. The sacred history of God's liberation of his people would be (or was being) reenacted in the American South. A white chaplain in the Union army working among the freedmen in Decatur, Alabama noted the power of the Exodus in the religion of the slaves: "There is no part of the Bible with which they are so familiar as the story of the deliverance of Israel. Moses is their ideal of all that is high, and noble, and perfect, in man. I think they have been accustomed to regard Christ not so much in the light of a *spiritual* Deliverer, as that of a second Moses who would eventually lead them out of their prison-house of bondage."[2]

The identity that African Americans felt with the children of Israel could take intensely emotional expression, as African Methodist Episcopal pastor William Paul Quinn demonstrated in 1834, when he exhorted the members of his congregation to "comfort and encourage one another, and keep singing and shouting, great is the Holy One of Israel in the midst of us. Come thou Great Deliverer, once more awake thine almighty arm, and set thy African captives free."[3] The Exodus came alive dramatically, especially in the spiritual songs and prayer meetings of the slaves who reenacted the story as they shuffled around in the holy ring dance called "the shout." In the ecstasy of worship, time and distance were bridged and the slaves became the Israelites. They travelled dry-shod, like the Hebrews, through the Red Sea; they too saw Pharaoh's army "get drownded"; they stood beside

[2]William G. Kephart, Letter of 9 May 1864, Decatur, AL, American Missionary Association Archives, Amistad Research Center, Tulane University, New Orleans, LA.

[3]William Paul Quinn, *The Sword of Truth Going "Forth Conqering and to Conquer"*. . . (1834), reprinted in Dorothy Porter, ed., *Early Negro Writing, 1760–1837* (Boston: Beacon, 1971) 635.

Moses on Mount Pisgah and caught sight of the Promised Land; they crossed Jordan under Joshua and marched with him round the walls of Jericho. Their prayers for deliverance resonated with the experiential power of these liturgical dramas.

Thus, in the story of Israel's exodus from Egypt the slaves predicted a future radically different from their present and so gave meaning and purpose to lives threatened by senseless and demeaning brutality. In times of despair they recalled the Exodus and in that story found hope to endure. As a slave named Polly poignantly explained to her mistress, "We poor creatures have need to believe in God, for if God Almighty will not be good to us some day, why were we born? When I heard of his delivering his people from bondage, I know it means the poor Africans."[4]

The Exodus epitomized the dichotomy between the Christianity of the master and that of the slave. The division was described by a white Methodist minister who was pastor of a black congregation in Charleston, South Carolina, in 1862. He recalled that when he preached "the law of liberty" and "freedom from Egyptian bondage" he meant it figuratively, as "relief from the servitude of sin, and freedom from the bondage of the devil," whereas they "interpreted it literally in the good time coming, which of course could not but make their ebony complexion attractive, very."[5] The Exodus, the Promised Land, and Canaan meant freedom in the vocabularies of the slaves. Canaan sometimes referred not only to the condition of freedom but also to the geography of freedom, the North or Canada. As Frederick Douglass recalled, when he and several companions had plotted to escape from slavery, their "repeated singing of 'O Canaan, sweet Canaan, / I am bound for the land of Canaan,'" meant "something more than a hope of reaching heaven. We meant to reach the North, and the North was our Canaan."[6] To be sure, the major import of the Exodus was to

---

[4]Diary entry of 12 December 1857 in Barbara Leigh Smith Bodichon, *An American Diary, 1857–1858* (ed. Joseph W. Reed, Jr.; London: Routledge & Kegan Paul, 1972) 65.

[5]A. M. Chreitzberg, *Early Methodism in the Carolinas* (Nashville: Methodist Episcopal Church, South, 1897) 158–59.

[6]Frederick Douglass, *Life and Times of Frederick Douglass: Written by Himself* (1892; reprinted New York: Crowell-Collier, 1969) 159–60.

nurture internal resistance, not external acts of rebellion, but the symbolic resistance extrapolated from the Exodus story was real. It took no genius to identify the revolution in status envisaged in the slave song "My army cross ober, My army cross ober / O Pharaoh's army drownded."

Identification with Israel, moreover, constituted an assertion by slaves and free blacks that they were a special, divinely favored people. This was an identity in stark contrast to the racist propaganda of the dominant culture, which degraded them as members of an inferior race. The appropriation of the Exodus story by African Americans inverted one of the oldest and most pervasive myths of national identity. From the earliest years of settlement, European colonists had represented their journey across the Atlantic to America as the exodus of a new Israel from the bondage of an old-world Egypt into the Promised Land of milk and honey. For Africans, the narrative was reversed: the Middle Passage had brought them to an American Egypt where they suffered bondage under a new Pharaoh. White Americans saw themselves as the new Israel; black Americans identified themselves as the old. The nation's claim to be the new Israel was contradicted by old Israel still enslaved in her midst.[7]

American preachers and orators mined Exodus as a rich source of metaphors to describe the unfolding history of the nation. Each section of the narrative, the bondage in Egypt, the rescue at the Red Sea, the wandering in the Wilderness, and the entrance into the Promised Land, provided a typological map to reconnoiter the moral terrain of American society. John Winthrop, the leader of the great Puritan expedition to the Massachusetts Bay Colony, set the pattern in 1630 in his sermon, "A Model of Christian Charity." Its evocative image of a "city upon a hill" still echoes in contemporary presidential addresses. By the end of the eighteenth century, an increasingly confident, prosperous, and newly independent country was becoming the redeemer nation. Antebellum Americans proclaimed that the destiny of the new Israel was to reach the pinnacle of perfection and carry liberty and

[7]This point is articulated well by Vincent Harding in "The Uses of the Afro-American Past," in Donald R. Cutler, ed., *The Religious Situation, 1969* (Boston: Beacon, 1969) 829–40.

Christianity around the globe.[8] But the other, darker, Israel found a voice as well:

> America, America, foul and indelible is thy stain! Dark and dismal is the cloud that hangs over thee, for thy cruel wrongs and injuries to the fallen sons of Africa. The blood of her murdered ones cries to heaven for vengeance against Thee.... You may kill, tyrannize, and oppress as much as you choose, until our cry shall come up before the throne of God; for I am firmly persuaded, that he will not suffer you to quell the proud, fearless and undaunted spirits of the Africans forever; for in his own time, he is able to plead our cause against you, and to pour out upon you the ten plagues of Egypt.[9]

So wrote Maria Stewart, a free black reform activist in Boston during the 1830s. These words, written in 1831, were addressed to Americans, many of whom believed that their nation was the probable site of the coming millennium, Christ's thousand-year reign of peace and justice.

Free blacks like Maria Stewart, in scores of addresses, sermons, and pamphlets, located America in a part of the Exodus story different from that cited by their white countrymen. From their perspective America was Egypt, and as long as the country continued to enslave and oppress black Israel, its destiny was in jeopardy. America stood under the judgment of God, and unless it repented speedily, the death and destruction visited upon biblical Egypt would be visited upon the nation. God, they insisted, would act again, as he had of old, to save his people; he would destroy their oppressors. In the words of a widely

---

[8]See Conrad Cherry, ed., *God's New Israel: Religious Interpretations of American Destiny* (Englewood Cliffs, NJ: Prentice-Hall, 1971) 25–92. As Theodore Dwight Bozeman has pointed out, this later rhetoric has "echoed" a good deal more world-saving zeal than was actually expressed by Winthrop and his generation. See Bozeman, "The Puritans' 'Errand Into the Wilderness' Reconsidered," *New England Quarterly* 59 (1986) 231–51.

[9]Maria Stewart, "Religion and the Pure Principles of Morality, the Sure Foundation on Which We Must Build," in Marilyn Richardson, ed., *Maria Stewart, America's First Black Woman Political Writer: Essays and Speeches* (Bloomington: Indiana University Press, 1987) 39–40.

circulated jeremiad published by a free black Bostonian, David Walker, in 1829, "God rules in the armies of heaven and among the inhabitants of the earth, having his ears continually open to the cries, tears and groans of his oppressed people, and being. . . just and holy. . . will. . . one day appear fully in behalf of the oppressed, and arrest the progress of the avaricious." In terms strikingly prophetic of the Civil War, Walker warned Americans that racial oppression would lead "them to rise up one against another, to be split and divided. . . to oppress each other, and. . . to open hostilities with sword in hand."[10]

The Civil War and emancipation seemed to validate the African American interpretation of Exodus. "Shout the glad tidings o'er Egypt's dark sea / Jehovah has triumphed, his people are free!" the exslaves sang in celebration of emancipation. It did not take long, however, for the freedmen to realize that the Promised Land still lay somewhere far in the distance. As time went on and slavery was succeeded by other forms of racial oppression, black Americans seemed trapped in the wilderness no matter how hard they tried to reach Canaan. The former slave Charles Davenport voiced the disappointment and skepticism of many when he recalled in the 1930s, "De preachers would exhort us dat us was de chillen o' Israel in de wilderness an' de Lord done sent us to take Dis land o' milk and honey. But how us gwine-a take land what's already been took?"[11] Slavery had indeed ended, but in the late nineteenth century the situation of blacks in America seemed to be worsening instead of improving. Against the backdrop of disenfranchisement, lynching, pseudoscientific racism, and institutionalized segregation, emigration to Africa appealed to some African Americans, as it had in the 1830s and 1850s. The largest mass movement based upon the ideal of an African Zion arose in the early twentieth century under the leadership of Marcus Garvey. While the ideal of African emigration has provided a perennial and powerful challenge to African American identity, few black Americans heeded the call to emigrate; most continued to search for their Promised Land

[10]David Walker, *Appeal to the Coloured Citizens of the World* (3d ed.; Boston: Walker, 1830) reprinted in Herbert Aptheker, ed., *One Continual Cry* (New York: Humanities Press, 1965) 65–66.

[11]Norman R. Yetman, ed., *Voices From Slavery* (New York: Holt, Rinehart and Winston, 1970) 75.

in America. As decade succeeded decade, the Exodus story continued to symbolize their unique experience of American slavery as well as their deferred aspirations for full freedom.

As it was transmitted in black culture, song, literature, and oratory, the symbol of the Exodus continued to carry emotional power even for those African Americans whose view of human history no longer included the possibility of divine intervention. The Exodus still elicited within African Americans a sense of special identity and historic destiny whenever black preachers and orators evoked its resonance, as did Martin Luther King, Jr. on the night before his assassination: "We've got some difficult days ahead. But it really doesn't matter with me now. Because I've been to the mountaintop. . . . And I've seen the Promised Land. And I may not get there with you. But I want you to know tonight that we as a people will get to the Promised Land."[12]

Ethiopia

While the Exodus story is clearly applicable to freedom from slavery, Ps 68:31—"Princes shall come out of Egypt and Ethiopia shall soon stretch forth her hands unto God"—is more obscure. Yet the open-ended vagueness of the prediction served to extend its explanatory range to cover the most varied circumstances of African American history. From at least 1774, when the poet Phillis Wheatley cited the verse, Ps 68:31 has been interpreted as a prophecy of the divinely appointed destiny of black people.[13] The explications of the prophecy varied widely, but in the nineteenth and early twentieth centuries, three major themes evolved: the African race, the redemption of Africa, and the mission of the darker races.

All interpreters agreed that Egypt and Ethiopia referred to the African race. African Americans appropriated Egypt and Ethiopia as

[12]Martin Luther King, Jr., Sermon of 3 April 1968, Mason Temple, Memphis, TN, reprinted in James Melvin Washington, ed., *A Testament of Hope: The Essential Writings of Martin Luther King, Jr.* (San Francisco: Harper & Row, 1986) 286.

[13]Phillis Wheatley, Letter to the Rev. Samuel Hopkins, 9 February 1774, reprinted in John Shields, ed., *The Collected Works of Phillis Wheatley* (New York: Oxford University Press, 1988) 175–76.

their African origins and looked to those ancient civilizations as exemplars of a glorious African past. "Ancient history, as well as holy writ, informs us of the national greatness of our progenitors," boasted African Methodist minister William Miller in 1810.[14] Biblical, archaeological, and historical evidence was marshalled by black scholars to prove that descendants of Africa had nothing to fear from comparisons with the descendants of Europe. The vaunted superiority of Anglo-Saxon civilization was based on ignorance. The historical record showed that the "children of Ham were clearly the first to lead off in the march of civilization." While the Egyptians were establishing law and political institutions, the sons of Japhet, the Europeans, were still "a savage race of men, inhabiting the rocks and caverns, a wretched prey to wild beast and to one another."[15]

African Americans needed to reclaim for themselves a civilized African past in order to refute the charge that they were inherently inferior, especially because they assumed that modern Africans and African Americans were less civilized than Anglo Americans. "I admit," wrote William Wells Brown, an escaped slave, novelist, and historian, in 1863, "that the condition of my race. . . at the present time cannot compare favorably with the Anglo-Saxon."[16] The disability of the race, however, was due to the circumstances of enslavement and oppression forced upon it by whites. The historical evidence proved that the reverse had once been the case. But Egypt and Ethiopia had fallen. Why? Grown prosperous, they had forgotten God and turned to idolatry, claimed William Miller.[17] "Where nations have turned aside to idolatry they have lost their civilization," explained black historian George Washington Williams.[18] Hosea Easton, a minister in Hartford,

[14]William Miller, *A Sermon on the Abolition of the Slave Trade: Delivered in the African Church, New York on the First of January, 1810* (New York: Totten, 1810) 4.

[15]William T. Alexander, *History of the Colored Race in America* (1887; reprinted New York: Greenwood, 1968) 8.

[16]William Wells Brown, *The Black Man: His Antecedents, His Genius, and His Achievements* (Boston: Redpath, 1863) 32.

[17]Miller, *A Sermon*, 5–6.

[18]George Washington Williams, *History of the Negro Race in America* (2 vols.; New York: n.p., 1883) 1. 109.

Connecticut, placed the blame on warfare. Whatever the cause, the fall from former glory had been great. African Americans, lamented Easton, are "the remnant of a once noble but now heathenish people," as different from their ancestors as they are from other races.[19] Williams speculated that "the genuine African has gradually degenerated into the typical Negro, the lowest strata" of the once great African race.[20]

And yet, if princes had once ruled wisely in Egypt and if Ethiopia had once inaugurated civilization, might not their descendants in America restore their rightful dignity among the nations, so that once again "princes shall come out of Egypt and Ethiopia shall soon stretch forth her hands to God"? Could this have been the purpose of slavery: the education, elevation, and regeneration of the descendants of Africa? A number of articulate black leaders thought so.

As early as 1808, in one of the earliest black sermons extant, Absalom Jones, pastor of St. Thomas African Episcopal Church in Philadelphia, broached the question of why God had permitted slavery. "It has always been a mystery," he confessed, "why the impartial Father of the human race should have permitted the transformation of so many millions of our fellow creatures to this country, to endure all the miseries of slavery. Perhaps his design was, that a knowledge of the gospel might be acquired by some of their descendants, in order that they might become qualified to be the messengers of it, to the land of their fathers."[21] The problem with this answer, as Jones and other black leaders knew well, was that the evangelization and civilization of blacks was *the* rationalization used by Europeans, from the mid-fifteenth century on, to justify enslaving Africans. In effect, this explanation came dangerously close to absolving whites of the sin of slavery. Blacks refused absolution by distinguishing between

---

[19]Hosea Easton, *A Treatise on the Intellectual Character, and Civil and Political Condition of the Colored People of the United States* (Boston: Knapp, 1837) 19–20.

[20]Williams, *History*, 1. 109.

[21]Absalom Jones, *A Thanksgiving Sermon Preached January 1, 1808, in St. Thomas's or the African Episcopal Church, Philadelphia: On Account of the Abolition of the African Slave Trade, on That Day, By the Congress of the United States* (Philadelphia: Fry & Kammerer, 1808) 18.

the divine will and divine permission. God wills good; he only permits evil, and from evil draws good. Although "God permitted these things to come to pass," Miller preached, "it does not follow that the oppressors of Africa are less culpable for their savage treatment to the unoffending Africans."[22] George Washington Williams reiterated the sentiment two generations later: "God often permits evil on the ground of man's free agency but he does not commit evil. The Negro of this country can turn to his Saxon brothers and say, as Joseph said to his brethren who wickedly sold him, 'As for you, ye meant it unto evil, but God meant it unto good; that we, after learning your arts and sciences, might return to Egypt and deliver the rest of our brethren who are yet in the house of bondage.'"[23]

The purpose of God, revealing itself in human history, was the redemption of the African race. Slavery was his means for achieving this end—drawing good out of evil. The sons of Ethiopia, now enlightened by the Christian gospel, would return to Africa and rekindle the flame of religion and civilization snuffed out by idolatry long ago. This civilizing mission rested firmly upon nineteenth-century Christian assumptions about African "paganism." The African, according to an article published in the influential *AME Church Review* in 1890,

> has made few strides along the line of intelligence; his sight has long become dimmed to apprehend his Maker. He has declined in the scale of human intelligence. He gropes in darkness. He has wandered from the shining face of his God into gross ignorance. The twentieth century of his Redeemer's advent dawns upon him sunk in superstition, and worshipping the creature more than the Creator.[24]

Alexander Crummell, one of the major late nineteenth-century advocates of the evangelization of Africa and himself an Episcopal missionary to Liberia for twenty years, reminded African Americans of their duty to assist the simple, childlike Africans to the higher level

[22]Miller, *A Sermon*, 7–9.
[23]Williams, *History*, 1. 113–14.
[24]George B. Peabody, "The Hope of Africa," *AME Church Review* 7 (1890) 58–59.

of civilization to which blacks in America had already attained. Although Crummell praised the natural modesty and generosity of the Africans as superior to the moral corruption of the English and the Americans, he was confident that Africa stood in need of the blessings of technological civilization. In this regard, Crummell and other proponents of African missions revealed an ambivalent attitude about Africans. On the one hand, they presumed that Africans were backward pagans; on the other, they viewed Americans as racist, imperialistic, and materialistic. Americans were superior in civilization, Africans in natural religiosity.[25]

It was the proper mission of the African American, not the European American, to bring the gospel to the African. As Emmanuel K. Love observed before the black Baptist Foreign Mission Convention in 1889, "There is no doubt in my mind that Africa is our field of operation and that [as] Moses was sent to deliver his brethren, and as the prophets were members of the race to whom they were sent, so I am convinced that God's purpose is to redeem Africa through us." "This work," he concluded, "is ours by appointment, by inheritance, and by choice."[26] Europeans had failed to Christianize the "dark continent" despite previous attempts. Edward Wilmot Blyden, a missionary and cabinet minister in Liberia, argued that God intended Africa for black missionaries. By allowing slavery, he converted them; by permitting racism, he directed them back; and by completely shutting up the vast interior of Africa from exploration, "until the time arrived for the emancipation of her children in the Western World," God had clearly singled out black people as His chosen instrument to redeem Africa.[27] A few dissenting voices denied that the redemption of Af-

---

[25]Alexander Crummell, *Christian Recorder*, 23 September 1865; idem, "The Obligation of American Black Men for the Redemption of Africa," *African Repository* 48 (1872) 162–68; idem, *The Future of Africa* (1862; reprinted New York: Greenwood, 1969); and idem, *Africa and America* (1891; reprinted New York: Greenwood, 1969).

[26]Cited in James Melvin Washington, *Frustrated Fellowship: The Black Quest for Social Power* (Macon, GA: Mercer University Press, 1986) 137–38.

[27]Edward W. Blyden, "The African Problem and the Method of Its Solution," *AME Church Review* 7 (1890) 205, 213. See also St. Clair Drake, *The Redemption of Africa and Black Religion* (Chicago: Third World, 1970) for the fullest study of this theme.

rica was the divinely appointed destiny of black Americans. For example, T. Thomas Fortune, the militant editor of the *New York Age* complained, "The talk about black people being brought to this country to prepare themselves to evangelize Africa is so much religious nonsense boiled down to a sycophantic platitude. The Lord who is eminently just, had no hand in their forcibly coming here. It was preeminently the work of the devil. Africa will have to be evangelized from *within*, not *from without*."[28] Fortune had economics, if not symbolism on his side. Black churches were too poor to mount large-scale African campaigns, and attempts to work with the missionary boards of white denominations encountered difficulties over racial discrimination. Nevertheless, by the 1870s the idea of African missions loomed large in the consciousness of black Christians. Relatively few African Americans ventured the trip physically, but symbolically the mission to redeem Africa confirmed their destiny as a people.

Indeed, some nineteenth-century black Americans extended their redemptive mission beyond Africa. "It is my solemn belief, that if ever the world becomes Christianized. . . it will be through the means, under the God of the *Blacks*, who are now held in wretchedness and degradation, by the white *Christians* of the world," claimed David Walker in 1829.[29] The peak of racial exceptionalism was reached by an A.M.E. minister who announced that African Americans were "the instruments in the hands of God for the redemption of Africa, the subjugation of America, and for bringing the world unto God and his Christ."[30] The mission of black Christians to be the bearers of true Christian civilization was elaborated in greatest detail by two black clergymen in the late nineteenth century. Theophilus Gould Steward and James Theodore Holly interpreted Ps 68:31 in a global perspective. Steward, a minister of the A.M.E. Church, published his treatise *The End of the World* in 1888 in order to debunk Josiah Strong's paean to the mission of the Anglo-Saxon race, *Our Country*, published in 1885. Scripture and history, he argued, demonstrated that

---

[28]T. Thomas Fortune, *Black and White: Land, Labor, and Politics in the South* (1884; reprinted Chicago: Johnson, 1970) 86–87.

[29]Walker, *Appeal*, 104.

[30]James Porter, "Afro-American Methodism as a Factor in the Progress of Our Race," *AME Church Review* 7 (1891) 321.

America had been displaced in the drama of salvation. It was impossible for America to convert the world to Christianity, because America had turned Christianity from a world religion into a clan cult. Americans preached and practiced Anglo-Saxonism, not Christianity. Assessing the militarism, nationalism, and materialism of the age, he concluded that the civilization epitomized by Europeans and Americans would soon destroy itself in fratricidal warfare. A new age was about to begin, during which the darker peoples of the world, long oppressed by Western civilization, would create a raceless, classless, weaponless Christianity that would convert the world and welcome the arrival of "the universal Christ."[31]

James Theodore Holly, a black Episcopal priest and missionary to Haiti, also defined a universal role for the darker races at the end time of human history. In a striking reversal of the biblical curse of Canaan by Noah, which had been used for centuries to justify African slavery, Holly wrote in 1884 that the "divine plan of human redemption" was unfolding in three historic periods or dispensations. The first dispensation belonged to the Semitic race whose task was to formulate and preserve the word of God. The second or Japhetic phase coincided with the apostolic or evangelical period, the age of the Europeans who were commissioned to spread the gospel. The Hebrew dispensation ended with the destruction of the temple in 70 CE. The Japhetic phase would soon end in warfare, after which the millennium would commence. During this thousand-year reign of peace and justice, the Hamitic race would bring to completion the divine plan of human redemption only imperfectly realized by the Semitic and Japhetic races. To the sons of Ham, "the elect among nations," "the crowning work of the will of God is reserved."[32] The Semites preserved the word of God; the Japhites preached it; during the last and greatest dispensation, the Hamites would finally put the word of God into practice. Holly explained why the Hamites had been so favored:

---

[31]Theophilus Gould Steward, *The End of the World; Or, Clearing the Way for the Fullness of the Gentiles* (Philadelphia: A.M.E. Church Book Rooms, 1888) 119–27.

[32]James Theodore Holly, "The Divine Plan of Human Redemption, In Its Ethnological Development," *AME Church Review* 1 (1884) 79–85.

The African race has been the servant of servants to their brethren of the other races during all the long and dreary ages of the Hebrew and Christian dispensations. And it is this service that they have so patiently rendered through blood and tears that shall finally obtain for them the noblest places of service in the Coming Kingdom. That what has been a curse to them under Gentile tyranny will become a blessing to them under the mild and beneficent reign of Christ, and thus will be realized the double but adverse significations of the Hebrew word *barak*. . . which signifies "to bless," and also "to curse." . . . The curse of Canaan, dooming him to be a servant of servants unto his brethren, which lowered him to a place of dishonor under the earthly governments of men, will turn to a blessing unto him and exalt him to the posts of honor under the heavenly government of God.[33]

During the nineteenth century, African Americans had spun out of Ps 68:31 a theology of history that extolled their past, valorized their present, and magnified their future as the people chosen by God for the leading role in the drama of human salvation. By the beginning of the twentieth century, the religious symbolism of the verse had expanded to include the political rhetoric of a developing pan-African movement.

Pan-African ideas had been circulating for quite some time—invariably supported by references to Ps 68:31—in the sermons and speeches of nineteenth-century proponents of African emigration. Pan-Africanism emphasized some familiar themes—ancient African civilization, the redemption of Africa, and the glorious African future—but it gave them a new political urgency that impelled black intellectuals and activists from America, Europe, and Africa to organize an international movement. The goals of the movement included race pride, race unity, "Africa for Africans," and the formation of an African national homeland for the continent's far-flung exiles. Against the background of the "European scramble for Africa," the partition of the continent among rival European powers, black delegates articulated pan-African sentiments at congresses on Africa that met in Chicago in 1893, Atlanta in 1895, and London in 1900, with the last forming a short-lived Pan-African Association. The largest and most

[33]Ibid., 83–84.

influential pan-African movement, the Universal Negro Improvement Association (UNIA), founded by Marcus Mosiah Garvey, carried the gospel of race pride, race unity, and African nationalism not only to its enrolled membership but also to black communities all over the United States and beyond.[34] Black Americans, whose race caused them to be treated as aliens in their own land, found in Garvey's UNIA the comfort of a black national identity free of ambivalence and alien-ation, regardless of whether or not they actually went "back to Af-rica." The UNIA created its own flag, national anthem, provisional government, and steamship line, all to reinforce a sense of national identity among its members. For those who were disaffected with Christian churches, the UNIA supplied a weekly Sunday service, a baptismal ritual, a hymnal, a creed, a catechism, and the image of Jesus Christ as a "Black Man of Sorrows" and the Virgin Mary as a "Black Madonna." The creed read in part, "We believe in God, the Creator of all things and people, in Jesus Christ, His Son, the Spiri-tual Savior of all mankind. We believe in Marcus Garvey, the leader of the Negro peoples of the world, and in the program enunciated by him through the UNIA."[35] This put Garvey on a plane with divine authority. The question and answer format of the *Universal Negro Catechism* (1921) served to overcome deeply ingrained feelings of black inferiority by instilling within members the certainty of their special destiny as a race. The catechism, a summary of the biblical and historical "proofs" for pan-African doctrine, provided members with ammunition against the race's detractors. For example,

> Q. Is it true that Noah cursed his son Ham? A. No; he cursed Canaan, the youngest son of Ham. . . . Q. Who are the descen-dants of Canaan? A. The Canaanites who dwelt in Palestine before the Jews took possession of it. Q. Are Negroes concerned in this curse of Noah? A. Certainly not. . . . Q. What prediction

---

[34]A useful summary of pan-African ideas and movements is P. Olisanwuche Esedebe, *Pan-Africanism: The Idea and Movement, 1776–1963* (Washington, DC: Howard University Press, 1982).

[35]Quoted in Tony Martin, *Race First: The Ideological and Organizational Struggles of Marcus Garvey and the Universal Negro Improvement Associa-tion* (Dover, MA: Majority Press, 1976) 69–70.

made in the 68th Psalm and the 31st verse is now being fulfilled? A. "Princes shall come out of Egypt, Ethiopia shall soon
stretch out her hands unto God." Q. What does this verse prove?
A. That Black Men will set up their own government in Africa,
with rulers of their own race.[36]

Under the twin banners of "Up You Mighty Race" and "One God,
One Aim, One Destiny," Garvey succeeded, as no one before or since,
in awakening the black masses to the ideal of black exceptionalism
and mobilizing them to realize the providential destiny of the race.
After his arrest, incarceration, and eventual deportation by the federal
government for mail fraud, the UNIA dispersed, but the ideals of pan-
African identity, articulated so effectively by Garvey, lived on in a
variety of movements and figures into the late twentieth century. Their
influence can still be seen in the cultural nationalism of the 1960s and
1970s, the Rastafarianism of Garvey's own Jamaica, and the Afro-
centrism promulgated by some Black Studies programs. While pan-
Africanists believed that the chosenness of black people consisted in
their African nationality, other African Americans discovered their
exceptionalism in new religious options.

Racial Messianism

In the twentieth century, many of the historic expressions of African American chosenness have culminated in the theme of racial
messianism—the idea that black people and societies have been chosen not just for deliverance from bondage, not only for a redemptive
role in Africa, but as a "redeemer nation" in world history. Although
this more recent development falls beyond the scope of the present
volume, it may be useful to summarize its most important characteristics.

Clearly, since the days of slavery black Americans had identified
themselves metaphorically with biblical Israel. The first organization

---

[36]*Universal Negro Catechism* ([New York]: privately printed by the Universal Negro Improvement Association, 1921) 7, 11. The catechism was com-
piled by the Rev. George Alexander McGuire, a black Episcopal priest, who
served for a time as chaplain of the UNIA before founding the African Orthodox Church.

to take this identification literally, however, was the Church of God
and Saints of Christ, founded in 1896 by William S. Crowdy in
Lawrence, Kansas. Crowdy preached a heterodox version of Judaism
based upon his assertion that black people were descended from the
ten lost tribes of Israel. Similar beliefs inspired the development of
other black Jewish congregations. In the 1920s, Wentworth A. Matthew formed around a nucleus of West Indian immigrants the Commandment Keepers Congregation of the Living God, for years Harlem's
largest congregation of black Jews. The Commandment Keepers believed that African Americans were "Ethiopian Hebrews," or Falashas,
who had been stripped of their true religion by slavery. Judaism was
the ancestral heritage of the Ethiopians, whereas Christianity was the
religion of the "gentiles," i.e., the whites.[37]

Messianism, however, could and did take a different tack. In 1913,
the first organized movement of black Americans to identify itself as
Muslim was founded by Timothy Drew in Newark, New Jersey. The
Noble Drew Ali, as his followers called him, taught that African
Americans were not Negroes but Asiatics. Their original home was
Morocco; their true nationality was Moorish American. To symbolize
the recovery of their true identity, members of the Moorish Science
Temple received new names and identity cards issued by Noble Drew
Ali. Knowledge of their true selves, Ali taught, would empower them
to overcome racial oppression. The Moorish Science Temple survived
Ali's death in 1929, only to be eclipsed by another esoteric Muslim
group that claimed much more national attention.[38]

This organization was the Nation of Islam, which grew from two
small congregations in Detroit and Chicago to dozens of mosques
embracing thousands of members in every section of the country.
Under the leadership first of W. D. Fard, and then of Elijah Muhammad

---

[37]Howard M. Brotz, *The Black Jews of Harlem: Negro Nationalism and
the Dilemmas of Negro Leadership* (New York: Schocken, 1964); Deanne
Shapiro, "Double Damnation, Double Salvation: The Sources and Varieties
of Black Judaism in the United States" (M.A. diss., Columbia University,
1970).

[38]Arthur Huff Fauset, *Black Gods of the Metropolis: Negro Religious Cults
in the Urban North* (1944; reprinted Philadelphia: University of Pennsylvania
Press, 1971) 41–51.

and Malcolm X, black Muslims invented new racial, national, and religious identities that rejected both America and Christianity, although doing so required them to deny significant aspects of their own history as African Americans, as well as to invert the myth of American exceptionalism. America, they claimed, was indeed special; America was Satan![39]

For most black Americans this rejection was too high a price to pay, even to be free of the American dilemma. Nor did most of them believe that Christianity was a white man's religion. Distinguishing between true Christianity and false, they continued to embrace the gospel of Jesus even as they condemned its American perversions; this too blazed a trail for twentieth-century messianism. Blacks had earlier condemned "slaveholding religion" and uttered jeremiads against the apostasy of America over slavery. Had not the Redeemer himself, as Isaiah had predicted of old, come as a "suffering servant"? If so, who in America resembled him more, the master or the slave? It was the destiny of those who had been "buked and scorned" to save "the soul of the nation," as the motto of the Southern Christian Leadership Conference expressed it a century later.

Scholars have recently emphasized that the fundamental views and attitudes of Martin Luther King, Jr. were deeply rooted in the black culture of his home and church.[40] King's belief in redemptive suffering derived initially not from Gandhi but from his predecessors in the pulpit, generations of black preachers who had appealed to Isaiah 53 to prove that the African Americans' history of suffering was replicating the biblical pattern: the servants of God may have to suffer, but their suffering leads to salvation. King's allusions to the suffering

[39]C. Eric Lincoln, *The Black Muslims in America* (Boston: Beacon, 1961); Essien Udosen Essien-Udom, *Black Nationalism: A Search for Identity in America* (Chicago: University of Chicago Press, 1962).

[40]Lewis V. Baldwin, "Martin Luther King, Jr., The Black Church and the Black Messianic Vision," *Journal of the Interdenominational Theological Center* 12 (1984–85) 93–108; James H. Cone, "Martin Luther King Jr., Black Theology—Black Church," *TToday* 41 (1989) 409–20; idem, "The Theology of Martin Luther King, Jr.," *USQR* 40 (1986) 5–20; Clayborne Carson, "Introduction," in idem, ed., *The Papers of Martin Luther King* (Berkeley: University of California Press, 1992) 1. i–xxiii

servant motif heightened the sense of racial identity in his black audiences by evoking their common history of slavery and oppression, a history that bespoke a special destiny.

The civil rights movement, at least its nonviolent wing, revitalized the nineteenth-century belief that America's moral leadership lay with black people. Blacks in both centuries asserted their claim to moral leadership in biblical and messianic terms. This is not to say that African Americans had simply created a black version of American exceptionalism. King, Howard Thurman, and others insisted that the particular history of black Americans represented the suffering of the poor and oppressed everywhere. According to the suffering servant version of exceptionalism, God's chosen people were not the rich and powerful, but the despised and disinherited.

Nonviolence, redemptive suffering, and the identification of black people as suffering servants were vehemently rejected by Malcolm X and others as dangerous forms of racial masochism and passivity. But there is no denying the pervasiveness and endurance of this version of exceptionalism in African American culture. Perhaps its rhetorical and symbolic power was most accurately captured in James Baldwin's fictional account of a black teenager's coming to acceptance of his racial identity in *Go Tell It on the Mountain*, published in 1952. The novel culminates in an all-night conversion scene in a Harlem storefront church, and the themes and images convey, in their own religious idiom, the sense of chosenness that enabled blacks to endure brutal suffering with dignity, pride, and hope.

Conclusion

Over the last two centuries African Americans have invented a myth of their own exceptionalism based largely upon biblical themes and religious imagery. Given the centrality of religion in black American culture this is not surprising. Many black Americans have not accepted the myth of chosenness in any of its varied forms. Yet, despite abundant reasons for skepticism about God's intentions for the race, the myth of African American chosenness has continued to exert a powerful intellectual and emotional appeal. Whether this would be the case if racial discrimination was ended is a question that will not likely be answered soon. Certainly the continuing power of exceptionalism as a rhetorical strategy for black Americans is attributable to the intransigence of a racism that still requires them to assert their equal status as human beings. African Americans, moreover, undoubtedly share the tendency of all ethnic groups to maintain identity by distinguishing their cultural legacies.

The myth may have endured for another reason, however: African American chosenness still conveys a message that desperately needs to be heard: All people are chosen, because we are all "children of God."

Response

*Silke Lehmann**

In 1903, a cartoon appeared in the *Boston Record* showing Booker T. Washington's skill and success in tapping the wealth of Andrew Carnegie. Carnegie's face is depicted as part of a rock formation, and the cartoon is titled "The Modern Moses Strikes Rocks."[1] In 1886 Sarah Bradford's biography of Harriet Tubman, the slave woman who was the most outstanding black conductor on the underground railroad, appeared under the title *Harriet Tubman: The Moses of Her People*.[2] One of the most comprehensive and serious studies on Marcus Garvey and his movement, published by E. D. Cronon in 1955, carries the title *Black Moses*.[3]

The history of African Americans is full both of images and direct quotations from the Hebrew scriptures and of parallels drawn between black Americans and Israel. By utilizing the larger time frame of nineteenth- and twentieth-century history rather than the narrow time scale of 1880–1920, Albert Raboteau has demonstrated the continuity and the varieties of the chosen people theme in African American history. He rightly points to the fact that the Exodus story took on the dimensions of an archetypal myth for African Americans in the nineteenth century. The story of Israel's Exodus supported the slaves' hope for a radically different future; in times of despair they could turn for relief to the idea of Exodus. Exodus epitomized the dichotomy between the Christianity of the masters and that of the slaves. Raboteau, supporting Vincent Harding, makes the important statement that one

---

*Silke Lehmann, D.Phil, is currently based in Göttingen, Germany.

[1] Louis R. Harlan, *Booker T. Washington: The Wizard of Tuskegee, 1901–1915* (New York/Oxford: Oxford University Press, 1986) 270.

[2] Sarah Bradford, *Harriet Tubman: The Moses of Her People* (1886; reprinted Secaucus, NJ: Citadel, 1974).

[3] E. David Cronon, *Black Moses: The Story of Marcus Garvey and the Universal Negro Improvement Association* (Madison: University of Wisconsin Press, 1955).

of the oldest and most pervasive myths of American national identity becomes inverted by the appropriation of the Exodus story by African Americans. While white Americans portrayed the colonists' journey across the Atlantic as the Exodus of a new Israel from an old world Egypt to the new Promised Land, black Americans believed that they had experienced a different story: the slave trade had brought them to an American Egypt. White Americans regarded themselves as the new Israel, but black Americans saw themselves as members of the old and still suffering Israel. For that matter, white America's claim to be the new Israel was opposed by old Israel still in bondage.

For nineteenth-century black Americans, the Promised Land lay ahead. Many of them considered the American North their Promised Land. For others, albeit a minority, a return to Africa held the promise of solving their problems. With regard to the idea of a chosen people, however, both destinations posed special problems. The early nineteenth-century campaign to return free blacks to Africa was first and foremost a white idea. Except for Paul Cuffe, who accompanied thirty-eight emigrants in 1815, no black Moses was prepared personally to lead his people to Africa. Rather, organizations dominated by white Americans attempted to ship free blacks back to Africa. To these philanthropists it seemed impossible that black Americans should remain in a nation that whites perceived as forever white, Protestant, and "civilized."

What could have been the most convincing reincarnation of the idea of chosenness among African Americans—a migration from the American Egypt to the African Promised Land—was therefore corrupted from the start, despite the support it received from Ps 68:31 ("Let bronze be brought from Egypt; let Ethiopia hasten to stretch out its hands to God") and from pan-Africanism. Such a solution, moreover, was to remain unacceptable for the majority of blacks, even though Marcus Garvey with his Universal Negro Improvement Association (UNIA) came close to reviving this dream at the beginning of the twentieth century. Garvey pleaded: "Wake up Ethiopia! Wake up Africa! Let us work toward the one glorious end of a free, redeemed and mighty nation. Let Africa be a bright star among the constellations of nations." Garvey also appealed to race pride: "To be a Negro is no disgrace, but an honor, and we of the UNIA do not want to become white. . . . We are proud and honorable. We love our race and respect and adore our mothers."[4] Outcries such as these made his movement the first real mass movement among blacks in the history of the United States. Garvey's whole argumentation definitely implied the notion of chosenness.

The vision of the North as the Promised Land was much more widely accepted than any dream of a return to Africa.[5] Before and after the Civil War, and before and after the First World War, African Americans from the South saw the North as the Promised Land of freedom, racial justice, and economic opportunity. We know, however—and those who migrated soon had to realize—that the North was, to say the least, not the land of milk and honey. In the North, African Americans not only found themselves in a society filled with many religions and ethnic groups, but also in a society full of social tensions and racism. Since the discrepancy between their dreams of the Promised Land and the realities of life in the North was painful, arguments for chosenness have lived on in the twentieth century as well. They have been accompanied by various forms of racial messianism that have stressed black specialness and promised to offer solutions to the American dilemma.

Albert Raboteau's question—whether the myth of chosenness would lose its appeal among African Americans if racial discrimination were to be ended—is indeed a question for the future. Perhaps we could come closer to an answer if, building on existing studies of Africa and America, we looked for the theme of chosenness—or its absence— in those societies where black Africans have been able to shape political affairs or in those parts of the West Indies where black people have been able to participate in government. Other studies could probe ideas of chosenness and redemption in countries like Brazil or even South Africa, where blacks form a majority but have been excluded from sharing political responsibility.[6] Since none of these cases would

---

[4]Quotations are taken from John Hope Franklin, *From Slavery to Freedom: A History of Negro Americans* (New York: Knopf, 1967) 490–91.

[5]Nicholas Lemann, *The Promised Land: The Great Black Migration and How It Changed America* (New York: Knopf, 1991).

[6]In recent years, some comparative work has been done in this field; see,

replicate the very special political, cultural, and economic conditions in the United States, however, we would presumably be dealing as much with contrasts as with comparisons.

Martin Luther King, Jr., had, among his many capabilities, a special degree of insight into the problems and potential of American society and politics. On the one hand, he appealed to black pride and asked his people to unite in an implicitly (and often explicitly) adversarial relation to the oppressing society. On the other hand, he knew that justice for blacks could only be realized as one element in a more just American society. In 1963, in his most famous speech, King proclaimed that

> even though we must face the difficulties of today and tomorrow, I still have a dream. It is a dream deeply rooted in the American dream that one day this nation will rise up and live out the true meaning of its creed—we hold these truths to be self-evident, that all men are created equal.[7]

For King, the Promised Land was neither Africa nor a separate black state, but a better America. In his last speech, on 3 April 1968, the

---

for example, J. Mutero Chirenje, *Ethiopianism and Afro-Americans in Southern Africa, 1893–1916* (Baton Rouge: Louisiana State University Press, 1987); Carl Degler, *Neither Black nor White: Slavery and Race Relations in Brazil and the United States* (Madison: University of Wisconsin Press, 1986); George M. Fredrickson, *White Supremacy: A Comparative Study in American and South African History* (New York/Oxford: Oxford University Press, 1981); idem, *The Arrogance of Race: Historical Perspectives on Slavery, Racism and Social Inequality* (Middletown, CT: Wesleyan University Press, 1988); idem, *Black Liberation: Ideology and Leadership in American and South African Freedom Struggles, 1880–1976* (forthcoming); Dwight N. Hopkins, *Black Theology USA and South Africa: Politics, Culture and Liberation* (Maryknoll, NY: Orbis, 1989); Sylvia M. Jacobs, *Black Americans and the Missionary Movement in Africa* (Westport, CT: Greenwood, 1982); and Orlando Patterson, *Slavery and Social Death: A Comparative Study* (Cambridge, MA: Harvard University Press, 1982).

[7]*A Testament of Hope: The Essential Writings and Speeches of Martin Luther King, Jr.* (James Melvin Washington, ed.,; New York: Harper Collins, 1991) 219.

eve of his assassination, he again referred to the best in the American dream, to "those great wells of democracy which were dug deep by the Founding Fathers in the Declaration of Independence and the Constitution." Even more relevant here, however, is King's great peroration:

> We've got some difficult times ahead. But it doesn't matter with me now. Because I've been to the mountain top. . . . And I've looked over, and I've seen the Promised Land. I may not get there with you. But I want you to know tonight, that we as a people will get to the Promised Land.[8]

Albert Raboteau points to King's belief in redemptive suffering. King and generations of black preachers before him argued that the African Americans' suffering would eventually lead to salvation. Although this was a line of reasoning not accepted by the more radical Civil Rights activists, it remains a very moving argument. It is an argument, we should note, that draws not only from the Hebrew scriptures but also from the New Testament, from Jesus' assurances that the poor and the wretched of this earth will be saved.

Such argumentation was by no means singular. It had been pursued by the left wing of the Reformation, by eighteenth-century German Pietists, and, among others, as Paul Mendes-Flohr's article in this volume shows, also by Jews. Here again, in exploring the correlation between chosenness and suffering, a comparative approach may be most helpful and produce the most insights.

[8]Ibid., 286.

In Pursuit of Normalcy:
Zionism's Ambivalence toward Israel's Election

Paul Mendes-Flohr[*]

Introduction

In addressing the questions raised by the topic of this volume, I shall enlist the rabbinic principle of answering a question with yet another question. Animating this principle, of course, is the presupposition that before matters can be clarified, they must first be confounded. Salvation only comes from a healthy confusion.

It is undoubtedly a tacit assumption of the theme of this volume that the concept of a chosen people is biblical in origin and that modern Western nationalism is likely to be modeled, at least rhetorically, on the privileged status that Israel enjoyed as God's elect.

[*]Paul Mendes-Flohr is Professor of Modern Jewish Thought and Intellectual History at the Hebrew University of Jerusalem.

Ideationally, then, there would seem to be a direct line between "the Old Testament covenant" and Western nationalist movements that marched under a banner proclaiming that theirs was a chosen people. Accordingly, given the biblical provenance of the concept, one would assume that Zionism, the Jewish analogue of Western nationalism, was similarly nurtured by the concept of a chosen people.

Is the concept, however, a Jewish idea? Is it applicable to an examination of Jewish self-understanding? As I shall endeavor to show, the term "chosen people" is not found in classical Jewish sources and seems to have entered Jewish discourse only with Jewry's encounter with the modern world. At this juncture, the term "chosen people" was apparently borrowed from the Christian vocabulary as a lexical equivalent of the expression Jews traditionally used to refer to their relationship with God. To be sure, the concept may have existed in Judaism before the term itself; certainly the tradition testifies to the divine election of Israel. To complicate the picture still further, in all the various attempts in classical Judaism to delineate the beliefs and dogmas of Judaism, not once is election mentioned.[1] As Solomon Schechter once suggested, election may have been an "unformulated dogma," its truth being so self-evident that no one felt a need to record it.[2] This may, however, be begging the question, since the same could be said about the existence and oneness of God, which are stated in all formulations of Israel's essential creed.[3] The omission of the notion of Israel's chosenness from traditional Jewish dogmatics, moreover, raises the issue of the notion's cultural valence. Indeed, the role that election plays in crystallizing Jewish self-understanding may be less central than that which the concept of a chosen people fulfills in certain Christian communities.[4]

---

[1]See Menachem Kellner, *Dogma in Medieval Jewish Thought: From Maimonides to Abravanel* (New York: Oxford University Press, 1987).

[2]Solomon Schechter, "Election of Israel," in idem, *Aspects of Rabbinic Theology: Major Concepts of the Talmud* (New York: Macmillan, 1909) 57.

[3]For a succinct review of the subject, see Menachem Kellner, "Dogma," in Arthur A. Cohen and Paul Mendes-Flohr, eds., *Contemporary Jewish Religious Thought: Original Essays on Critical Concepts, Movements, and Beliefs* (New York: Free Press, 1987) 141–46.

[4]As a general observation, one may note that election, emboldened by

The question then is whether Israel's understanding of itself as God's elect is identical with the concept of a chosen people sponsored by Western Christianity. No semantic quibble is intended. Both the meaning of election and the way it functions in Israel's consciousness of itself as a people are of phenomenological significance, and as such may bear on the sensibilities and imaginative horizons of an ideology such as Zionism that claims to speak on behalf of the Jewish people.

Zionism, of course, is a coat of many colors, indeed a dizzying array of often calling together ideological hues. In calling together the First World Zionist Congress in 1897, Theodor Herzl (1860–1904) found himself a leader of bourgeois admirers as well as radical Marxists; his dream of renewed Jewish political sovereignty was embraced by religious Jews and militant atheists. Indeed, Herzl was baffled—if not perturbed—by the cacophonous medley of competing visions of a restored Zion. One voice, however, dominated in the founding decades of the movement, a period known in Zionist historiography as the first, second, and third *aliyot* (1882–1903, 1904–1914, and 1919–

---

feelings of superiority (see n. 25 below), plays a greater role in Jewish folk culture—and as such it may not differ from the popular culture of other oppressed minorities—than it does in Jewish theology, beholden as it is to the universal presuppositions of monotheism. Indeed, as I shall endeavor to show, Jewish religious thought tends to emphasize the covenantal obligations attendant on election. Further, in contrast to Christianity, traditional Judaism (with few exceptions) did not develop a theology of election. One significant exception occurs, perhaps not coincidentally, in the twentieth century with the mystical nationalism of Rabbi Abraham Isaac Kook (1865–1935), who, drawing inspiration from the kabbalah, attributed to the Jewish people an intrinsic holiness while lending an eschatological endorsement of Zionism. For a sociological analysis of the "structural" tension in Judaism between particularism and universalism, see Samuel N. Eisenstadt, "The Format of Jewish History: Some Reflections on Weber's Ancient Judaism." Parts 1, 2. *Modern Judaism* 1 (1981) 54–73, 217–34. The same theme is considered from the perspective of comparative religion, with pertinent remarks on Rabbi Kook's theology, in R. J. Zwi Werblowsky, *Beyond Tradition and Modernity: Changing Religions in a Changing World* (London: Athlone, 1976) 40–60. Many of the theoretical issues considered in this article were clarified in conversation with Sholomo Fischer of the Van Leer Jerusalem Institute. I gratefully acknowledge his erudition and wisdom.

1923)—in other words, the initial waves of Zionist immigration to the land of Israel.[5]

This voice, despite its varied nuances, was decidedly secular, placing emphasis on practical deeds toward the realization of a comprehensive revolution in all aspects of Jewish life. Some spoke of a revitalization of Judaism by a secular redefinition of pristine Jewish values that would allow them to engage the mind and soul of Jews drawn to the modern world. Others desired a more fundamental break with tradition.[6] Micah Joseph Berdichevski (1865–1921) called for a Nietzschean transvaluation of values: "We have come to a time of two worlds in conflict: To be or not to be! To be the last Jews or the first Hebrews. . . . We are the last Jews—or we are the first of a new nation."[7]

Virtually all Zionists—at least the overwhelmingly secular majority of the first three *aliyot*—shared an insistence that the Jews must be a "normal" people. In the name of the desired normalization, they consciously sought to jettison the idea of election. An acerbic diatribe against the apologetic theology of Western Jews, who were desperately trying to ingratiate themselves with liberal opinion, was penned in 1893 by the Zionist writer Ahad Ha‘am (1856–1927), then still a resident of czarist Russia. He asked bitingly, "Do I envy these fellow Jews their emancipation?" Replying to his own question, he bellowed,

---

[5]The hiatus between the second and third *aliyot* is explained by the fact that during World War I immigration to Palestine was virtually impossible. Overwhelmingly comprised of idealistic, often self-consciously antibourgeois youth, the first three *aliyot* regarded themselves as the vanguard of the people "reborn," intellectually and spiritually. Not all the thinkers and writers inspiring these *aliyot* necessarily joined them in the practical work of "redeeming" the land of Israel (and thereby also the Jewish people), but these intellectuals nonetheless served to articulate the pioneering ethos. Accordingly, not all the voices quoted in this essay were actual participants in the *aliyot*.

[6]For a critical and typological analysis of the various positions within secular Zionism, see Menahem Brinker, "Brenner's Jewishness," *Studies in Contemporary Jewry* 4 (1988) 232–49.

[7]Micah Joseph Berdichevski, "Wrecking and Building" (1900–1903), in Arthur Hertzberg, ed., *The Zionist Idea: A Historical Analysis and Reader* (Garden City, NY: Doubleday, 1959) 292, 294.

No! a thousand times No! I may not be emancipated but I have not sold my soul for emancipation. . . . *I at least have no need to exalt my people to Heaven, to trumpet its superiority above all other nations, in order to find a justification for its existence.* (my emphasis)[8]

Ahad Ha⁽am further stated that despite their newly acquired political liberties, Western Jews had actually become "spiritual slaves." This tragic paradox of emancipation, he contended, was only thinly veiled by the apologetic gyrations of a concocted theology that seeks to justify Jewry's abiding particularity in terms of its universal mission. In contrast, the Jews of autocratic Russia, although they still suffered the indignities of the ghetto, were "spiritually free." They saw no need to apologize for remaining Jews. Furthermore, Ahad Ha⁽am noted that, as a secular Jew, he felt no compunction whatsoever about criticizing Judaism, which he found reprehensible or outdated:

I at least can speak my mind concerning the beliefs and opinions which I have inherited from my ancestors, without fearing to snap the bond that unites me to my people. I can even adopt that "scientific heresy that bears the name Darwin," without any danger to my Judaism. In a word, I am my own, and my opinions and feelings are my own. I have no reason for concealing or denying them, for deceiving others or myself. And this spiritual freedom—scoff who will!—I would not exchange or barter for all the emancipation in the world.[9]

For Ahad Ha⁽am the normalization of the Jews sponsored by Zionism was precisely the securing of this "spiritual freedom," particularly in its secular expression. For other Zionists, the ideal of normalization entailed the return of the Jews to world history and the end of Jewish exceptionalism in all forms.[10]

[8] Ahad Ha⁽am, "Slavery in Freedom," in Hans Kohn, ed., *Nationalism and the Jewish Ethic: Basic Writings of Ahad Ha⁽am* (New York: Schocken, 1962) 64.

[9] Ibid., 65.

[10] This attitude is poignantly depicted in a short story by the Hebrew writer

All Zionists spoke of a rejection or negation of the Diaspora, called *galut* ("exile") in the traditional Jewish parlance they insistently retained when speaking of Israel's dispersion. "The Zionist attitude begins," as the historian Ben Halpern observed, "with a lively awareness and affirmation of Exile as a condition"—a condition that is inherently problematic for continued Jewish existence.[11] Through deliberate human effort—guided by social and political analysis—Jews were to dismantle the infamy of exile; they would no longer piously await the messiah whom God would graciously dispatch to redeem them. Exile, therefore, became the grand symbol of Jewish abnormality, and the return to Zion marked the reversal of this sorry condition.[12]

Zionism, therefore, was not simply a territorial movement dedicated to the restoration of a forlorn people to its ancestral homeland. Rather, it was preeminently a movement dedicated to the cultural and psychic healing of people suffering from the scourge of a bimillennial exile. Even for those Zionists—usually of a Western assimilated background—who regarded anti-Semitism as the most urgent issue facing the Jewish people, the psychic rehabilitation of the Jew was an exigent task. Thus, at the Second Zionist Congress, Max Nordau (1849–1923), a famed literary critic and Herzl's right-hand man, called for creating "once again a Jewry of Muscles":

> Once again! For history is our witness that such a Jewry once existed. . . . In the narrow Jewish street [of the ghetto] our poor limbs soon forgot their gay movements; in the dimness of sunless houses our eyes began to blink shyly; the fear of constant persecution turned our powerful voices into frightened whispers, which rose in a crescendo only when our martyrs on the stake

---

Haim Hazaz, "The Sermon" (1942), in Joel Blocker, ed., *Israeli Stories* (trans. Ben Halpern; New York: Schocken, 1962) 65–86.

[11]Ben Halpern, "Exile," *Jewish Frontier* (1954) 6.

[12]Halpern (Ibid., 9) states: "The intellectual substance of Zionism is the rejection of Exile: not the denial of Exile, please note, but its rejection. . . . There were two historical attitudes to which Zionism opposed itself, and in opposing, was defined. The first was the acceptance of Exile as a 'commitment'— the attitude, by and large, of Orthodox Jewry at the time. The other was the 'denial' of Exile as a condition—an attitude which arose in Reform Judaism."

cried out their dying prayers. . . . But now. . . let us once more become deep-chested, sturdy, sharp-eyed men.[13]

Nordau fantasized the new Jew as Simeon Bar Kokhbah redivivus, although the heroic exploits of this fearless leader of the revolt against the Roman emperor Hadrian were hardly noted by Jewish tradition but in fact cherished in Christian memory through writings rejected by the rabbis.

The Zionist vision of a new Jew and a new Judaism, a vision fanned by contradictory impulses, was replete with paradoxes. The most fundamental contradiction was perhaps inherent in the very quest for normalization, because a studied pursuit of normalcy may be as chimerical as the efforts of an individual who stands before a mirror practicing spontaneity. Normalization may also have been denied to the Zionist movement by the intrinsic ambiguity of its project. On the one hand, normalization was to signify the healing of a nation maimed by a tragic exile that had drained it of the vitality of a genuinely creative and proud people. Exile had putatively rendered the Jews an overspiritualized phantom, listlessly awaiting supernatural redemption. The cure proffered by the Zionists to lead the people to national health and a normal constitution amounted to a radical secularization and a break with the Jewish past, or at least with its enfeebling religious traditions. On the other hand, Zionism was bent on avoiding the sad experience of Western Jewry and the ignominy of assimilation, self-denial, and "self-liquidation" (*Entjudung*), as one of the leaders of Labor Zionism (and a future president of the state of Israel) put it.[14] The preservation of the Jewish people was a—indeed, *the*—cardinal value of Zionism.

The twin objectives of normalization and preservation were to be pursued by creating a culture grounded in the Hebrew language, which

[13]Max Nordau, "Muskeljudentum," in *Juedische Turnzeitung* (1903); translated in Paul Mendes-Flohr and Judah Reinharz, eds., *The Jew in the Modern World: A Documentary History* (New York: Oxford University Press, 1980) 434–35.

[14]Salman Rubaschof, "Erstlinge der Entjudung," *Der juedische Wille* 1 (1918) 30–35. Rubaschof, who later changed his name to Shazar, was the third president of the State of Israel.

in turn was cast anew as the colloquial idiom of the people. These objectives were centered in what Herzl aptly called an *Altneuland*.[15] Hence, as long as Zionism focused on Hebrew and the land of Israel, the break with Jewry's religious past could never be as clean as envisioned. One may say that the utopian aspect of Zionism always had a restorative dimension.[16] The resulting tension or even dialectic between the two, needless to say, was often unintended, as the young Gershom Scholem (1897–1982) observed with respect to Hebrew. Three years after he settled in Palestine full of enthusiasm to participate in the Zionist project, Scholem shared his apprehensions regarding the fate of Hebrew in a letter, dated December 1926, to the philosopher Franz Rosenzweig:

> This country is a volcano, and language is lodged within it. People here talk of many things that may lead to our ruin, and more than ever of the Arabs. But there is another danger, much more uncanny than the Arab [question], and it is a necessary result of the Zionist enterprise: What of the "actualization" of the Hebrew language? That sacred language on which we nurture our children, is it not an abyss that must open up one day? The people certainly don't know what they are doing. They think they have secularized the Hebrew language, have done away with its apocalyptic sting. But that, of course, is not true: [What is celebrated here as] the secularization of the language is no more than a *façon de parler*, a phrase! It is impossible to empty words so bursting with meaning, unless one sacrifices the language itself. The phantasmagoric gibberish we hear spoken in our streets precisely defines the faceless lingo which alone has permitted the "secularization" of the language. But if we transmit the language to our children as it was transmitted to us, if we, a generation of transition, revive the language of the ancient books for them, shall not the religious power of the language explode one day?[17]

[15]This was the title of Theodor Herzl's novel of 1902, published in English as *Old-New Land* (New York: Schocken, 1987).

[16]See Yosef Gorni, "Utopian Elements in Zionist Thought," *Studies in Zionism* 5 (1984) 19–27; and Ehud Luz, "Utopia and Return: On the Structure of Utopian Thinking and Its Relation to Jewish-Christian Tradition," *JR* 73(1993) 357–77.

[17]Quoted in Stephane Moses, "Scholem and Rosenzweig. On Our Lan-

The tragedy of Zionism, Scholem suggested, would be its failure to appreciate the dialectic that it had set in motion. The resulting secularization would lead not to the renewal of the people and its culture, but rather, he warned, to its vulgarization and ultimate ruin.

Eschewing such Cassandran speculations, it will suffice simply to note that the dialectical tension of which Scholem spoke was characteristic of virtually all aspects of Zionist culture.[19] In this article we shall explore the tension as it is manifest in Zionist attitudes toward Israel's election.

Chosenness in Classical Judaism

> For you are a people consecrated to the Lord your God: of all the peoples on earth, the Lord your God chose (*baḥar*) you to be His treasured people (*ʿam segulah*). (Deut 7:6)[19]

> Blessed art Thou, O Lord, who has chosen (*baḥar*) us from all the peoples by giving us Thy Torah. (*Traditional Jewish Prayer Book*)

As I have suggested, an appreciation of the role of the chosen people concept within classical Zionism requires first a clarification of the traditional Jewish understanding of chosenness. I shall begin, then, with a philological observation that is admittedly captious and perhaps even trivial. The term "chosen people" does not exist in the lexicon of classical Judaism. The Hebrew Bible speaks in Deut 7:6— the locus classicus for Israel's election—of *ʿam segulah*. This term is

---

guage: A Confession," *History and Memory: Studies in Representation of the Past* 2 (1990) 97. I have altered the translation slightly, consulting the original German manuscript in the Leo Baeck Institute, New York.

[18]For a detailed analysis of this tension as it pertains to modern Jewish thought in general, see Paul Mendes-Flohr, "The Dialectic of Atheism and Secularization in Modern Jewish Thought," in Albino Babolin, ed., *Ateismo e Societa* (Perugia: Editrice Benucci, 1992) 167–89.

[19]In citing the Hebrew Bible I shall follow the "New Translation of the Holy Scriptures" (3 vols; ed. Harry M. Orlinsky; Philadelphia: Jewish Publication Society, 1962–82).

a conjoining of two nouns, the first denoting "people" and the second "a special treasure." Thus the term denotes a people who are a special treasure to God, "a treasured people."[20] Until the modern period, Jewish tradition knew no other term but ʿam segulah to characterize Israel's graced relationship to God.[21] In the traditional Jewish imagination this relationship was intimately associated and even correlated with the covenant. This is made clear in the prologue to the revelation of the Ten Commandments: "Now then, if you will obey Me faithfully and keep My covenant, you shall be My treasured possession (ʿam segulah) among all the peoples. Indeed, all the earth is Mine, but you shall be to Me a kingdom of priests and a holy nation" (Exod 19:5–6). The covenantal character of Israel's election receives emblematic expression in the traditional Hebrew prayer book. In a liturgical formulation reaching back to the temple service,[22] the pious Jew recites various benedictions in which God is praised for having "chosen us. . . by giving us Thy Torah."[23]

---

[20]Regarding the translation of ʿam segulah, see Moshe Greenberg, "Hebrew segulla: Akkadian sikiltn," JAOS 71 (1951) 712–14.

[21]Modern Hebrew does speak of "chosen people"—ʿam nevḥar, or, alternately, ʿam beḥirah—but clearly as a translation from European languages. The question arises whether the translation bears with it the importation of meanings that may have been originally foreign to the Jewish understanding of election. To be sure, the adoption of a non-Jewish—that is, a Christian (traditional or laicized)—understanding of election may have already occurred with the Enlightenment and emancipation, when the Jews entered European culture. A comparative ideational and phenomenological study of Jewish and Christian notions of election is both desirable and needed. Assuming there are differences, a study of how Christian conceptions of election may have shaped modern Jewish perceptions of Israel's election would also be welcomed. For an important contribution toward such a study, see Arnold M. Eisen, The Chosen People in America: A Study of Jewish Religious Ideology (Bloomington: Indiana University Press, 1983).

[22]Ephraim E. Urbach, The Sages: Their Concepts and Beliefs (trans. Israel Abrahams; Cambridge, MA: Harvard University Press, 1987) 534; see also Meir Bar-Ilan, "The Idea of Election in Jewish Prayer," in Shmuel Almog and Michael Heyd, eds., Chosen People, Elect Nation and Universal Mission (Jerusalem: Zalman Shazar Center for Jewish History, 1991) 131 [Hebrew].

[23]Weekday Prayer Book (New York: Rabbinical Council of America, 1961) 83.

With reference to Israel's divine election, classical Judaism employs the term "choose" (*baḥar*) only as a verb, never as an adjective;[24] certainly, chosenness is not cited as an inalienable attribute.[25] God chooses Israel to receive his Torah and to obey its commandments: "The Lord your God commands you this day to observe these laws and rules; observe them faithfully with all your heart and soul" (Deut 26:16). This is the overarching image of Israel's election in

[24]A past participle based on this root does occur, usually with a possessive pronoun, namely, *beḥiri*, meaning "my chosen one," such as in Isa 42:1; 43:20; and 45:4. In these passages, as in Ps 89:4, the phrase reflects a relationship of affection, akin to saying "my dear one." Indeed, it might be more accurate to translate *beḥiri* as "my favorite one." It thus marks neither an exclusive relationship nor an ontological claim.

[25]To be sure, there are currents in classical Judaism that ascribe to Israel's election a primordial, even ontological entitlement, an unconditional privilege that therefore was free of the emotional ambiguity to which we have alluded. Some rabbis of the Talmud taught that in the very act of creation, God had already planned to elect Israel. Thus the election had an eternal, unconditional significance, which by implication was independent of the Jewish people's faithfulness to God and the covenant, although no one would dare suggest this explicitly. (See Urbach, *The Sages*, 525–41.) The Spanish Jewish philosopher Judah Halevi (b. before 1075, d. 1141) held that God fashioned a special "Jewish soul," one that was qualitatively superior to that of non-Jews. The Jew's soul, according to Halevi, allowed him or her to achieve a spiritual excellence—the ultimate expression of which was prophecy—that Gentiles, regardless of their intelligence and goodness, could never attain. It was by virtue of this unique spiritual faculty that the Jews were able to receive the Torah. "Therefore," Halevi concluded, "without the children of Israel there would be no Torah; moreover, they did not derive their uniquenes from Moses, but Moses derived his uniqueness from them" (Halevi *Sefer hakuzari* 2.56). One may find similar notions in the kabbalah and Hasidism. Perhaps reflecting this trend in Jewish theology, Jewish folk culture abounds with attitudes assuming Israel's innate superiority to Gentiles, especially in matters of the intellect and morality. Most Jews, however, would undoubtedly agree with Halevi that despite their inborn virtues, not all Jews are inevitably smart or upright. On the contrary, precisely because of their spiritual promise, when Jews fall they are truly degenerate. As one scholar recently noted, paraphrasing Halevi, "like the little girl in the jingle, when a Jew is good he is very good but when he is bad he is horrid" (Louis Jacobs, *God, Torah, Israel: Traditionalism without Fundamentalism* [Cincinnati: Hebrew Union College Press, 1990] 59).

traditional Judaism: Israel is *chosen* by God to bear the "yoke of Torah."[26] Indeed, although the Jews are enjoined to rejoice in their election, they are also exhorted to acknowledge that it is an onerous responsibility, entailing exceptional duties and an exacting, frightful accountability: "You alone have I singled out of all the families of the earth—that is why I will call you to account for all your iniquities" (Amos 3:8).

The Ambivalence of Israel's Election

The intention of the preceding philological excursus has been phenomenological rather than theological. In keeping with my introductory remarks, I have wished merely to highlight traditional Jewry's understanding concerning its election. I have also sought to point to the perplexity that often attended Israel's assumption of its covenantal responsibilities, beginning with that fateful day when Moses descended Mount Sinai with God's commandments. With the advent of Zionism, these conflicting emotions emerged as a tortured ambivalence.

In classical Judaism the emotional perplexity to which I am referring is perhaps no more powerfully captured than in an oft-told rabbinic midrash. Commenting on the scriptural passage, "And they took their places at the foot of the mountain" (Exod 19:17), the midrash explains that when the children of Israel gathered at the foot of Mount Sinai "the Holy One, blessed be He, hung the mountain over [them] like a pail, and declared: 'If you accept the Torah, fine; if not then this mountain will be your grave.'"[27] The midrash, in fact, boldly suggests that God's election of Israel was an aggressive act.[28]

Other rabbinic midrashim attribute the image of the "suffering servant" (Isaiah 53) to Israel;[29] because of its loyalty to the covenant, Israel must forever endure humiliation and anguish. The Hasidic master Rabbi Levi Yitzhak of Berditchev (1740–1809), who would often

[26] *m. ʾAbot* 3.5.
[27] *b. Šabbat* 88b.
[28] I am indebted to my colleague Galit Hasan Rokem for this insight.
[29] See, for example, *Midrash on Psalms* Psalm 113. Hermann Cohen, *Religion of Reason Out of the Sources of Judaism* (trans. Simon Kaplan; New York: Ungar, 1972) 282.

remonstrate with God regarding Israel's tribulations, is said to have once suddenly interrupted his prayers and cried,

> From the moment You concluded a covenant with Your people, you have consistently tried to break it by testing it; why? Remember: at Sinai You walked back and forth with Your Torah like a peddler unable to dispose of his rotten apples. Your Law, You offered it to every nation and each turned away contemptuously. Israel alone declared itself ready to accept it, to accept You. Where is its reward?[30]

In modern literature, Israel's ambiguous experience of its election was given poignant expression by Richard Beer-Hofmann (1866–1945), a colleague of Theodor Herzl's in the literary circle called Young Vienna. In his play written in 1918, *Jacob's Dream*, Beer-Hofmann explored the patriarch's inner crisis during the night at Beth-El when he accepted for himself and his descendants the burden of his father's blessing:

Rebecca [explaining to Edom why Jacob was chosen]:
Yes! Yes! Because—
Because he moves forever shadowed by deep
    questioning,
And you rejoice, happy and safe and sated! Because
    his father's doubts and dreams and longings,
In never-ceasing claims, resound in him!
Because he does not shroud his God in
    distant heavens,
But wrestles with Him daily, heart to heart!
. . .
And in every suffering he has a part
And speaks to all things, and all things
    to him. . . .
He bears the blessing—*and* the
    blessing's burden!. . . .
Jacob (bitterly): This is what chosen means:

---

[30]Quoted in Elie Wiesel, *Souls on Fire* (trans. Marion Wiesel; London: Weidenfeld & Nicolson, 1972) 109–10.

Not to know dreamless sleep,
Visions at night—and voices round by day!
Am I then chosen? Chosen that all suffering
Calls me, demands me, and complains to me?
That even the dumb look of the dying beast asks
    me: Why so?[31]

This ambivalence regarding Israel's election is at the core of Zionism and its attempt to recast—to "normalize" was the telling slogan—the image and self-consciousness of the Jewish people.

Normalization or Preservation?

Those bums [the Zionists] want to be happy![32]

In Zionism the ambivalence toward election is manifest as a grand paradox. On the one hand, Zionism was born of a rebellion against Israel's seemingly interminable exile and endless torment, a rebellion that often vented its fury against the religious values that seemed to conspire with the political and social forces that were keeping Israel in bondage. The poet laureate of modern Hebrew, Chaim Nachman Bialik (1873–1934), in "City of Slaughter," a poem written in the wake of the Kishinev pogroms that took place during Easter 1903, denounced neither God nor the venomous mobs. Instead, he berated the Jews themselves, beholden as they were to pious irrelevancies that had rendered them supinely accepting of exile and its humiliation:

Descend then, to the cellars of the town,
There where the virginal daughters of thy folk

---

[31]Richard Beer-Hofmann, *Jacob's Dream: A Prologue* (trans. Ida Bension Wynn; Philadelphia: Jewish Publication Society of America, 1946) 60–61, 121.

[32]"Die Kerls wollen glücklich sein!" Cited from a conversation with Hermann Cohen in Franz Rosenzweig, "Einleitung in die Akademieausgabe der Jüdischen Schriften Hermann Cohens," in idem, *Der Mensch und sein Werk: Gesammelte Schriften*, vol. 3: *Zweitromland: Kleinere Schriften zu Glauben und Denken* (eds. Reinhold Mayer and Annemarie Mayer; Dordecht: Nijhoff, 1984) 219.

were fouled,
Where seven heathens flung a woman down,
The daughter in the presence of her mother,
The mother in the presence of her daughter,
Before slaughter, during slaughter, and
after slaughter;
. . .
Note also, do not fail to note,
In that dark corner, and behind the cask
Crouched husbands, bridegrooms, brothers, peering from
the cracks,
Watching the sacred bodies struggling underneath
. . .
Crushed in their shame, they saw it all;
They did not stir nor move;
They did not pluck their eyes out; They
Beat not their brains against the wall!
Perhaps, perhaps, each watcher had in his
heart to pray:
*A miracle, O Lord—and spare my skin
this day!*[33]

On the other hand, Zionism sought not only to restore the political dignity of the Jews, but also to renew the pristine values of Israel, albeit laicized, often radically so.

I would characterize this paradox as a dialectic tension between utopian and restorative features of Zionism, a tension between the quest for normalization and the equally compelling desire to preserve the Jews as a nation wedded to their own distinctive culture. It is discerned most vividly with respect to the election of Israel. The premise of Zionism, as we have noted, was that in exile Jewry had become an abnormal, spiritually and socially deformed nation. As one of the fathers of Russian Zionism, Leo Pinsker (1821–1891) claimed in his seminal pamphlet of 1882, "Auto-emancipation: An Appeal to his People by a Russian Jew," the Jews had become a "ghostlike" people who marched through the Diaspora as phantoms bereft of real

---

[33]Hayyim Nahman Bialik, "City of Slaughter," in Israel Efros, ed., *The Complete Poetic Works of Hayyim Nahman Bialik* (trans. Abraham M. Klein; New York: Histadruth Ivrith of America, 1948) 133–34.

life, lacking the attributes of genuine and healthy nationhood. Worse, they had lost the will that would sustain a normal national life. He likened the Jews to an ailing individual desperately in need of healing.[34]

The novelist Joseph Hayyim Brenner (1881–1921), one of the most respected voices of the Second Aliyah, which established the creed of pioneering Zionism in Palestine, saw the concept of election as a vain attempt to glorify and disguise the illness afflicting the nation in exile. Thus, in his immensely popular novel, *From Here and There* (*Mi Kan u-mi-Kan*), Brenner's protagonist declares,

> With a burning and passionate pleasure I would blot out from the prayer book of the Jews of our day "Thou hast chosen us" in every shape and form. Even today I would do this: I would scratch out and remove every false nationalist passage until there remained no remembrance of them. For the vacuous national pride and contentless Jewish boasting will not heal our misfortune.[35]

With Nietzschean inflections, Berdichevski—who, like Brenner, was born in czarist Russia, raised in a pious home, and endowed with a rich traditional Jewish education—called for "a transvaluation of the values that have been the guidelines of our lives in the past":

> Our hearts ardent for life, sense that the resurrection of Israel depends on a revolution—the Jews must come first, before Judaism—the living man, before the legacy of his ancestors. . . . Such a choice promises us a noble future; the alternative is to remain a straying people following its erring shepherds. A great responsibility rests upon us, for everything is in our hands! We are the last Jews—or we are the first of a new nation.[36]

[34]See Leo Pinsker, "Auto-Emancipation: An Appeal to his People by a Russian Jew" (1882), in Herztberg, *The Zionist Idea*, 181–98.

[35]Joseph Hayyim Brenner, "*Mi Kan u-mi-Kan*," in M. Z. Wolpovski, ed., *Collected Works of Y. H. Brenner* (2 vols.; Tel Aviv: Kibbutz Ha-meʾuḥad, 1977) 2. 1280 [Hebrew].

[36]Berdichevski, "Wrecking and Building," 294–95.

The radical secularization implied by Berdichevski's envisioned "transvaluation of values" was—as was the restoration to Zion—merely the indispensable condition for the normalization of Jewry. Socialist Zionists like Brenner would also stipulate that the process of healing Israel required the fundamental restructuring of Jewish economic life: "Our urge for life, which stands above logic, says: All this is possible. Our urge for life whispers hopefully in our ear: Workers' Settlements, Workers' Settlements. . . Workers' Settlements—this is our revolution. The only one."[37] The Jews, Brenner reasoned, would also have to reacquaint themselves with power, including military might.[38] Only then, he concluded, could their pretensions to being a chosen people be properly tested.[39] Brenner formulated this proposition somewhat paradoxically: To vindicate their chosenness, the Jews must first "become a chosen people, become, that is, like all other nations, each of whom is chosen *by itself*."[40] Normalization, as Gershom Scholem affirmed, would probe the truth of all the pious litanies of Judaism.[41]

Zionism and Religious Tradition

Despite itself, the Zionist enterprise could not disengage totally from the religious tradition of Judaism, its symbolic and ideational universe.[42] This is seen most dramatically in the fierce debate surrounding the so-called Uganda Scheme, the offer made in 1903 by the British Empire to establish an autonomous Jewish settlement in East Africa. The founder of the World Zionist Organization, Herzl, presented the proposal to his fellow Zionists. He urged them, given the

[37]Joseph Hayyim Brenner, "Self-Criticism" (1914), in Hertzberg, *The Zionist Idea*, 312.

[38]See Ehud Luz, "The Moral Price of Sovereignty: The Dispute about the Use of Military Power within Zionism," *Modern Judaism* 7 (1987) 51–98.

[39]See Menachem Brinker, *Narrative Art and Social Thought in the Work of Y. H. Brenner* (Tel Aviv: ʿAm ʿOved, 1990) 178–84 [Hebrew].

[40]Brenner, "Self-Criticism," 308; my emphasis.

[41]See Gershom Scholem, "Judaism," in Cohen and Mendes-Flohr, *Contemporary Jewish Religious Thought*, 505–8.

[42]See Ehud Luz, *Parallels Meet: Religion and Nationalism in the Early Zionist Movement, 1882–1904* (trans. Lenn J. Schramm; Philadelphia: Jewish Publication Society of America, 1988).

poor prospects of attaining an international charter that would allow Jewry to reestablish its home in Palestine, to consider seriously the Uganda Scheme as a means of providing immediate relief to the oppressed Jewish masses in Eastern Europe. Herzl's close associate Max Nordau assured the movement that the proposed settlement in Uganda would be merely a *Nachtaysl* ("shelter for the night") on the road to Zion. To Herzl and Nordau's profound dismay, however, the Russian Zionists, most of whom were militantly secular, vigorously rejected the Uganda Scheme, insisting that the goal of reclaiming Israel's ancient patrimony in Palestine could not be compromised.

It is significant that the religious Zionists (*Mizrahi*), led by the pragmatic Rabbi Yitzhak Reines (1839–1915), endorsed the Uganda Scheme. For secular East European Zionists, the renewal of the Jewish people could be achieved only in the land of Israel. This renewal would consist of the reordering of Jewish economic and social structure, the rebirth of Hebrew as their national vernacular, and the reformation of their spiritual life as a comprehensive and secularly relevant culture. In their effort to achieve renewal, they were not prepared to wait for the Messiah or for the consent of diplomats; they therefore resolved—to use Herzl's derisive phrase—"to infiltrate into Palestine" in order to begin the work of Jewish redemption, which they, indeed, did not hesitate to call redemption (*ge'ulah*).

Indeed, to mobilize Jewish passion and fantasy for the "return to Zion"—a term central to the Zionist vocabulary and consciously borrowed from the Hebrew scriptures (Ps 126:1)—religious and even messianic images were evoked. In 1898, the ideological founder of Socialist Zionism, Nachman Syrkin (1868–1924), published a brochure, "Die Judenfrage und der sozialistische Judenstaat" ("The Jewish Question and the Socialist State"), which concluded with an appeal to the Jewish people to assume the task of creating the first socialist state and then "once again [to] become the chosen of peoples." He argued that by blending socialist ideals with Israel's ancient "messianic hope" of national restoration, Zionism would offer the Jews a unique opportunity to liberate themselves from the misery of exile, while at the same time being "the first to realize the socialist vision. This is the tragic element of [the Jews'] fate but it is also a unique mission. . . . Israel will once again become the chosen of the peoples!!"[43] The spiritual mentor both of the Second Aliyah and of the pioneers (*ḥalutsim*) of Syrkin's socialist vision, Aaron David Gordon (1856–1922), voiced grave reservations about celebrating the Jews once again as the chosen people. To him all peoples were unique and each had a distinctive vocation. Nonetheless, he assigned to Zionism and reborn Jewry a particularly elevated vocation, which he articulated with images reminiscent of biblical and rabbinic reflections on Israel's election:

> We were the first to proclaim that man is created in the image of God. We must go farther and say: the nation must be created in the image of God. Not because we are better than others, but because we have borne upon our shoulders and suffered all which calls for this. It is by paying the price of torments the likes of which the world has never known that we have won the right to be the first in this work of creation.[44]

In returning to its land, Gordon observed, Israel would perforce command the attention of the world. It ought to acknowledge its destiny and strive to be an exemplary nation by creating an *ʿAm-ʾAdam*, a "people-humanity." More precisely, it would be a people-incarnating humanity, by which he meant a nation that endeavors to infuse its institutions and communal ethos with humanity's most elevated virtues: morality and a reverence for nature.[45]

Having abandoned middle-class comfort in his native Russia at the age of forty-eight in order to settle in Palestine, Gordon had become a pioneer, even though he had never before engaged in physical labor. He became a legendary figure who enjoyed a unique moral authority among the far younger *ḥalutsim* of the Second Aliyah. Working at manual labor by day (eighteen hours a day, it is said) and writing at

---

[43]Nachman Syrkin, "The Jewish Problem and the Socialist-Jewish State" (1898), in Hertzberg, *The Zionist Idea*, 349–50.

[44]Aaron David Gordon, "ʿavodatenu meʿaṭah" (1920), in idem, *Ha-ʾomah ve-haʿavodah* (Jerusalem: Mosad Bialik, 1951) 240–41 [Hebrew].

[45]See Gad Ofaz, "The Creation of *Am-Adam*: The National Utopia of Aaron David Gordon," *Zionism: Studies in the History of the Zionist Movement and the Jewish Community in Palestine* 15 (1990) 77–106 [Hebrew].

night, he developed his views with a highly idiosyncratic blend of German romanticism, Russian populism (he was especially inspired by the teachings of Tolstoy), and the kabbalah.

Gordon's writings were, in fact, too ethereal to be accessible to most of his admirers. Far more influential and central was Berl Katznelson (1887–1944), the indomitable labor leader of Palestinian Jewry. He unhesitatingly and unapologetically employed religious language. In an address entitled "Facing the Days Ahead," which he gave at the Seventh Conference of the Judean Workers' Union in 1918, Katznelson sought to inspire anew the idealism of the pioneers and their commitment to "liberating and liberated labor," buffeted as they were by mounting hardships and apprehensions about the future. Beseeching his comrades, most of whom were raised in traditional homes in Eastern Europe, he expressly appealed to their primal Jewish sentiments. "What Jew with a generous heart would begrudge the prophetic promises, would renounce the destiny of being chosen and the [vision of] redemption, and would not rejoice that 'the Torah shall go forth from Zion?'"[46] Katznelson reminded his fellow *halutsim* that Israel's prophets—he actually used the pronoun "we"—were the first to proclaim the "ideals of justice and righteousness." Accordingly, he asked rhetorically, "who among us does not know that it is incumbent upon us to be a light unto the nations?" (see Isa 42:6). He concluded by urging his audience not to be estranged from the vision of the prophets and the obligations of election, even though these traditions had been usurped by a Jewish bourgeoisie that was in need of platitudinous slogans to camouflage its own moral bankruptcy:

> It is true that [the blessing] "Thou, God, has chosen us," together with all the other ideals [of our tradition], have for a long while become but prim top hats adorning the bald heads of "plutocrats" who occasionally deign to perform a religious rite. . . . But the prophets of truth and justice are now called upon to protest and secure the nation's way of life and workers' rule in the land [of Israel].[47]

[46]Berl Katznelson, "Li-krat ha-Yamim ha-Baʾim," in idem, *Collected Works* (12 vols.; ed. Shmuel Yaveneli; Tel Aviv: Workers' Party of Eretz Yisrael, 1944) 1. 66. See Isa 2:3 for the scriptural quotation.
[47]Ibid., 68.

What Katznelson seemed to be suggesting was a dialectic between the Zionist program of national normalization and a biblical or prophetic idealism. As he knew well, however, not only did the imperatives of normalization—the quest to be "a nation like all other nations"— threaten to vitiate the idealistic passion; there was also the danger that the very ideals from which he and his comrades sought to draw inspiration might come to be regarded as impediments on the path to Israel's renewed nationhood.

Legitimate versus False Nationalism

In November 1917, Great Britain issued the Balfour Declaration, inexorably linking Zionism's fortunes to the schemings of international politics and a tragic conflict with Arab and Palestinian national aspirations. The Zionist leadership was now obliged to steer the movement through the rough and uncertain seas of realpolitik. It was within this context that Israel's election was once again introduced. The intent was to restrain a tendency to allow the pursuit of the movement's political interests to promote a myopic nationalism.

The spiritual mentor of Central European Zionists, Martin Buber (1876–1965) often employed the theme of election as a foil against what he derisively called *Kleinzionismus*. In September 1921, he addressed the Twelfth Zionist Congress in Carlsbad, a meeting convened in the wake of the Balfour Declaration and the establishment of the British mandate over Palestine. He spoke of the dangers of nationalism attendant upon Zionism's entry into world politics and its alliance with the interests of an imperialist power. Buber suggested that there were two forms of nationalism. One of these comes to heal a particular nation's suffering. It serves to correct a fundamental lack in the life of the nation, its "lack of unity, freedom, or territorial security." This form of nationalism he considered "legitimate."

Unfortunately, according to Buber, nationalism can also become a "permanent principle" and exceed its proper limits. Such a "false nationalism" unabashedly trumpets a national egoism that considers all actions in the name of national interest to be sacred and morally self-evident. A lifelong Zionist, Buber warned his comrades of a such a danger. The establishment of an autonomous Jewish community in Palestine, he explained, was a necessary "station in [the] healing process" of the Jewish people. It should only be a "station," however, and the Jews must perforce be ever mindful that the restoration of nationhood in and of itself could not exhaust the meaning of Israel's yearning for Zion:

> That original yearning is back of all the disguises which modern national Judaism has borrowed from the modern nationalism of the West. To forget one's peculiar character, and accept the slogans and paroles of a nationalism that has nothing to do with the category of faith, means national assimilation. . . . When Jewish nationalism holds aloof from such procedures, which are alien to it, it is legitimate. . . . Here the question may arise as to what the idea of the election of Israel has to do with all this. This idea does not indicate a feeling of superiority, but a sense of destiny. It does not spring from a comparison with others, but from the concentrated devotion to a task. . . . The prophets formulated that task and never ceased uttering their warning: If you boast of being chosen instead of living up to it, if you turn election into a static object instead of obeying it as a command, you forfeit it![48]

Throughout the years Buber would return to this theme.[49] On one occasion he observed that the Zionist movement derived its name not from the people it served but from a place, Zion, "'the city of the great king' (Ps 48:3), that is of God as the King of Israel."[50] As such, he maintained that the very name of the movement would not allow it to forget the election with which Israel was called into being. We need not endorse Buber's theology or share his faith in the "hidden" power of the name Zion, but his observation serves to highlight the religious pedigree of the Zionist idea.

---

[48]Martin Buber, "Nationalism," in idem, *A Land of Two Peoples: Buber on Jews and Arabs* (ed. Paul Mendes-Flohr; New York: Oxford University Press, 1983) 55–56.

[49]See Manuel Duarte de Oliveira, "The Election of Israel in the Thought of Martin Buber" (Ph.D. diss., Hebrew University of Jerusalem, 1992).

[50]Martin Buber, *On Zion: The History of an Idea* (trans. Stanley Godman; New York: Schocken, 1973) xvii–xxii.

Response

*Robert T. Handy**

This learned article, written by a scholar of Jewish thought who is deeply versed in the primary sources and in a wide range of contemporary scholarly materials, is richly informative. As a church historian of the modern period who has been involved in studies of American Protestant life and thought in and about the Holy Land, I venture this comment on Professor Mendes-Flohr's fascinating and provocative thesis from a quite different perspective.

I am not convinced by his suggestion that since the term "chosen people" is not found in classical Jewish sources, the concept did not emerge early, indeed not until Jewry's encounter with the modern world. I find the word "may" no less than five times in the first few pages of his essay and am told that "the question then is whether Israel's understanding of itself as God's elect is identical with the concept of a chosen people sponsored by Western Christianity." "Identical" is a very strong word, and as a historian I expect the precise meanings of words and phrases to change over the decades, never mind the centuries. Can a claim for the identity of a concept across several millennia be supported by convincing evidence?

To take an illustration of how concepts quickly take on new meanings from the modern period (to which our author quickly moves in providing important insights into the rise of Zionism), the first sixteen words of the First Amendment of the Constitution of the United States read: "Congress shall make no law respecting an establishment of religion, or prohibiting the free exercise thereof." Nothing is said there about the separation of church and state, but "cultural valence" soon led the amendment's words to be so interpreted. On 1 January 1802, just after the tenth anniversary of the ratification of the amendment on 15 December 1791, Thomas Jefferson wrote, "I contemplate

*Robert T. Handy is Henry Sloane Coffin Professor Emeritus of Church History at Union Theological Seminary, New York.

with sovereign reverence that act of the whole American people which
declared that their legislature should 'make no law respecting an establishment of religion or prohibiting the free exercise thereof,' thus
building a wall of separation between church and state."[1] Nor was
Jefferson's remark a casual one; on the same day, referring to the
words just cited, Jefferson wrote, "Averse to receive addresses, yet
unable to prevent them, I have generally endeavored to turn them to
some account, by making them the occasion, by way of answer, of
sowing useful truths and principles among the people, which might
germinate and become rooted among their political tenets."[2]

Mendes-Flohr says openly that his philological observation that the
term "chosen people" does not exist in the lexicon of classical Judaism is admittedly captious, and perhaps even trivial. He mentions,
however, words that do occur in such passages of the Hebrew scriptures as Deut 7:6 and Exod 19:5–6, as well as in the traditional Jewish prayer book, words that are related to Israel's understanding of
election and covenant. I am thus not persuaded that the *concept* of
what the English words "chosen people" convey did not emerge in
various and changing forms before that concept surfaced explicitly in
the course of contacts with Western Christianity. His twenty-fifth footnote refers to certain currents in classical Judaism that seem to illus-
trate that the chosen people context as it has been widely understood
did link Israel with ontological entitlement and a people's superiority.
How to assess the importance of such currents and the extent of their
influence on Jewish thought and life in the past seems to me to
require further reflection and debate.

I am much indebted to Mendes-Flohr for deepening and enriching
my understanding of the complex, many-sided movement of Zionism.
It is hard but nevertheless extremely important for Christians and
Christian scholars to learn and relearn the roles that their tradition

---

[1]Thomas Jefferson, reply to an address by a committee of the Danbury
Baptist Association, 1 January 1802; quoted in Robert M. Healey, "Thomas
Jefferson's 'Wall': Absolute or Serpentine?" *Journal of Church and State* 30
(1988) 442.

[2]Thomas Jefferson to Levi Lincoln, 1 January 1802, in Paul L. Ford, ed.,
Writings of Thomas Jefferson (10 vols.; New York: G. P. Putnam's Sons,
1892–99) 8. 129; quoted in Healey, "Thomas Jefferson's 'Wall,'" 441.

exercised in the long, tragic exile of the Jewish people, with its terrible suffering through many centuries; Christians must again face the fact that persons nurtured in various strands of the complex Christian tradition mingled with others in the terror of the Holocaust. The author's analysis of the profound, agonizing tensions and ambivalences within Zionism between the longing for "normalization" (modernization, secularization, independent nationhood) and the preservation of the Jewish people, their piety, and their language is profoundly moving to me. I think that even as an outsider I do understand and to an extent feel the longing of the Jewish people for a secure space of their own where their unity (however imperfect) and their piety (however diversified) can be expressed in a nation state. Although the analogies are certainly not precise, various Christian churches across history have often claimed immense geographical areas for Christ and succeeded in establishing themselves as the one religious tradition to be recognized and supported by particular nations with their armies and treasuries. Churches working with governments have persecuted Christian dissenters and other religious traditions with varying degrees of suppression and brutality, the realities described by such words as crusades, inquisitions, and pogroms. Repeatedly, churches and nations of Christian background, even after recognizing religious freedom under the law, have sought to mold national cultures after the old, familiar patterns of Christendom. All too easily they have assumed that the rights of majorities take precedence over the rights of minorities and individuals.

Many twentieth-century Christians, among them people in high places, have hoped that the Jewish people might find new patterns in the continuing tension between particular religions and modern states. Thus Woodrow Wilson, whose approval of the Balfour Declaration of 1917 before its publication became public knowledge a year later, could say in the presence of Rabbi Stephen S. Wise, "To think that I, a son of the manse, should be able to help restore the Holy Land to its people."[3] Another American president provided de facto recognition of Israel eleven minutes after it declared its independence in

[3]Stephen S. Wise, *Challenging Years: The Autobiography of Stephen Wise* (New York: Putnam, 1949) 186–87.

1948; a recent biographer of Harry S. Truman summarized the situation by saying that "as would sometimes be forgotten, it was not just American Jews who were stirred by the prospect of a new nation for the Jewish people, it was most of America."[4] Later, when Truman visited the Jewish Theological Seminary in New York and his longtime friend and former partner Eddie Jacobson proclaimed him as "the man who helped create the State of Israel," Truman blurted out, "What do you mean 'helped create'? I am Cyrus, I am Cyrus!"[5] He thus identified himself with an ancient king of Persia who believed himself called to erect a house of God at Jerusalem in Judah.

Not only Jewish hopes are invested in Israel's future; many others are concerned about the way Israel can deal with the serious tensions that arise in part out of the history traced by Mendes-Flohr. In the course of his article, he calls attention to traditional Jewry's self-understanding of its election as a call to obedience, responsibility, suffering, and servanthood, as well as to the problems that these "calls" posed for Zionism, especially secularized Zionism. The deeper religious traditions of Judaism continued to echo through the cry of those who put the emphasis on "once again a Jewry of Muscles," a conviction understandable enough after two millennia of exile and torment. There were those, nonetheless, who called for a commitment to biblical or prophetic idealism and urged that Israel be more than a nation among nations. As a Christian, I remember how often I have heard sermons that have emphasized in various ways that chosenness, election, or divine calling is precisely a summons to obedience, responsibility, suffering, and servanthood, not to privilege, wealth, or earthly power.

Alas, such words among us are all too often not matched with deeds. The Christian-Jewish tragedy obviously fell most heavily on the people of the Hebrew scriptures and traditions, but has not been without damage to many Christians' understanding of the deeper roots

---

[4]David McCullough, *Truman* (New York: Simon & Schuster, 1992) 596; see p. 618 on the speed of Truman's recognition of Israel.

[5]As quoted by Moshe Davis, "Reflections on Harry S. Truman and the State of Israel," in Allen Weinstein, ed., *Truman and the Commitment to Israel* (Jerusalem: Magnes, 1981) 82–85.

of their own tradition. If, as Mendes-Flohr contends, the familiar concept of chosen people came from Western Christianity (of which I am not convinced at this point), certainly aspects of the historic biblical understanding of chosenness and election to obedience and responsibility have been frequently retained in rhetoric (although all too often slighted in practice) among many church people. In any event, Mendes-Flohr has sparked a debate that can deepen our understanding, whatever our backgrounds or attitudes, of our own traditions and those traditions of others which concern chosenness and election.

Chosenness, Nationalism, and the Young Church Movement:
Sweden 1880–1920

Stephen A. Mitchell*
and
Alf Tergel

"Gothicism," Chosenness, and Nationalism

When August Strindberg, Sweden's most renowned man of letters, was asked in 1897 what reform he most wanted to see in his lifetime, he replied, "Disarmament."[1] Here, as in many other ways,

*Stephen A. Mitchell is Professor of Scandinavian and Folklore at Harvard University; he is also Curator of the Milman Parry Collection of Oral Literature. Alf Tergel is Associate Professor in Church History at Uppsala University in Sweden. The authors acknowledge the invaluable assistance of Maria Erling in the preparation of this article.
[1]Quoted in Elizabeth Sprigge, *The Strange Life of August Strindberg* (London: Hamish Hamilton, 1949) 231.

Strindberg's thinking ran counter to the prevailing sentiments of his time and his nation. In Sweden, the waning decades of the nineteenth century and the first decades of the twentieth were filled not with thoughts of disarmament, but rather with the question of how Sweden could protect its status as a neutral and independent country amid the growing pace of European armament. Indeed, the whole question of Swedish chosenness—and of how the nation's fragile position could be defended among the jostling egos of European superpowers—played a prominent role in Swedish intellectual life; the argument concerning chosenness would propel itself into the arena of national politics and religious debate as well, particularly with respect to the Young Church Movement (*Ungkyrkorörelsen*).

The language and substance of the prewar defense debate, with its implicit belief in chosenness, was not cut from whole cloth, for the country had a lengthy history of being seen, and seeing itself, as "elect." The roots of this idea are discernible in late medieval associations of Sweden with the Goths of antiquity, and "Gothicism" reached its zenith in the seventeenth century during Swedish participation in the Thirty Years' War under the leadership of Gustavus Adolphus.[2] The effects of this historical confection on Swedish perceptions of self may be surmised, for example, from the attempt a half-century later to identify Sweden as the Garden of Eden described in Genesis.[3] Swedish history is marked at various points by the reappearance of the chosenness theme, for example in the attempts of Karl XII to contain Russia; the role Gustav IV conceived for himself against the Antichrist, Napoleon; and perhaps even the moral posture that Sweden has taken in international affairs during the last fifty years. In the five-hundred-year history of Swedish chosenness, however, few examples are more pronounced than the sense of national mission that emerged around the turn of this century, when cultural, political, and religious nationalism came together in a frenzied symbiosis. At that time, Sweden was particularly prone to relish her

[2]See, for example, Josef Svennung, *Zur Geschichte des Goticismus* (Skrifter utgivna av Kungliga Humanistiska Vetenskapssamfundet i Uppsala 44:2B; Stockholm: Almqvist och Wiksell, 1967).

[3]Olof Rudbeck, *Atland eller Manheim* (4 vols.; Uppsala: Curio, 1675–1702).

vaunted past. She had long since been stripped of her once far-flung Baltic empire, and now the union with Norway, the last vestige of her former status as a European power, was under increasing stress. Rapid industrialization, together with large-scale emigration to America, had radically altered the character of traditional provincial life, and the threat of war—especially against Russia, the traditional enemy—seemed very real, particularly as this threat was often manipulated in popular culture.[4]

Of the many elements of Swedish intellectual life involved in the chosenness debate of the prewar period, several interrelated spheres— literature, politics, and religion—are useful areas for exploring the rhetoric of chosenness. In the case of Sweden's literary establishment, it is particularly illuminating to examine works by two of its most ardent nationalists, Viktor Rydberg (1828–1895) and Werner von Heidenstam (1859–1940),[5] whose works exhibit sentiments that strongly

[4]Representative works in the early period would include Ludwig Douglas's inflammatory brochure "Hur vi förlorade Norrland" ("How we lost Norrland," [1889; 3d ed.; Stockholm: Nordin & Josephon i Kommission, 1890]), which portrayed a Russian invasion of the province, and in the later period, Sven Hedin's two brochures, "Ett varningsord" ("A Word of Warning," [Stockholm: Bonniers, 1912]) and "Andra varningen" ("Another Warning," [Stockholm: Kungl. Boktryckeriet, P. A. Norsted & E- söner, 1914]), which likewise promoted the idea of Russian designs on Sweden. The question of Russian *sågofilare* ("saw sharpeners"), in which large numbers of itinerant Russian tradesmen were portrayed as spies, offers particularly clear instances of the near hysteria that prevailed at the time. See Sten Carlsson and Jerker Rosén, *Svensk Historia*, vol. 2: *Tiden efter 1718* (Stockholm: Svenska Bokförlaget, 1961) 577, 617, 619. Few books give a clearer view of the nationalist frenzy that reigned than Sven Hedin's own retrospective, *Försvarsstriden 1912–14* (Stockholm: Fahlcrantz och Gumælius, 1951).

[5]The works of other poets and novelists from this period (for example, Gustav Fröding and Selma Lagerlöf), while generally milder in tone, also promoted cultural nationalism. Reviews of Rydberg and Heidenstam—as well as of the period in general—written in English are found in Lars Warme, ed., *A History of Swedish Literature* (Lincoln: University of Nebraska Press, forthcoming). Detailed examinations are found in Olle Holmberg, *Viktor Rydbergs lyrik* (Stockholm: Bonniers, 1935); Staffan Björck, *Heidenstam och sekelskiftets Sverige: Studier i hans nationella och sociala författarskap* (Stockholm: Natur och Kultur, 1946); and Jan Stenkvist, *Nationalskalden: Heidenstam och politiken från och med 1909* (Stockholm: Bonniers, 1982).

parallel those found among the religious nationalists affiliated with the Young Church Movement. Typically, although not uniformly, these visions of Sweden's special status were packaged in the pseudohistorical guise of early Germanic culture, Viking Age Scandinavia, or Sweden's period as a great power (*Stormaktstiden*). To a lesser degree, presentations of Sweden's elect character allude to biblical notions of chosenness.

The Literature of Chosenness

As journalist, author, and professor of cultural history, Viktor Rydberg set the parameters of the Swedish chosenness discussion with his writings on the question of national defense. Inspired by his studies of the Swedish Middle Ages, Rydberg saw the issue of guaranteeing Sweden's independence in highly romantic terms. Sweden's military might, he contended, depended upon her peasants. Against the rising power of well-equipped European armies, he envisioned the Swedish peasantry armed as a militia that he frequently compared to the Swiss pikesmen of the late medieval and early modern periods.[6] One of the most prominent exponents of latter-day "Gothicism," Rydberg drew images from Nordic mythological materials, as well as from the nation's real and imagined history, in order to bolster his pleas for the defense of the motherland. For example, in 1888 Rydberg published "Vård-trädet," an alliterative poem composed in conscious imitation of Old Norse poetry; in it he combines the image of Yggdrasill, the world-tree of Scandinavian mythology, with that of a familial tree.[7] When a storm blows the tree down, the family gathers around and the father calls for the tree, a symbol of the family's strength and durability, to be turned into weapons for the defense of the motherland, law, and freedom, traits associated with the imagined democratic yeomen society of the Swedish Middle Ages:

[6]Rydberg articulated this view both in his literary works (for example, *Vapensmeden: häringar från reformationstiden* [Stockholm: Bonniers, 1891]) and in his political tracts (for example, "Huru kan Sverige bevara sin själfstä ndighet?" ["How can Sweden maintain its independence?"] 1859).

[7]Viktor Rydberg, "Vårdträdet," in *Viktor Rydbergs Skrifter: Dikter* (14 vols.; ed. Karl Warburg; Stockholm: Bonniers, 1919) 1. 275–86.

Ditt virke skall slöjdas	Your timber shall be carved
till värnande sköldar	into protective shields
att lyftas framför	to be lifted before
lag och frihet;	law and freedom;
med järnet spetsas	with iron are sharpened
till spjutstänger	the spear-shafts
att föras i fejd	to be carried into the fray
för fosterjorden	for the native soil
av mina söners	by my sons'
modige söner	bold sons
i Svealandens	in the ranks
kämpars led.	of Sweden's warriors.[8]

Such expressions, along with Rydberg's other romantic mythological and cultural-historical writings—for example, *Undersökningar i germansk mythologi* ("Investigations into Germanic Mythology", translated into English as *Teutonic Mythology* [1906])—exerted a great impact on the Swedish public, especially after 1887. In that year he published *Fädernas gudasaga* ("Our Fathers' Mythology"), which the Swedish school system used well into the twentieth century as the standard introduction to native mythological traditions.[9] That the conservative student association to which many of the Young Churchmen belonged named itself after the watchman of the ancient Nordic gods, Heimdal, surely betokens the influence of this handbook and of the larger "Nordic revival." Rydberg characterized Heimdal as a god whose tasks demanded "strength, wisdom, and hardiness" ("styrka, visdom, och härdighet").[10] Such a description was undoubtedly congenial to the students of the Conservative Party. Nor can it be coincidental that the same text maintained that the great eschatological event of Nordic mythology, Ragnarök, would begin when "Heimdall's horn-blast, ringing throughout the world, awakens [the gods] to the final battle between good and evil" ("Heimdallslurens världsgenomträngande klang väcker dem till den sista striden mellan det goda och det onda"), a

---

[8]Ibid., 280–81.
[9]Viktor Rydberg, *Undersökningar i germansk mythologi* (2 vols.; Stockholm: Bonniers, 1886–89); idem, *Fädernas gudasaga. Berättad för ungdomen* (Stockholm: Bonniers, 1887).
[10]Rydberg, *Fädernas gudasaga*, 23.

concept of obvious relevance to the Young Conservatives' view of themselves.[11]

When Rydberg's died in 1895, the foremost neoromantic and nationalist figure in Swedish belles lettres, especially with respect to the theme of chosenness and the country's connections to its glorious past was Werner von Heidenstam. The author of a series of historical works treating national themes, Heidenstam published in 1899 a poetic cyle entitled "Ett Folk" ("A People"). The text, which fantasizes the emergence of a Swedish nation, begins with the prophet Nahum speaking to the Assyrian king, and suggests (following an old formula in Scandinavian historiography) that the Swedes have emigrated from the ancient Middle East. At Odin's command, bards sing of their forgotten *urhem* ("ancestral home"), Viking exploits are valorized, and around a bloodstained altar, Odin sets up the pagan gods. The cycle continues:

> Sverige, Sverige, Sverige, fosterland,
> vår längtan bygd, vårt hem på jorden!
> Nu spela skällorna, där härar lysts av brand,
> och dåd blev saga, men med hand vid hand
> svär än ditt folk som förr de gamla trohetsorden.

> Oh Sweden, Sweden, Sweden, native land,
> The home and haven of our longing!
> The cow-bells ring where armies used to stand,
> Whose deeds are story, but with hand in hand
> To swear the ancient troth again thy sons are thronging.[12]

Using a unique blend of patriotism, conservatism, and radicalism that appealed to its *fin de siècle* audience, the poem continues with the

---

[11]Ibid., 147.

[12]Werner von Heidenstam, "Ett Folk," in Kate Bang and Fredrik Böök, eds., *Verner von Heidenstams samlade verk*, vol. 19: *Nya dikter* (Stockholm: Bonniers, 1944) 13. The translations here and below are taken from *Sweden's Laureate: Selected Poems of Werner von Heidenstam* (C. W. Stork, trans.; New Haven: Yale University Press, 1919) 137. "Ett Folk" originally appeared in *Svenska Dagbladet* and was published in a slightly modified form in *Nya Dikter* (1915).

sections "Sweden" ("Sverige"), "Fellow-citizens" ("Medborgarsång"), "The Ballot" ("Röstsedeln"), "Soldiers' Song" ("Soldatsång"), and, most importantly, "Invocation and Promise" ("Åkallan och löfte"). In this last section of the poem, in response to proposals that Sweden should forget its bygone greatness, the poet exhorts the nation to rise up and fulfill the dream of dominion in the North (*herraväldet i Norden*); he claims that "it is finer to hear the bow-string snap / Than never the bow to have bended" ("Det är skönare lyss till en sträng, som brast, / än att aldrig spänna en båge"). The poet throws himself on the ground and prays "like a soldier of Judah" ("som en bedjande stridsman av Juda").[13] In "Ett Folk," the concatenation of Swedish patriotism, Germanic mythology, Old Testament imagery, and national defense is explicit and raised to high art. Although its view may be extreme, it is not unrepresentative of the chosenness theme in Swedish literature of the period.

Nationalism and patriotism were experiencing a renaissance in Swedish literary and aesthetic life at the turn of this century. This point is amply illustrated by the cases of Rydberg and Heidenstam, as well as by the fact that the Swedish national anthem achieved its definitive form at the beginning of the twentieth century. Parallel to this cultural nationalism, Swedish society was also experiencing political nationalism. This phenomenon was conditioned in particular by the country's foreign relations, especially the fear of Russia that resulted from attempts at russification in Finland, and the widespread ill will that came with efforts toward Norwegian independence. When the union between Sweden and Norway was dissolved in 1905, nationalist sentiment flowed uninterrupted into the political landscape.

Chosenness and the Young Church Movement

From this ground swell of nationalism, the Young Church Movement emerged among university students in Uppsala and took the offensive in addressing the intellectual and popular challenges facing the Church of Sweden.[14] In their defense of the national church, the

---

[13]Heidenstam, "Ett Folk," 16–17.
[14]On the Young Church Movement, see Alf Tergel, *Ungkyrkomännen, Arbetarfrågan och Nationalismen 1901–1911* ("The Young Churchmen, the

Young Church leaders borrowed important themes from the nationalist movement, while the Young Church Movement, in turn, provided
a religious point of departure for those pursuing a nationalist ideology.[15] Although the Young Church Movement did not have grass
roots support and therefore cannot be seen as a popular movement in
the tradition of labor, temperance, or the Free Church, it did have
great influence on the Church of Sweden. The Young Church Movement also made itself felt more broadly through its religious and
theological justification of a nationalist political ideology—especially
a stronger defense policy—in the decades preceding the First World
War.

The most immediate threat to the national church was the Free
Church revival movement, which advocated separation from the Church
of Sweden and the formation, based on a model imported from Anglo-
American traditions, of pure congregations of converted believers. In
response, the Young Church Movement dedicated itself to a revival of
Sweden's historic national church. Fundamental to the Young Church
Movement was the notion of a "Folk Church," or "People's Church,"
especially as it was developed by the theological leader of the move-

---

Worker Problem and Nationalism 1901–1911") (Acta Universitatis Upsaliensia.
Studia Historico-Ecclesiatica Upsaliensia 15; Uppsala: Almqvist och Wiksell,
1969); and idem, *Från Konfrontation till Institution, Ungkyrkorörelsen 1912–
1917* ("From Confrontation to Institution, The Young Church Movement from
1912–1917") (Acta Universitatis Upsaliensia. Studia Historico-Ecclesiatica
Upsaliensia 25; Uppsala: Almqvist och Wiksell, 1974).

[15]On the cultural, religious, and political climate of this period, see, for example, Gustaf Aulén, *Hundra års svensk kyrkodebatt: Drama i tre akter* (Stockholm: Svenska kyrkans diakonistyrelses bokförlag, 1953); Ragnar Ekstrom,
Gudsfolk och folkkyrka (Lund: Gleerups, 1963); Nils Elvander, *Harald Hjärne
och konservatismen: konservativ idédebatt i Sverige 1865–1922* (Skrifter utg.
av Statsvetenskapliga föreningen i Uppsala 42; Stockholm: Almqvist och Wiksell,
1961); Karl G. Hammar, *Liberalteologi och kyrkopolitik. Kretsen kring
Kristendomen och vår tid 1906–omkr. 1920* (Bibliotheca historico-ecclesiastica
Lundensis 1. Acta Universitatis Lundensis, Sectio I, Theologica, juridica,
humaniora 15; Lund: Gleerups, 1972); Gunnar Richardson, *Kulturkamp och
klasskamp: Ideologiska och sociala motsättningar i svensk skol-och kulturpolitik
under 1880-talet* (Studia historica Gothoburgensis 2; Göteborg: Akademiför-
laget, 1963); and Edvard Rodhe, *Svenska kyrkan omkring sekelskiftet* (Stockholm:
Svenska kyrkans diakonistyrelses bokförlag, 1930).

ment, Einar Billing, a professor of theology at Uppsala. The Young Church Movement's Christian interpretation of national identity took shape within the concept of this "Folk Church," while at the same time the "Folk Church" concept provided a convenient framework for national interpretations of Christian identity. Moreover, Billing's formulation of this idea positioned the Young Church Movement in direct opposition to the Free Church advocates: in contrast to their attempts to separate the church from the world, he maintained that the church must be the occasion for connecting the world, and particularly the Swedish people, with the gospel of the forgiveness of sins.

Billing's major theological contribution was to subject Lutheran teaching to historical critical analysis, and in doing so he laid a foundation for much of later Swedish theology.[16] The relationship between revelation and history, especially as set out in his 1907 book *De etiska tankarna i urkristendomen* ("The Ethical Ideas in Early Christianity"), was fundamental for Billing. In this book, he pointed out that the Bible bears witness to God through his works. Billing contrasted what he called the Israelite or prophetic outlook on life with the Hellenistic view. There is no history in Hellas; the world there is static and god is a *deus otiosus* who does not intervene in the world of humans. Existence is understood as a cycle; there is nothing new under the sun. In Israel, on the other hand, the prophets see existence as a history shaped during God's battle against destructive forces in creation. Billing perceived the prophets' preaching as an interpretation of history. God reveals himself as the God of history. The crucial divine act is the rescue from Egypt, and Israel's history is interpreted in the light of the Exodus.

Jesus, the gospel, and the church were placed in this perspective by Billing: they were God's works, which contributed to God's objectives for humankind. He saw divine revelation as taking place continually by way of history within history. Thus, Billing understood the Bible as history and drama, not as a collection of doctrines and

[16]On Billing's views and influence, see Gustaf Wingren, *An Exodus Theology: Einar Billing and the Development of Modern Swedish Theology* (trans. Eric Wahlstrom; Philadelphia: Fortress, 1968); and Gösta Wrede, *Kyrkosynen i Einar Billings teologi* (Studia doctrinae Christianae Upsaliensia 5; Stockholm: Svenska kyrkans diakonistyrelses bokförlag, 1966).

dogmas. The biblical message is to be understood as a testimony of God's love. For Billing, the gospel offers humanity as a whole its "exodus" from "captivity" and drew humans into God's covenantal history.[17]

Billing's hypothesis about a "Folk Church" was rooted, among other influences, in his study of prophecy in the Hebrew scriptures, which led him to draw attention to individuals in the history of Israel as objects of God's works. Billing placed the church at the center of God's relationship to humanity. He then focused primarily on the Church of Sweden and her territorial parishes. The church is God's own handiwork and a direct continuation of Christ's work. The church's task, Billing pointed out, is to proclaim "the forgiveness of sins to the Swedish people."[18] For Billing, the church by its existence manifests the universality of grace and its foundation in God's prevenient grace. The Church of Sweden with its territorial parishes was God's creation, built from the gospel; by its openness, Billing maintained, it expressed the universality of grace.

Any view of the church that insisted on a personal declaration of belief for denominational affinity led in Billing's eyes to an exclusivity that impeded the universality of prevenient grace. For Billing, the church was not merely an association of believers, and he consistently emphasized that the gospel is the foundation of the communion.

Other Young Churchmen formulated the "Folk Church" concept differently, but in general this idea was the form that nationalism took in church life. Although the notion of the "Folk Church" took shape primarily under the influence of the territorial parish churches of the countryside, Swedish society—traditionally agrarian—was gradually being transformed into a society based on industry. Here lay an inner tension in the vision of the Swedish national church: it was principally inspired by the traditions of the countryside and the rural church,

---

[17]See Einar Billing, *De etiska tankarna i urkristendomen i deras samband med dess religiösa tro* ("The Ethical Ideas in Early Christianity in the Context of Its Religious Faith") (2 vols.; Uppsala: Sveriges kristliga studentrörelses bokförlag, 1907) 1. 79, 81; 2. 19, 48, 63–65; (2d rev. ed.; Stockholm: Sveriges kristliga studentrörelses bokförlag, 1936) 352.

[18]Einar Billing, *Folkkyrkan och den frikyrkliga församlingsprincipen* (Uppsala: n.p., 1912) 51.

but it was to be realized in new industrial areas. Still, the idea of the "Folk Church" served two purposes. In addition to the fact that it distinguished the Church of Sweden from the Free Churches, whose New Testament view of congregations denied the national church its status as a true Christian church, it sought to reach out to the breakaway workers' movement, whose members were frequently estranged from the very church to which they formally belonged.

Furthermore, the Young Churchmen used the idea of "The People of Sweden—A People of God," realized in the idea of the "Folk Church," as an instrument by which they might demonstrate that the Church of Sweden was religiously motivated and not merely a state function. In addition, they sought to inspire secular Swedes, especially the industrial workers, and make them aware that they belonged to this church. The "Folk Church" was to be a church for all people, a church whose design was intimately bound to the rhythms of life—particularly to the landscape—and a place to which the Swedish people could always come to meet God. Central to the purposes of the Young Church Movement was the maintenance and strengthening of a single church for the entire country. In this respect the "Folk Church" ideal resonated with the national romantic movements of the nineteenth century, which had maintained that people with the same history, culture, religion, language, and traditions constituted a nation.

Manfred Björkquist, although hardly a theological innovator in the mold of Billing, nevertheless emerged as a key leader of the Young Church Movement. While a student, his critical confrontation with the new theology promoted by Einar Billing, Nathan Söderblom, and others nurtured in Björkquist a taste for combat. He proposed, for example, a crusade for the summer of 1909 in which students would go in pairs to the parishes of central and northern Sweden and testify to what "burns in our hearts." His articles in *Vår Lösen* ("Our Watchword") throughout the next decade provided a theological and spiritual call to arms for an energetic generation of emerging leaders. Especially in his 1909 pamphlet "Kyrkotanken" ("The Idea of the Church"), Björkquist gave form to the ideas that had been generated among the students in Uppsala.[19] The Young Church Movement's

---

[19]Manfred Björkquist, "Kyrkotaken" (Uppsala: Sveriges kristliga studentrö relses bokförlag, 1909).

slogan, *Sveriges folk—ett Guds folk* ("The People of Sweden—A
People of God"), with its nationalist overtones, implied that Christianity should be realized in the lives not only of individuals but also
of the nation as a whole. Björkquist derived the justification for the
people's cardinal role in the church chiefly from Billing, whose expo-
sitions of prophetism had made the people a central concept and whose
presentation of God's action with the people of Israel, the chosen
people, gave the Young Church Movement the incentive to a nationalist emphasis. Here the broader scope of the Young Church Movement began to narrow, however, as the influence of Nathan Söderblom's
ecumenical internationalism and Einar Billing's Lutheran theology of
Christianity vocation gave way to an increasingly fervid concern for
a religiously grounded Swedish nationalism promoted by Björkquist
and Johan Eklund.

In Johan Alfred Eklund, bishop, hymnist, and poet, the Young
Church Movement found its primary advocate of nationalism and
chosenness.[20] His deep involvement in the national coalition movement dated from the dissolution of the Union in 1905, and it was
Eklund who projected into the Young Church Movement the ideas
prevailing among the political Young Conservatives. He also gave the
Young Church Movement its battle hymn, "Fädernas kyrka" ("Our
Fathers' Church"), with its multiple echoes of, or at least parallels to,
the sentiments of Rydberg and Heidenstam. Following several direct
allusions to Sweden's decisive part in the Thirty Years' War under
Gustavus Adolphus—"Frid åt Guds kyrka var kampen värd" ("Peace
for God's church was worth the fight" [stanza 5])—the hymn suggested modern parallels for Sweden's most famous historical role:

Ädel är skaran, sen tusen år
Gud i vår kyrka fått frälsa.
Framåt vår hoppfyllda längtan går:
Ungdomen kristnad är Sveriges vår,
Sveriges framtid och hälsa.

Komme nuåter till strid för Gud
Skaran sin Konung till möte,

---

[20]On Eklund, see Hans Börje Hammar, *Personlighet och samfund. J. A.
Eklund och hans tillflöden* (Stockholm: Verbum, 1971).

Väpnad och villig, i helig skrud,
Samlad, som daggen på ljusets bud
Flödar ur morgonens sköte.

Kristnade ungdom, dig gånge väl.
Strid för Guds ära i Norden.
Kämpa för frihet åt bunden träl.
Gud bringe friden till Sveriges själ,
Gud bjude frid över jorden.

Noble is the troop, for a thousand years
God has been able to redeem in our church.
Forward our hope-filled longing goes:
A Christian youth is Sweden's spring,
Sweden's future and health.

Come again to battle for God,
The troop to meet its King,
Armed and willing, in holy apparel,
Gathered, as dew at light's command
Floods from the morning's bosom.

Christian youth, may you proceed well.
Battle for God's glory in the North.
Fight for freedom for the bound thrall.
May God bring peace to Sweden's soul,
May God grant peace throughout the world.[21]

In the years before the First World War, Eklund advocated a strong defense policy on the ground that Sweden was the outpost of the Christian evangelical world against the Orthodox Slavs to the east. Eklund viewed Russian expansion toward the Atlantic as a real threat, and he was not alone in this fear; if Sweden were to stand sentinel on Europe's cultural frontier, guarding against the immanent danger of

[21]"Fådernaskyrka," Hymn 169, stanzas 7–9, in *Den svenska Psalmboken* (Stockholm: Svenska kyrkans diakonistyrelses bokförlaget, 1957). Although translated here as "troop," it should be noted that the full range of *skara* includes not only this military interpretation, but also a more general implication of "multitude," as well as the narrower "tribe."

expansion from the East, she needed a strong defense, which would constitute the self-defense of both the church and the population. The most consistent advocate within the Young Church Movement of a national, conservative outlook with Christian overtones, Eklund saw Sweden as a nation chosen by God with a special vocation similar to that of the Israelites. By reason of the country's geographical position, its historical mission since the time of the Thirty Years' War had consisted of protecting Germanic culture against the Orthodox Slavs to the East and the Gallic Catholics to the South. From this view of Sweden's calling, which Eklund perceived as a task divinely imposed on Sweden by God, it followed that his sympathies in the prewar antagonism between the great powers lay with Germany; he was correspondingly hostile to France and Russia. Eklund derived the pattern for his nationalism chiefly from the Hebrew scriptures, where God entrusts to the Israelites a special task in history, namely, to be a light to the Gentiles and to be the people by whom God will bring Gentiles to the faith. Thus, the principal source of his nationalism was the idea of the chosen people as found in the Hebrew scriptures. Furthermore, Eklund interpreted Sweden's history in categories of thought taken from the Hebrew Bible, and thus as God's history with his chosen people.

If racist and confessional themes were interwoven in Eklund's thought with conservative and nationalist ideas, he was not alone in this regard. Björkquist developed nationalist and religious concepts reminiscent of Eklund's; he, too, maintained that every people has its god-given vocation. Distinctive national character must be safeguarded; otherwise a people cannot fulfill the task imposed on it by God. Against this view of divinely appointed national tasks, a few voices cried out. One of the most vocal was Arthur Engberg, the leader of Verdandi, the Social Democratic student association and later ecclesiastical minister in Social Democratic governments.[22] Consistently critical of the focus on military spending that the conservatives advocated, he proposed that the church would be well advised to remem-

---

[22]It should be noted that the principal liberal, as well as conservative, student organization named itself after a figure from Nordic mythology: Verdandi is one of the norns, or fates, of Scandinavian mythology.

ber what he believed was an ethical responsibility to use its resources for productive ends.[23]

The Young Church Movement engaged actively in the prewar national defense movement by instigating a collection for a warship in 1912 and by participating in the Farmers' March in 1914, in which farmers waited upon the king with demands for a stronger defense. Whereas conservative, middle-class groups contended that national defense needed strengthening against what they perceived as the Russian threat, the Social Democratic workers gave priority to social reforms and argued that they had no homeland to defend. Liberals, who were in office in the years before the First World War, were divided about the need to strengthen defense.

The inspiration for the defense movement came from Young Conservatives who at the same time were active in the Young Church Movement. The Young Churchmen attributed their commitment to defense to their perception of the church: in order to realize the Young Church program, "The People of Sweden—A People of God," there had to be an autonomous Swedish nation. The Farmers' March and its consequences underscored how deeply the nation was divided on defense, and events confirmed that the Young Church Movement did not represent the whole nation. Young Churchmen intervened in the defense dispute in order to effect national unity, but their efforts led to the opposite result: national dissension. The Young Church vision of a united Swedish people under God's leadership thus proved to be illusory when tested against a concrete social issue.

Just as such attempts by conservative forces to use Christianity and the Church of Sweden for the purposes of power politics were rejected by Engberg, so they were also rejected by Nathan Söderblom, who became archbishop of Sweden in 1914.[24] At the outbreak of the war, Söderblom stood aloof from the Young Church talk of "The People of Sweden—A People of God," if that motto was understood as denying that other people also had a place in God's plan for the

---

[23]See, for example, Arthur Engberg, "Maktfilosofin," *Tiden* (1916) 331–32.

[24]Bengt Sundkler, *Nathan Söderblom: His Life and Work* (Lund: Gleerups, 1968) 100–216.

world. Söderblom spoke of two gods, the god of nationalism and the God of Christianity. The god of nationalism he repudiated, for God was not the God of Russia, France, Germany, or Sweden alone. Primarily under the influence of Söderblom's international orientation, made topical by the war, nationalism in the Young Church Movement waned. The potential for genuine extremism had always been great, but the commitment to missionary activity within the Young Church Movement, especially as it was advocated by several of its leading members, had tended to restrain any drift toward extreme nationalism within the Movement and to balance the pull in this direction, which Eklund in particular encouraged. For example, Björkquist, although one of the most ardent nationalists, had originally intended to become a missionary and as a result of the international orientation that this interest involved for most Swedish participants, he was never caught in the undertow of national extremism. Similarly, K. B. Westman and Gunnar Dahlquist had early on evinced a strong missionary interest, and both later held leading posts in the Church of Sweden's Mission (*Svenska kyrkans mission*).

The decline in nationalist ideology and rhetoric with the outbreak of the war was marked in Björkquist, who emphasized that the slogan "The People of Sweden—A People of God" was also a vision of peace. The church was necessary in order to instill in people a sense of world community, and of familial obligations toward other nations. According to this thinking, the "Folk Church" should not serve popular egoism and national pride, but rather must be a tool by which people were turned into servants in the world of nations; furthermore, it must support the international legal system. Björkquist also referred to nationalism as a religion, repudiating nationalism both when it embraced one people at the expense of others and when it strove for power. He replaced the old watchword "The People of Sweden—A People of God" with "The Nations—God's Peoples" ("folken—Guds folk"). Previously he had maintained that the people of Sweden would be transformed into the people of God; as a result of the war, this optimistic view widened to include all peoples, and instead of "the people," Björkquist spoke of "the peoples."[25] Although the different

---

[25]Manfred Björkquist, *Vårens oro* (Uppsala: n.p., 1915) 44–45.

nations would remain intact, the wills of their people were subjected to the will of God: the devout of each land would serve humanity through their own people. The cooperation between the Young Conservatives and the Young Church Movement displayed in the prewar defense movement ceased under the influence of the First World War and the international peace movement. Just how far the Young Church Movement had shifted from its prewar stance can be gauged by the fact that it was actively involved in Nathan Söderblom's efforts to construct an international legal system for the peaceful resolution of conflict.

Transforming the Rhetoric of Chosenness

National political debate in Sweden in the prewar years was largely characterized by the synergism of the self-induced image of chosenness that both supported and found support in the search for a national defense strategy. In the end, the war transformed the character of the Young Church Movement: while neither the church nor its leaders stepped out of the ring of public policy, its alignment with the conservative defense agenda was effectively disrupted. The tension between the Young Church Movement and the political left gradually diminished during the First World War, when the Young Churchmen curtailed their commitment to defense and, together with workers, struggled for peace; rather than devoting itself to nationalist causes, the Young Church Movement turned its energies to assisting Nathan Söderblom's internationalist efforts. Thus, although the defense issue set the Young Church Movement and the political left at odds with each other, the peace issue brought them closer together.

Such internationalism was not new to the Young Church Movement. Missionary activity had, for example, played a significant role in the split between the "nationalists" and the "internationalists" in the Young Church Movement, and even the question of "pan-Scandinavianism" had been raised within the Movement. The breakup of the Union between Norway and Sweden at the turn of the century, however, had dampened enthusiasm for Nordic cooperation. Nor did the Young Church Movement, in general, provide fertile ground for the growth of "pan-Scandinavianism." Members of the Movement were principally engaged in making the people of Sweden into a people of

God, and this national orientation stifled enthusiasm for work intended to promote Nordic cooperation. The First World War, however, riveted attention on what was happening beyond the country's borders and opened wide the windows within the Young Church Movement toward the Nordic countries and Europe.

In the years immediately preceding the war, during which the debate over nationalism, defense, and the nation's mission was reaching a climax, the question was visited by two of the nation's most celebrated writers in a way that paralleled the developments already observed among the Young Churchmen. Ill, despondent, and isolated in the period just before his death, Strindberg devoted much of his energy to attacks on the conservatives and the monarchy. Significantly, Strindberg's last published work was an article entitled "Farliga gåvor" ("Dangerous Gifts") which appeared in *Social-demokraten* on 23 March 1912, less than two months before his death. In it, Strindberg decried Sven Hedin's saber rattling on behalf of a public subscription for a warship.[26]

If Strindberg was adamant in his opposition to the military escalation, Heidenstam's embrace of the pending conflict was fanatical, and his rhetoric increasingly inflammatory. In February 1914, he offered Swedes a catalogue of "what we want." What Swedes wanted, according to Heidenstam, was "to swear the oath that our ancient land should never fall into the hands of the barbarians" ("svära den eden att vårt gamla land aldrig någonsin i tiderna skall falla i barbarers händer"); what Swedes feared was "the threatening danger from the East" ("den hotande faran från öster").[27] Perhaps the clearest indication of the mood in intellectual circles is seen in Heidenstam's triumphant reception in Uppsala on 12 and 13 March 1914. Here, particularly in his address

---

[26]August Strindberg, "Farliga gåvor," *Social-demokraten*, 23 March 1912; cited in idem, *Samlade skrifter av August Strindberg*, vol. 53: *Tal til svenska nationen samt andratidningsartiklar 1910–1912* (ed. John Landquist; Stockholm: Bonniers, 1919) 546–48. With this article and his other attacks on conservative issues, Strindberg managed to create a storm of protest. See the collected articles in Harry Järv, ed., *Strindbergs fejden. 456 debattinlägg och kommentarer* (2 vols.; n.p.: Cavefors, 1968).

[27]Werner von Heidenstam, *Verner von Heidenstams samlade verk*, vol. 23: *Uppsatser och tal* (ed. Kate Bang and Fredrik Böök; Stockholm: Bonniers, 1943) 117.

to Heimdal,[28] the conservative student association so intimately bound to the Young Church Movement, Heidenstam tied together the historical, political, national, and religious themes which he had helped bring to the forefront of national consciousness. For conscientious citizens, he declared, there is but one question: the nation's security (*landets yttre säkerhet*).[29]

The moral confidence that Heidenstam exuded in the immediate prewar period was much shaken in Sweden, as elsewhere in Europe, by the actual events of the war. The Young Church Movement had made common cause with the internationalists by the end of the war, and when Heidenstam addressed the Nordic student meeting in Oslo some years after the war, he did so by calling on the members of this pan-Nordic forum not to be divided by misunderstanding. He urged them to shut out foreign entanglements, to promote friendship among themselves, and not to bear weapons against each other.[30] The rhetoric of a lifetime, however, was not easily put to rest. In this speech the old arsenal was trotted out again, but with a new goal apparently in mind. Whereas before the war, Sweden's history had been seen as giving it "the least decadent people in Scandinavia" ("det minst dekadenta folket i Skandinavien"),[31] Heidenstam now called on Norwegians, Danes, Finns, and Swedes to respond to their shared cultural and linguistic heritage and to "the ancient Scandinavian religion which still has a corner deep in our breasts" ("den nordiska urreligion, som har en vrå kvar djupt i vårt bröst"). They should imagine how they might collectively form "a high, yes, a new civilization" ("en hög, ja, en ny civilization").[32] Just as Björkquist altered the Young Church Movement's slogan, "The People of Sweden—A People of God" to "The Nations—God's Peoples," similarly, in the postwar era Heidenstam renewed the language of chosenness; it became the language, if not of internationalism, then at least of pan-Scandinavianism.

[28]Ibid., 121–32.
[29]The specification *yttre* ("outer," "exterior") related to the more narow question of what sort of defense the country should have: one that defended the perimeter, or one that, like Russia's, used its geography as a form of natural defense.
[30]Heidenstam, *Uppsatser och tal*, 153.
[31]Ibid., 116.
[32]Ibid., 152–53.

Response

*Knut Aukrust**

When we encounter, in one setting after another, the idea of a certain covenant between God and one nation or ethnic group, we often find that we are dealing with almost the same words, phrases, and sentences, with very few variations. If we take the rhetoric literally, it looks very similar from place to place and from time to time. When we try to interpret the message, therefore, it is important not only to listen closely to what we hear, but also to identify from where and from whom it is coming.

There are, of course, many reasonable ways to describe and identify the origin of the voice of a message. What are its historical, political, cultural, and sociological surroundings or contexts? What about gender? We have a number of parameters among which to choose. I shall try to describe one way we might handle these problems, making use of the research of Norwegian social scientist Stein Rokkan, who has been working on several political and cultural issues in both the United States and Europe. Rokkan has developed a model based upon what he calls center-periphery structures.[1]

Center can be described in terms of power on different levels and in different fields. Periphery, on the other hand, suggests the opposite characteristics; lack of power and influence in matters that are important for people as individuals and as a group. There are many centers,

*Knut Aukrust is Associate Professor in the Department of Society and Culture at the University of Oslo.

[1]See, for example, the volume of essays edited by Per Torsvik, *Mobilization, Center-Periphery Structures, and Nation-Building: A Volume in Commemoration of Stein Rokkan* (Bergen: Universitetsforlaget and Irvington-on-Hudson, NY: Columbia University Press, 1981); and Stein Rokkan's *Center-Periphery Structures In Europe: An International Social Science Council Workbook in Comparative Analysis* (Frankfurt/New York: Campus Verlag, 1987).

just as there are different peripheries. One location can be both center and periphery at the same time, depending on what we relate it to. For instance, Oslo, the capital of Norway, is in central Norway, with its own periphery; at the same time, however, we could also describe the city as peripheral if we are dealing with European politics and economics as a whole.

While the center tries to dominate, control, and even suppress the periphery in various ways, the periphery, on the other hand, often attempts to minimize, eliminate, and, in certain situations, fight against this domination. The structure here is dynamic rather than static; the periphery can try actively to influence and, by revolutionary actions, even put aside an old regime and replace it. The old periphery is then converted into a new center or, in matters of nation building, it creates its own center independent of the earlier power. In other words, such a model can be used to describe conflicts both within one nation or group and between nations and groups.

Clearly, the idea of chosenness can be described and analyzed in terms of center-periphery. Instances recorded in this volume demonstrate that chosenness in the hands of those at the center is significantly different from chosenness at the periphery, even when the vocabulary is almost the same. The idea has played an important role in creating and increasing the influence, domination, and even suppression, by one center or power, of people and countries at the periphery; but it has also been used to resist the suppression and domination of powerful nations and to give this resistance legitimacy.

The Swedish voice apparently belongs on the periphery, as a voice of a small country on the outskirts of Europe on the Scandinavian peninsula. The case is actually not so simple, however. In this part of the world, Sweden has actually played a major role. During the times of Gustav Vasa and for long after, Sweden had nurtured strong ambitions to be a central power in Europe, as Stephen Mitchell and Alf Tergel have pointed out.

As the twentieth century opened, these ambitions still seemed related to reality, but after 1905 we see Sweden stripped of external possessions and its influence further reduced. Mitchell and Tergel, exploring the nationalistic responses to this turn of events, focus on a relatively small group, the Young Church Movement. As they make clear, however, this movement gained influence, despite its lack of numerical strength, because of much wider connections to intellectuals and church leaders.

The Young Church Movement can be understood as the result of frustration that overtook a nation that had lost its earlier influence beyond its own geographical borders. It was now the time to strengthen the position of the country from within, in terms of Christianity and conservatism. In this situation, the threat from Russia appeared to be useful, since, in the face of domestic trouble, there is nothing better than an external enemy, real or imagined. The threat from Russia in this part of the world has often been exaggerated. A recent study has shown that in Norway as well, such a threat was used at the turn of the century to gain increases in military defense and to pursue other goals in domestic politics.[2]

Russia of course tried to maintain control over different parts of Eastern Europe during the czarist regime. Panslavism developed the idea of Russia's God-given mission to the world. This ideology played an important role in the works of Fyodor Dostoyevsky and was clearly expressed in *The Brothers Karamazov*. The full story of chosen people themes in Europe cannot be written without the Russian version. This idea of Panslavism, however, is not the same as military aggression.

Tergel and Mitchell's article is interesting in the way it reveals both the roots and the transformation of the rhetoric of chosenness. The combination of Nordic mythological materials and biblical myths as they appear in the poems of Viktor Rydberg and Werner von Heidenstam is typical not only for Sweden, but for all the Scandinavian countries.

The strong nationalist ideology we find in Sweden, particularly in the years before the First World War, is connected with the situation after the breakdown of the union with Norway. Sweden, as the former center, tried to maintain control, but did not succeed. Norway, however, on the periphery of the Scandinavian peninsula, represented quite another view. While the Swedish ideology of chosenness was conservative in this era, seemingly parallel ideas in the neighboring country,

---

[2]Knut Einar Eriksen and Einer Niemi, *Den finske fare: sikkerhetsproblemer of Minoritetspolitikk i nord 1860–1940* (Oslo: Universitetsforlaget, 1981).

which for several years had struggled for independence, meant something quite different. Here the notion of chosenness played a progressive and radical role both within the church and in politics.

Since the Middle Ages, Norway had been dominated by the other Scandinavian countries. The first union with Denmark lasted for four hundred years, until 1814. Henrik Ibsen, in his ironic way, described this period and its consequences for Norwegians—or "the monkey people," as he preferred to call them—in *Peer Gynt*:

> Four hundred years of unbroken night
> Brooded over the monkey world;
> And, as we know, a night of that length
> Leaves its mark on a population.[3]

As a result of the collapse in Europe after the Napoleonic Wars, Norway was given away to Sweden. For a short period in 1814, however, the Norwegian people managed to create a constitution and declare themselves independent. This new birth of Norway has been described as a sort of gift given to the nation quite unexpectedly and rather undeservedly. It is noteworthy that the constitution of 1814 was a very liberal one compared to others. It gave the right to vote in free elections to almost fifteen percent of the population, while the French constitution, for example, allowed only one percent of the population this right.

After the union with Sweden was established in the fall of 1814, the Norwegians managed to preserve their constitution from much interference by the Swedish throne. It was a challenge to Norwegian liberals to motivate the peasants to use the possibility the constitution gave them. Here the idea of chosenness was important.

In the beginning of the nineteenth century, there were several Norwegian catechisms in the Lutheran tradition. They included a commentary on the Ten Commandments, in which the fourth commandment—"Honor thy father and thy mother"—was reinterpreted so as to convey a promise of chosenness: God does not just give the

---

[3]Henrik Ibsen, *Peer Gynt* (trans. Christopher Fry and Johan Fillinger; Oxford: Oxford University Press, 1989) 116.

obedient a long life, but also gives them a nation and a fatherland where they can fulfill their lives.

As the century advanced, the idea of chosenness developed into the idea that, first of all, it was the Norwegian peasants who embodied this special task of being chosen. The idea of making the lower class into the chosen people was not new, and in Norway theologians sympathetic to the Social Democratic Party specifically reasserted this idea as an affirmation about the working class.

In coalition with intellectuals in the cities, the peasants and laity within the church formed the backbone of the first liberal government in 1884. The Norwegian periphery had moved to a position of influence at the center. When the union with Sweden was broken in 1905, this was partly as a result of the events of 1884.

As in Sweden, the rhetoric of chosenness in Norway had two main sources. One was the Bible, particularly the Torah and the prophets. The New Testament, especially the Book of Revelation, was also used. Various interpreters connected Revelation 2 and the description of the "seven golden lampstands" to the Norwegian mission against Europe. Peripheral status was not a weakness; on the contrary, it had suddenly become a strength.

The other main source of rhetoric was the Germanic mythological universe. The Edda poems were frequently used, both the older ones—the collection of old Norwegian poems of gnomic, heroic, and mythical content—and the newer ones—the sagas written by Snorri Sturluson. The heroic past was an inspiration for the new nation.

The combination of biblical and national sources was not without danger and risks. In the 1920s and 1930s some nationalists were talking loudly about taking back earlier Norwegian possessions: Greenland, Iceland, the Hebrides, the Orkneys, and even Vinland should be part of Norway someday. The liberal idea of freedom as a task given to the Norwegians by God was at this point left behind and corrupted by ordinary aspirations to power.

The Norwegian language has contributed very little to the international vocabulary, but among its contributions are two words: *quisling* and to *quisle*. To quisle is to be a traitor who collaborates with an invading enemy, especially as a member of a puppet government. Vidkun Quisling, the eponym for these dreadful terms, was a local

Norwegian Nazi leader who cooperated with Germany during the Second World War, in pursuit of his own vision of Norwegian national destiny. During his trial after the war, Quisling described his adolescence in an old-fashioned parsonage in the Norwegian countryside at the turn of the century. Reading was one of his favorite occupations. And what was he reading? The Hebrew scriptures and the Edda. A dangerous combination indeed.

The Swiss: A Chosen People?

Ulrich Gäbler[*]

The religious basis of the Confederation is a constant topic in
Swiss history. In the framework of this general theme I wish to
deal with the following questions: Is the idea that God had something
special in mind for Switzerland found in Swiss history? Among all
the peoples of the world has God provided the Confederation with a
special task? In other words, have the Swiss understood or do they
understand themselves as a chosen people?

The answer to these questions can contribute to a better understanding of Swiss history and Swiss identity, as is suggested by parallel studies of the United States and England. In these societies the
consciousness of being chosen peoples unleashed enormous cultural

[*]Ulrich Gäbler is Professor of Church History at the University of Basel in
Switzerland.

The author is indebted to Catherine E. Hutchison, Thomas K. Kuhn, and
John O'Brien for their help and advice.

and political forces.[1] The English and Americans claimed for themselves a special association with God that corresponded to the alliance between God and Israel in the Old Testament. It was supposed that because of this selection these nations had a distinctive place in salvation history—that God was using them as instruments in his holy work on earth.

This Anglo-American sense of chosenness originated in England during the second half of the sixteenth century and was tied to a concrete historical situation. England felt threatened by Catholicism's growing strength. Catholicism was resisted, and the conviction grew that God had chosen England as a new Israel to act against a powerful Spain. This sense of England as a new Israel remained lively. As is well known, it traveled with the Puritans to America; it is also true, however, that more than two centuries later the English were convinced that God had given them the task of Christianizing the heathen world.

In America, seventeenth-century Puritans and their successors were convinced that the promised kingdom of God, the reign of peace named in the Bible, would be built on the newly discovered continent. The Puritan plantation was the city on a hill that Jesus had described as the light of the world (Matt 5:14). The hope of the people focused on this city; the Puritans were convinced that the restructuring of church and society begun in America would succeed and that the history of salvation would reach its goal there.

In the nineteenth century, this Anglo-American consciousness of a mission of bringing salvation to the world became detached from its religious roots and took a more worldly, secular form. England and

---

[1]The following is based in part upon André du Toit, "Puritans in Africa? Afrikaner 'Calvinism' and Kuyperian Neo-Calvinism in Late Nineteenth-Century South Africa," *Comparative Studies in Society and History* 27 (1985) 236–37. The literature on the earlier English and American formulations is no longer easy to survey; the most important works are still Michael Walzer, *The Revolution of the Saints: A Study in the Origins of Radical Politics* (New York: Atheneum, 1968); Conrad Cherry, *God's New Israel: Religious Interpretations of American Destiny* (Englewood Cliffs, NJ: Prentice-Hall, 1971); and Ernest Lee Tuveson, *Redeemer Nation: The Idea of America's Millennial Role* (Chicago: University of Chicago Press, 1968).

America by then understood themselves as heralds and agents of democracy, freedom, and peace.

The question is whether similar motifs emerged in Switzerland during the period—the end of the nineteenth and the beginning of the twentieth centuries—when forms of nationalism that had been shaped by religion became intense in many other Western countries. At this time Switzerland was not facing major political or social problems. Instead, the country was undergoing a transition from a Confederation based mainly on the power of the cantons to a federal state with strong central institutions. The political consciousness of the Swiss shifted slowly from the frame of one's town or canton to the Swiss confederacy as a whole. Informing and promoting this process were various conceptions that served to strengthen national unity and a perception of Swiss uniqueness. Surprisingly, however, ideas of chosenness were not prominent among these nationalistic conceptions. This may be due to the fact that Swiss identity itself was not in dispute. The basis for it had already been laid in earlier times of crisis for the Swiss, especially during the Reformation period, when the conflict between Protestants and Catholics had threatened the continuance of the Confederation. In the eighteenth century, Swiss society had been shaken by serious social tensions, and the so-called Helvetian Society had tried to overcome them. Swiss identity can be said, therefore, to have been defined in the sixteenth and eighteenth centuries rather than during the period prior to the First World War.

Given this background, I shall ask first of all whether the motif of chosenness was used by the main representatives of the Reformation and the Enlightenment in Switzerland, Huldrych Zwingli and Johann Caspar Lavater. I shall then return to the nineteenth century to give some examples of the conceptions used to support growing national consciousness, and I shall deal finally with two texts that defined Swiss uniqueness in the 1920s and 1930s. It seems that the problems evident in other countries prior to the First World War had to be solved in Switzerland in the face of the menace of Italian fascism and German national socialism. Religious motifs indeed became much more important in those later decades; in this sense, attitudes in Switzerland after 1920 can be compared to attitudes in other countries immediately before the First World War.

Zwingli

Huldrych Zwingli's reformist critique dealt with faith and life; the Zürich reformer wanted a renewal of theology as well as of private and public life.[2] He denounced the mercenary and pension systems as creating a particularly deplorable state of affairs. The practice of recruiting mercenaries in the Confederation had been generally adopted by foreign powers such as France and the Papal States in order to pursue their military campaigns. To facilitate recruitment, the foreign rulers signed guaranteed contracts with the Swiss cantons or individuals. Financial support for the recruiting officers was provided in yearly payments, the so-called pensions. Thus, foreign money flowed into the country through at least two channels. Pensioners and mercenaries were the ones who profited.

Zwingli knew what he was talking about when he attacked the pension system, since he had set up recruiting contracts with the Papal States and had drawn a papal pension for many years. Stamped in this sense as a partisan of the pope, he came to Zürich in 1519 and soon not only acted against the imminent renewal of the mercenary contract with France, but also attacked the mercenary and pension system on principle. Possibly under the pressure of his opposition, the Council of Zürich decided in 1521 to renounce mercenary alliances entirely. Zwingli saw in this decision the first step toward the moral recovery of Zürich and of the Confederation in general. To be sure, rural Switzerland did not follow Zürich's step, and the pension system continued unchanged there. In any case, adverse judgment on this practice was an important element in the conflict between Zürich and the rural cantons.

In 1522 and again in 1524, Zwingli sent passionate appeals to the rural Swiss confederates to convince them to give up the pension system. Nowhere else did Zwingli express himself so fully and fundamentally about Swiss history and its principles.[3] This is certainly no accident; in order to win the confederates to his point of view, he

---

[2]See Gottfried W. Locher, "Zwinglis Politik: Gründe und Ziele," *ThZ* 36 (1980) 84–102.

[3]See Eduard J. Kobelt, *Die Bedeutung der Eidgenossenschaft für Huldrych Zwingli* (Zürich: Leemann, 1970); and Gottfried W. Locher, "Das Geschichtsbild Huldrych Zwinglis," in idem, *Huldrych Zwingli in neuer Sicht: Zehn Beiträge*

emphasized the historical reality of the Confederation as the common ground between the Swiss of central Switzerland and the citizens of Zürich. The people of Zürich and the rural Swiss were bound to a common heritage so powerful that the current conflict could only be regarded as the kind of discord that flares up between spouses or brothers.[4]

Zwingli showed only a scant knowledge of Swiss history. A few basic dates were sufficient for him. With concise lines, he drew a simple and unified picture.[5] Through God's help the ancestors had driven out the nobility and the foreigners. Because God had been with the Swiss, the princes of Habsburg had been unable to defeat them in the battles of Morgarten (1315), Sempach (1386), and Näfels (1388),[6] in which the Swiss peasantry had maintained its freedom from aristocratic oppression. Because of their liberation from servitude to the nobles and king, the Swiss had lived with one another "in brotherhood," allowing law and justice to rule.[7] For two hundred years peace had reigned in the country because people had led pious and God-fearing lives.[8] The same promise that God had made to the children of Israel applied to them: because they had fulfilled the commandments, God had given them peace.[9] Zwingli called on the venerated monk of the fifteenth century, Niklaus of Flüe, as his witness that the Swiss Confederation could not be conquered through violence, but could well come to an end through moral decay.[10] The advance of injustice and the rule of obstinacy and self-interest would endanger the survival of the country.

Zwingli argued that although the earlier Swiss had lived modestly, without luxurious clothing or food, the land had produced people stronger than any other. Now this accomplishment had become dam-

---

zur Theologie der Zürcher Reformation (Zürich/Stuttgart: Zwingli Verlag, 1969) 75–103.

[4]Huldrych Zwingli, *Sämtliche Werke* (16 vols.; Leipzig: Heinsius, 1905–91) 3. 111.

[5]Ibid., 105–6.

[6]Ibid., 1. 171.

[7]Ibid., 3. 103–4.

[8]Ibid., 1. 171.

[9]Ibid., 187.

[10]Ibid., 3. 103.

aging to Switzerland, since foreign powers sought to recruit these strong people for their military campaigns. This was an immeasurable misfortune. Switzerland had constantly won its own wars; in foreign wars, however, the Swiss often were denied victory.[11] Zwingli turned his fellow citizens back to the way of their "pious" ancestors, who had not let themselves be dazzled by money and luxury, and who had stayed in their country. Admittedly, the Swiss soil bore "neither cinnamon nor ginger, neither malmsey nor cloves, nor bitter oranges, silk and such women's goods, but did produce butter, . . . milk, horses, sheep, livestock, cloth, wine, and grain in abundance."[12] What the foreign princes did not manage through violence and war, their money could achieve: division among the Swiss was at hand. A new nobility was rising because of the money flowing into the country. Instead of community spirit, self-interest reigned, and young people bled in foreign wars.

Zwingli's words bespoke the farmer's son and the critic of his times; like all moralists, he prized the past and castigated the present. His judgments were based on a simple picture of the history and character of the Swiss: the alliance owed its origins and survival to godly care. This would be preserved only if Switzerland did not betray its character. Switzerland must seek freedom from servitude and—linked inseparably to this—the cultivation of justice.[13] Here Zwingli pointed beyond the borders of the Swiss Confederation. Switzerland had become a place of refuge for people who were in desperate situations and had been deprived of their rights.[14] Even the great princes feared the Swiss Confederation because of its sense of justice. Freedom and law, given to the Swiss by God, were meant not only for them, but also for other peoples.

[11]Ibid., 1. 174.
[12]Ibid., 3. 106.
[13]See Berndt Hamm, *Zwinglis Reformation der Freiheit* (Neukirchen-Vluyn: Neukirchener Verlag, 1988) 10–16, the section entitled "Die eidgenössische Freiheit."
[14]Zwingli, *Sämtliche Werke*, 3. 104. The special role of Switzerland as a refuge for the persecuted and as a stronghold of justice is even more strongly emphasized by Heinrich Bullinger in his manuscript, written in 1525 or 1526, entitled "Accusation and Exhortation," where he has God say: "This I had commanded, that our country should be free for the weak and a house of

Despite all of this, I would argue that Zwingli avoided the specific idea of chosenness. Although he laid great emphasis upon God's solicitude for the Swiss, there is no evidence that because of this he saw Switzerland as standing out from other peoples. Zwingli said nothing of Switzerland's being chosen, nor of anything closely resembling that claim.

This conclusion can be substantiated by Zwingli's references to Israel. To be sure, Zwingli often compared the history of the liberation of the Swiss Confederation with that of Israel's emergence from servitude to the Egyptian rulers. For the Swiss, equipped with godly power, things had progressed as they had for the children of Israel. Zwingli gave the example of Israel to explain that freedom from servitude was due not to one's own ability, but to God's care. The example of Israel, moreover, showed what would happen when law and justice fell into disrepute and weakness, envy, and discord ruled.[15] Again, things would progress for the Swiss as they had for the people of Israel; warnings and calls for repentance would make no impression until the people were led away into captivity and came to sit, lamenting, by the waters of Babylon.[16]

Yet, for Zwingli, Israel served solely as an example. He did not identify the Swiss Confederation with Israel. He did not recognize the idea of the Swiss as a chosen people.

Johann Caspar Lavater and the Helvetian Society

The Helvetian Society, an organization of individuals who espoused political and literary Enlightenment ideas, came into being in 1761.[17]

---

justice. For this our ancestors were known by the fearful and all those without rights." Quoted in Fritz Büsser, "Bullinger als Prophet: Zu seiner Frühschrift 'Anklag und Ermahnen,'" in Irmgard Buck and Georg Kurt Schauer, eds., *Alles Lebendige meinet den Menschen: Gedenkbuch für Max Niehans* (Bern: Francke, 1972) 252. The original publication can be found in Heinrich Bullinger, *Accusation and Exhortation* (Zürich: Froschauer, 1528) see esp. fol. A2r–A3r.

[15]Zwingli, *Sämtliche Werke*, 1. 185.

[16]Ibid.

[17]The following general remarks on the Helvetian Society are based on Ulrich Im Hof, "Die Helvetische Gesellschaft 1761–1798," in Rudolf Vierhaus, ed., *Deutsche Patriotische und gemeinnützige Gesellschaften* (Wolfenbütteler

The founders were in agreement about the critique of the political conditions in the Confederation. The initiated complained about the lack of solidarity among the cantons, and they regretted the division into confessional blocs of Protestantism and Catholicism. The coexistence of aristocratic-urban and rural-democratic republics caused further offense. In addition, the ambitions of Zürich and Bern for hegemony over the weaker cantons appeared to endanger the balance of power in the Confederation. In its statutes of 1766, as a contribution toward overcoming these tensions, the Society took upon itself a mission "to establish and preserve love, union, and harmony among the Swiss."[18]

The foundation of the Society was not welcomed everywhere. Its members were suspected of political radicalism. One who was thought to be especially subversive was a young theologian from Zürich, Johann Caspar Lavater (1741–1801). At the formal "founding" meeting of the Society in 1766, he had already been critical of the prevailing political system. A year later, in 1767, Lavater took up a suggestion of the Society and published a collection of patriotic songs with the impressive title *Swiss Songs* (*Schweizerlieder*).[19] Further editions were hastily issued, enriched with new pieces by Lavater himself.

The history of this text need not be elaborated here, except to note that the fourth edition consisted of two major parts. First, Lavater presented songs about the illustrious past of Switzerland. These were

<hr />

Forschungen 8; München: Kraus, 1980) 223–40; see also Ulrich Im Hof and François de Capitani, *Die Helvetische Gesellschaft: Spätaufklärung und Vorrevolution in der Schweiz* (2 vols.; Frauenfeld/Stuttgart: Huber, 1983).

[18]Quoted in Im Hof, "Die Helvetische Gesellschaft 1761–1798," 225.

[19]First published as Johann Caspar Lavater, *Schweizerlieder* (Bern: Walthard, 1767), and reissued many times. A selection is offered in Ernst Staehelin, ed., *Johann Caspar Lavater: Ausgewählte Werke* (4 vols.; Zürich: Zwingli Verlag, 1943) 1. 68–80. I used the following edition: Johann Caspar Lavater, *Schweizerlieder* (4th ed.; Zürich: Bürckli, 1775). For the interpretation of the *Swiss Songs*, see Oskar von Arx, *Lavater's "Schweizerlieder"* (Phil. diss., Zürich University; Olten: Oltner Tagblatt, 1897); and in particular, Ulrich Im Hof, "Pietismus und ökumenischer Patriotismus: Zu Lavaters 'Schweizerliedern,'" *Pietismus und Neuzeit* 11 (1985) 94–110. On Lavater, see Horst Weigelt, *Johann Kaspar Lavater: Leben, Werk und Wirkung* (Göttingen: Vandenhoeck & Ruprecht, 1991).

followed in the second part by a collection of general patriotic songs such as a "Song of Praise to Helvetian Peace" and the "Hymn of a Swiss." Among others, William Tell was accorded a place of honor. Lavater's glorification of Swiss history left, it seemed, no massacres of heroes unrecorded and no heroic deed of the Swiss unmentioned.

Lavater made visible to his own times the memorable evidences of Swiss desire for liberty and of Helvetian community spirit. It is true—and this should be stressed—that Lavater's record of renowned deeds came to an end with the Swabian War of 1499, when the Swiss Confederation fought for the last time against a foreign enemy. He did not even mention the later conflicts between Protestants and Catholics within Switzerland, which had reached the level of an actual war in 1531. The history of Switzerland had lost its normative significance for Lavater with the division of the country along confessional lines.

If one looks for the religious content of songs, especially for statements about the relationship between God and Switzerland, the scarcity of comments about God and religion is immediately apparent. Some songs lacked any such allusions.[20] If Lavater touched upon religious themes, he did so without stirring up the special interests of confessional groups. Catholics as well as Protestants would find themselves included in his declarations. Lavater consciously leveled confessional strife. Although Protestant, he could, like Zwingli, praise the contributions of the monk Niklaus of Flüe to understanding and reconciliation among the Swiss. This conciliatory attitude is unmistakably expressed in one hymn: "Uprightness pleases God / With or without a rosary."[21] It was not important to Lavater whether as a Catholic one prayed the rosary or as a Protestant one rejected it; what was crucial was the virtue of uprightness. Lavater's understanding of God was dictated by similar tendencies. All confessional characteristics were absent. God was much more a "protective God"[22] who had stood by the whole Confederation as well as protected its individual

[20]For example, see the "Lied für Schweizermädchen," in Lavater, *Schweizerlieder*, 233–38.

[21]Lavater, *Schweizerlieder*, 184.

[22]Ibid., 163.

branches: "He, he in bloody storms breathes / Power into Swiss veins."[23]

Lavater designated the prayer of supplication as the prerequisite for such aid. William Tell looked to God[24] before he subdued the oppressor Gessler with his liberating shot; the heroes of the battle of Morgarten against the house of Habsburg and those of the battle of Grandson against Burgundy in 1475 all went down on their knees before battle.[25] After they had completed an act of liberation, they thanked God in the same way. Prayers of solicitation and thanks were an important component of the public religion of the Swiss confederates.

Although Lavater, whenever he spoke of the aid of God, thought above all of God's help to individuals, he also held that the Confederation as a whole owed its liberty to God. Thus the poet exclaimed in his song on the battle of Sempach: "O rejoice Sempach! God's power / Has freed you and freed us."[26] God also made the Swiss happy in their liberty: "He, he allowed us to become Swiss! / He, he sets us and our children / Free from tyranny."[27]

To be sure, God could take liberty away again should the Swiss prove ungrateful.[28] The crucial test of freedom lay in the virtuousness and uprightness expected of them.[29] Only a simple life without luxury was fitting for the Swiss:[30] trips to Paris and French ways of thinking would be enervating.[31] The most important thing for Lavater was that the Swiss keep their union; that is, that they live in harmony.[32] This admonition reflects more clearly than anything else the contemporary political and social situation of the Swiss Confederation.

The demands that Lavater made on his fellow citizens in a religious context corresponded exactly to the ideal of the enlightened

[23]Ibid., 297.
[24]Ibid., 27.
[25]Ibid., 46, 110.
[26]Ibid., 85.
[27]Ibid., 213.
[28]Ibid., 259, 298.
[29]Ibid., 270.
[30]Ibid., 179.
[31]Ibid., 275.
[32]Ibid., 183, 187.

citizen and patriot.[33] The religion of the Swiss songs came without a church, without a sermon, and without the sacraments, yet it served the public interest. Such an understanding of religion in a European intellectual around the year 1770 is not a surprise; it even corresponds rather precisely to the positive traits of Jean Jacques Rousseau's bourgeois religion as described in *The Social Contract*.[34] This so-called civil religion has without question remained influential in Switzerland up to the present time.

In his ideas about the relationship between God and the Swiss Confederation, Lavater developed motifs already found in Zwingli. He reiterated the desire for liberty and the tradition of community spirit, and he found the proof of God's favor in the uprightness of individuals. Like Zwingli, moreover, he refrained from calling the Swiss a chosen people. Lavater, however, did emphasize the relationship between the Swiss and their surroundings. He mentioned the foreigners who might enter Switzerland and who, he said, should be taken in hospitably. The needy should be able to say, "No! Such good people as the Swiss I never saw!"[35] The notion of political asylum shone through here,[36] as it had in Zwingli. More important is another passage where, alluding to Jesus' Sermon on the Mount, Lavater spoke of the light that "we" should be. "We"—the Swiss—should be an

[33]See Rudolf Vierhaus, "'Patriotismus'—Begriff und Realität einer moralisch-politischen Haltung," in idem, *Deutsche patriotische und gemeinnützige Gesellschaften*, 9–29; reprinted in idem, *Deutschland im 18. Jahrhundert: Politische Verfassung, soziales Gefüge, geistige Bewegungen: Ausgewählte Aufsätze* (Göttingen: Vandenhoeck & Ruprecht, 1987) 96–109.

[34]See Jean Jacques Rousseau, "Vom Gesellschaftsvertrag oder Principien des Staatsrechtes," in idem, *Politische Schriften* (1 vol.; Paderborn: Schöningh, 1977) 1. 195–208. It is particularly revealing that in Lavater, as in Rousseau, God's important protective function is invoked, which leads both writers to use the phrase "protective God." I find that Gerhard Kaiser's attempt to take Lavater's relevant insights back to Pietism misses the mark; Gerhard Kaiser, *Pietismus und Patriotismus im literarischen Deutschland: Ein Beitrag zum Problem der Säkularisation* (2d ed.; Frankfurt a.M.: Athenäum, 1973). See Hartmut Lehmann, "Pietism and Nationalism: The Relationship of Protestant Revivalism and National Renewal in Nineteenth-Century Germany," *CH* 51 (1982) 39–53.

[35]Lavater, *Schweizerlieder*, 270–71.

[36]See Im Hof, "Die Helvetische Gesellschaft 1761–1798," 108.

example of faithfulness; others should be free, too, to be as free as "we" are. With this Lavater gave one of his rare glimpses of the future. If all people could live securely until the end of time, then all nations would become one. What had already been reached as a possibility in Switzerland—liberty and concord—would then reign over the whole world. With words such as these Lavater alluded to the apocalyptic, godly kingdom of peace,[37] which he thought was merely in its beginning stage. Lavater's allusion is extremely restrained; as far as I can see, moreover, it is unique in his Swiss songs.

As with Zwingli, we can pursue our inquiry further by analyzing references to Israel. The poet Lavater mentioned Israel twice in describing the heroic deeds of the Swiss forebears. At one point he said that God led the "fathers" like sheep, "like the sons of Israel."[38] At another he pointed to an encounter in the Swabian War in which there were very few losses in Switzerland's army:

> Eleven Swiss, eleven only, fell;
> No army has won in this way
> Since Israel with its God
> Fought the heathen world.[39]

With such references to Israel, however, Lavater wanted to underline the greatness of the deed; an explicit identification of the Confederation with Israel was the least of his intentions.

Lavater had defined Swiss identity by using a historical myth. He traced the rise of the Confederation back to 1291, and he then interpreted the history of the next two centuries as a chain of liberating deeds. The enemies were identified with the aristocracy: the Swabians, the Habsburgs, Milan, or Burgundy. The successful resistance of the plain people became an essential element of the historical myth. At the beginning of the eighteenth century, this interpretation of history was expanded by an appropriate Alpine myth. The Swiss lived at the top of Europe; therefore they enjoyed the healthiest environment, and

[37]Im Hof (Ibid., 106–7) is justified in his assertion of this.
[38]Lavater, *Schweizerlieder*, 298.
[39]Ibid., 161.

the mountains protected this Alpine people physically as well as spiritually. They could hardly be touched by pernicious foreign influence. They were, therefore, "better" human beings.

In other words, Swiss identity was based on a myth designed geographically and historically. This ideology has retained its significance up to this very day.

Centralization and the Myth of Switzerland

With the French Revolution and the subjugation of Switzerland by Napoleon, the political situation of the country underwent a fundamental change. All the cantons were put on an equal footing, and privileges based on birth were abolished. Centrifugal tendencies remained, fueled by linguistic and ethnic differences as well as by a desire for cantonal self-assertion in opposition to a central power. The need to overcome these tendencies resulted in an emphasis on the "myth of Switzerland."

In this myth, a military motif was especially important. The heroic Swiss past could easily be linked with the people's unique readiness to defend themselves in the present as in the past. This warlike component of the myth was also given a religious garnish. The novelist Jeremias Gotthelf (1797–1854) extolled the deadly aim of the Swiss with their weapons of righteousness; he pictured them striking the distant enemy dead as if by a divine thunderbolt. The army was the bearer of the patriotic movement; it was understood to be both the expression of Switzerland's national unity and its school of democratic virtues. Alongside it, Confederation-wide societies of riflemen, gymnasts, and singers were established.

In the schools, history lessons propagated the tales of the country's heroic forefathers, whose history was a joint possession of all the cantons; these lessons emphasized that tolerance between Catholics and Protestants had been established as early as 1529, when the so-called First Kappel War was ended without bloodshed by a bilateral peace treaty. At the same time, common Confederate state symbols were being developed. Although these ranged from the Swiss cross to the figure of Helvetia, none had as much symbolic power as that of William Tell. Any faint murmurs of doubt as to Tell's historicity gained no hearing amidst the tumult and pageantry of the country's patriotic appropriation of its past.

The liberal state that emerged in 1848 implemented basic rights— for example, equality before the law, freedom to choose one's place of domicile, and freedom of foreign and domestic trade—within a national framework. Nevertheless, the sharp social contrasts recognized in the eighteenth century were not yet leveled. Another century would have to pass before a broad middle class would come to characterize Swiss society. The "state" did not intervene in this process of broadening the country's political base; deficiencies persisted, such as the denial of women's right to vote.

By the end of the nineteenth century, the feeling of "nationality" seemed to have been definitively transferred from the canton to the Swiss Confederation. The federal government had become increasingly visible throughout the country in the form of military barracks, post offices, and other official establishments; this newer federative thinking was reflected in the 1891 celebration of the sixth centenary of the country's founding. Both Switzerland's small size and its neutrality became matters of intense pride, as did its reputation as a place of asylum for the persecuted. Similarly, the Swiss prided themselves on their work ethic and their concern for hygiene. The Swiss "myth of cleanliness" took its place beside the "myth of freedom."

In this time of growing nationalism, theorists tried to account for Switzerland's special character. A statement made in 1875 by Carl Hilty, a Bernese professor of law, is indicative:

> It is not race or membership in a tribe, not a common language or customs, and not nature or history, that have founded the state of the Swiss Confederation. . . . Rather, in complete contrast to all the great powers, Switzerland originated from an idea, from a political concept and will, developing to ever greater clarity. This is what the country has been based on for five hundred years, today just as much as on the very first day. . . . In fact, everything that nature, language, blood, and tribal membership is capable of actually tends to drive the Swiss apart. . . . On the contrary, from the first day of its existence, the Swiss Confederation has set itself the high goal of forming out of the different peoples that make it up a new nationality of its own

with a defined character through benevolent intermingling in a free community—not German and not Latin—that is stronger than all the natural force of tribal membership and capable of making the latter forgotten.[40]

This statement of a liberal thinker may be considered a program rather than an observation of historical facts. It is nonetheless true that, given the ethnic, linguistic, and religious diversity of the country, neither race, literature, nor religion can be asserted as its characteristic or unifying element. Thus it made some sense, especially in this stage of national formation, to suppose that "political will" sufficed both to characterize the Swiss national essence and to conserve it.

The Early Twentieth Century

Before the First World War, however, tensions arose that would take their full effect after the war.[41] The political and economic antagonisms that led to a general strike in 1918 revealed a deep rift between middle class values and socialism. In addition, the alienation between the French- and German-speaking parts of Switzerland became visible. These manifestations of inner strife in society, moreover, were bound up with uncertainty about the spiritual foundations of state and culture. The situation was intensified by developments abroad. Italian fascism and German national socialism beckoned seductively. Inevitably, the question of the political or spiritual foundations of the Swiss Confederation arose. The Swiss national character had to be defined: the call for true patriotic attitudes was the other side of a debate concerning the character of Switzerland. The correct patriotic attitude, however, was as contested as the national character.

A flood of statements in literature, science, art, and politics attempted to clarify these questions. A number of religious voices joined in this discussion, but I shall restrict myself to a single text that lays claim to common sense as well as a certain degree of representative-

---

[40]Carl Hilty, *Vorlesungen über die Politik der Eidgenossenschaft* (Bern: Fiala, 1875) 28–29.

[41]See Ulrich Im Hof, *Geschichte der Schweiz und der Schweizer* (Basel/Frankfurt a.M.: Helbing & Lichtenhahn, 1986) 749–73.

ness. It consists of the address made by the Swiss Catholic bishops on the Swiss Day of Prayer in 1929.[42] In their position on the twofold question of the time—Swiss national character and the correct patriotic attitude—the bishops accented a love of fatherland. Their conservative understanding of the state was clearly shown as they called for a battle against the teaching of revolution and the so-called immorality of books, theater presentations, moving pictures, and fashion. Traditions should not be shaken: "Hold on in faith to our national arrangements and do not let yourselves be caught by those who decry them without knowing why."[43]

In this statement, the bishops repeated their antilabor position of 1920 and identified themselves as a part of the antisocialist bourgeois bloc of liberalism, political Catholicism, and conservative Protestant peasantry.[44] At the same time, they had to defend themselves from the reproach of being—in a fashion contradictory to Swiss identity— "obedient to Rome" and thereby ultramontane; they tried to prove that "we Catholics are better patriots and citizens, the more exactly we carry out the teachings of our faith."[45] They asserted that Catholics had always provided proof of such a love of the fatherland in the past; to prove their point, they named the founding heroes of the Confederation who had been brothers in faith.[46] As for the present, the Catholic Church was acting against the religious enthusiasts who wanted to do away with the army and were striving to extirpate patriotic thinking and feeling by treating such sentiments with scorn and mockery.

The bishops held that the example of the Israelites in the Old Testament should teach the meaning of the love of fatherland. This example, moreover, would teach what kind of treatment the mockers might expect: "Whoever spoke differently among the Israelites was

---

[42]*Die Vaterlandsliebe: Ansprache der hochwst. schweizerischen Bischöfe an die Gläubigen ihrer Diözesen auf den Eidgenössischen Bettag 1929* (Chur: Casanova's Erben, 1929).

[43]Ibid., 9.

[44]Urs Altermatt, *Katholizismus und Moderne: Zur Sozial- und Mentalitätsgeschichte der Schweizer Katholiken im 19. und 20. Jahrhundert* (Zürich: Benziger, 1989) 156.

[45]*Die Vaterlandsliebe*, 5.

[46]Ibid., 5–6.

treated as an enemy and perished wretchedly in the desert."[47] The bishops also warned, of course, against chauvinism and contempt for other peoples. On this day of prayer, however, God was to be thanked for his good deeds and asked to continue to hold his hand "protectively" over the homeland. Above all, however, the fatherly hand should "preserve reverence for his name and submission to his holy laws."[48]

The bishops stood decisively by the Christian definition of the basic values of the state. It is striking, nonetheless, that specific Roman Catholic religious convictions were completely in the background. Here we are dealing, instead, with a variant of the civil religion championed by Lavater. The notion of a special task for Switzerland among the peoples is not to be found.

In the second half of the 1930s, the tensions within the country lessened under increasing external pressure. The so-called "spiritual defense of the country" bore fruit. Self-reflection led to a patriotic consensus that found a powerful, duly thoughtful expression in the national exhibition of 1939 in Zürich.[49] The appeal of the Swiss Day of Prayer in 1939 was related to the Second World War, which had broken out two weeks before. This was the reason the Zürich professor of theology, Emil Brunner, gave a lecture with the characteristic title, "Swiss Freedom and the Rule of God."[50]

In Brunner's description of Swiss history and the character of the Confederation, certain slogans, examples, and motifs that we have already discovered in Zwingli and Lavater appear again: the "freedom of Switzerland" as the gift of God,[51] the prayer of the war heroes before and after battle,[52] Niklaus of Flüe as a fearless Swiss,[53] the endangering of Switzerland more from "inner enemies" of selfishness

[47]Ibid., 5.

[48]Ibid., 9.

[49]See Werner Möckli, "Schweizergeist, Landigeist? Das schweizerische Selbstverständnis beim Ausbruch des Zweiten Weltkrieges" (Phil. diss., Zürich University, 1973).

[50]Emil Brunner, *Schweizerfreiheit und Gottesherrschaft* (Zürich: Zwingli Verlag, 1939).

[51]Ibid., 4–5.

[52]Ibid., 12.

[53]Ibid., 10–11.

and materialism than from external threat,[54] and finally, the thought that Switzerland must give asylum to refugees.[55] Brunner, however, went one step further. Switzerland did not just arise through God's providence. Through God, the Swiss people had been placed at the sources of "the streams of Europe"[56] and were their guardians. This was also to be understood in the spiritual sense: "We should be guardians of the sources of the best European spiritual tradition."[57] This task consisted of testifying to one's reverence before the creator, because "if the Swiss people stop being a praying, believing people obedient to God, their mission in the world is over."[58] On religious grounds, Brunner claimed a special place for Switzerland among the peoples of the world. Not only did Switzerland owe its existence to godly providence; this providence had assigned to Switzerland a special task. The Swiss people should be an example to others of a humble, prayerful, and faithful people.

It is obvious that with this statement Brunner wanted to give a religious basis to the "spiritual defense of the country." To this extent, religion here serves political aims directly. I must refrain at this point from integrating Brunner's statements into the whole of his thought or from putting them in a contemporary framework. This would produce nothing for our inquiry, because what is striking is not

[54]Ibid., 7–10.
[55]Ibid., 13.
[56]Ibid. This idea—that the special distinction of Switzerland relates to the fact that the source of European rivers lies in the Saint Gotthard range—is already found in Johann Jakob Scheuchzer in 1706 and is then repeated in the writings of Gonzague de Reynold, Leonhard Ragaz, and Philipp Etter. This motif was included in the Federal Council message for 1938 for the protection and promotion of Swiss culture, which was to mould the offical basis of the "spiritual defense of the land." See Guy P. Marchal, "Die 'Alten Eidgenossen' im Wandel der Zeiten: Das Bild der frühen Eidgenossen im Traditionsbewußtsein und in der Identitätsvorstellung der Schweizer vom 15. bis ins 20. Jahrhundert," in Hansjakob Achermann, Josef Brülisauer, Peter Hoppe, eds., *Innerschweiz und frühe Eidgenossenschaft: Jubiläumsschrift 700 Jahre Eidgenossenschaft,* vol. 2: *Gesellschaft, Alltag, Geschichtsbild* (Olten: Walter, 1990) 343–44, 373, 376, 377–79.
[57]Brunner, *Schweizerfreiheit,* 13.
[58]Ibid., 14.

the fact that the motif of the chosen people now emerges, nor that the mission of this people, as Brunner construed it, consists in being an example of faithfulness to God. To me, what is most striking is that the motif of the chosen people is not found more frequently or earlier in Swiss history.

Conclusion

It is noteworthy that in the history of other Western countries the use of the motif of the chosen people almost always signifies an identification with Israel. The English or North American people are described as the "new Israel"; in the Netherlands of the seventeenth century, one speaks of these peoples as the property of God, whom he selected for himself in a special way.[59] In South Africa around 1880, the "specially selected people of Israel" are mentioned; next to this, the godly distinction of the white inhabitants in the midst of the blacks was the second highest distinction.[60] In Swiss history, all such identification with Israel is lacking.

The explanation for this phenomenon seems both amazing and simple. Self-designation as a chosen people is possible only when there is a fundamental correspondence between the people described in the Bible and God's "new" people. Experienced readers of scripture, however, cannot overlook the fact that the Confederation did not demonstrate the essential constitutive characteristics of the people of Israel. The Swiss lacked a common ethnic origin, and they had no firmly unified political organization. A central authority or a king was

---

[59]E. H. Kossmann, "In Praise of the Dutch Republic: Some Seventeenth-Century Attitudes," in idem, *Politieke Theorie en Geschiedenis: Verspreide opstellen en Voordrachten* (Amsterdam: Bakker, 1987) 161–75, esp. 169–71. See also Leo Layendecker, "Zivilreligion in den Niederlanden," in Heinz Kleger and Alois Müller, eds., *Religion des Bürgers: Zivilreligion in Amerika und Europa* (Religion, Wissen, Kultur 3; München: Kaiser, 1986) 64–84, esp. 73–76.

[60]In South Africa, after the conquests in Transvaal in 1880–1881, the motif of a chosen people is grasped for the first time; see André du Toit, "Puritans in Africa?" 232; see also idem, "No Chosen People: The Myth of the Calvinist Origins of Afrikaner Nationalism and Racial Ideology," *AHR* 88 (1983) 920–52.

abhorred, and there was no one language binding all the people together. Most importantly, even in religion they were not unified.

As a whole, then, the Confederation was too different from the Israel of the Bible for the Swiss to be able to identify with Israel. For precisely this reason, in Zwingli, Lavater, and the episcopal appeal, only comparative references to single parallels between Israel and Switzerland are found. One could not speak of God's people or God's chosen people because the Swiss as a whole did not understand themselves as one people. They were thereby hindered from identifying with the people of Israel, and I am convinced that for a long time this protected Switzerland from an exuberant nationalism.

Response

Robert P. Ericksen*

In 1931, Karl Barth criticized Emanuel Hirsch for excessive nationalism in his theology. Hirsch countered, charging that Barth, being Swiss, could not understand the issue:

> Whoever is not in the position with us to bring tremblingly before God the fate of Germany and to stake his own and his children's existence on that fate. . . that person also cannot stand in judgment on whether our will is bound on God or not.[1]

I had always assumed Hirsch simply meant that Barth, although teaching in a German university, did not have a German heart beating in his breast. Barth therefore could not feel what was important to a true German. Ulrich Gäbler's paper suggests it may be just as important to know that Barth was Swiss, not just that he was non-German.

Is there something in Swiss history and identity that protects against arrogance, aggrandizement, and excessive nationalism? Gäbler argues that the Swiss have never considered themselves a chosen people. He suggests this is because they do not have a common ethnic background, religion, or language—the necessary ingredients of a *völkisch*, nationalistic world view. These factors almost certainly help to explain the Swiss disinclination to proclaim themselves a new Israel or to make trouble for their neighbors.

*Robert P. Ericksen is Professor of History at Olympic College in Bremerton, Washington.
[1]See Robert P. Ericksen, *Theologians under Hitler: Gerhard Kittel, Paul Althaus, and Emanuel Hirsch* (New Haven: Yale University Press, 1985) 145. This exchange erupted with the Gunther Dehn affair in 1931. Hirsch attacked Dehn's right to teach German students because of Dehn's pacifism and lack of nationalist commitment. Hirsch, of course, soon threw his support to Adolf Hitler and became the most significant theologian to back the Nazi regime.

I agree with Gäbler's approach, that of scrutinizing moments of national controversy about the meaning of the Swiss Confederation. I accept his analysis of Zwingli and Lavater. Each of them believed in a God who acts within human history and a relationship with God in which the Swiss should do God's will and thereby be rewarded. This is also the understanding that Israel had with the God of history. Zwingli and Lavater, however, did not claim that the Swiss version involved a "special" relationship with God, nor did they claim that Switzerland replaced Israel in God's eyes.

There is no national aggrandizement in such an ideology. Zwingli stressed that the Swiss Confederation began when the "pious" forefathers freed themselves from oppression from outside. God rewarded them for their piety and simplicity, but it was necessary for the Swiss to continue to nurture piety, simplicity, *and justice* in order to continue to receive God's favor. Zwingli did posit uniqueness, claiming a land that, in Gäbler's paraphrase, "produced people stronger than any other." His image of the ideal Switzerland, however, involved justice for outsiders as well as members of the Confederation and included the assumption that this nation should be a refuge for the politically oppressed of other lands.

With Lavater an eighteenth-century cosmopolitanism emerged, as is evident in his willingness to rise above Catholic-Protestant divisions and in the resulting "civil religion," without a "church, without a sermon, and without the sacraments." In his collection of patriotic songs, Lavater praised Swiss battles and heroes, but only for their preservation of Swiss freedom and harmony. He too saw Switzerland as a land of refuge for the oppressed and as a model to other nations. He imagined a future in which the entire world would enjoy the freedom and harmony already present in the Swiss Confederation. He *did* claim uniqueness. As Gäbler summarizes Lavater, "The Swiss lived at the top of Europe. . . [and] enjoyed the healthiest environment. . . . Therefore they were 'better' human beings." According to Gäbler's argument, however, there is still no claim to being a chosen people, no identification with Israel, and no suggestion of an aggressive role for Switzerland in the world.

When we move to the nineteenth century, after Napoleon had demonstrated to Europe the power of nationalism, we find that Swiss intellectuals emulated their counterparts in Germany and elsewhere in cultivating a national myth. Gäbler shows us this and acknowledges that the myth had a military component, as in the novels of Jeremias Gotthelf and the semihistorical but much-loved story of William Tell. Their program of national consciousness raising worked and was also propagated through the developing schools of the nineteenth century. By the late nineteenth century it created a stronger Swiss identity that replaced identification with one's canton.

Emphasis on the uniqueness of the Swiss—the physical strength, the straight-shooting arrow—was a part of this message. As with Zwingli and Lavater, the nineteenth-century Swiss seemed to claim a "good" relationship with the God of history, if not a "special" relationship, earning his good rewards by their strength and good behavior. How does this differ from more malignant examples of nationalism? Once again we find an emphasis on justice, on Switzerland as a place of "asylum for the persecuted." More important, perhaps, Gäbler notes that "Switzerland's small size and its neutrality became matters of intense pride." Malignant nationalism rarely if ever celebrates these two virtues.

In the period after the First World War, many German theologians moved in a direction that both exhibited and endorsed malignant nationalism. These theologians simply expressed a conservative opposition to the social accompaniments of modern society. Gerhard Kittel, for example, in a speech in 1921, castigated the Enlightenment and secularism. He complained about rampant immorality in Germany, as seen in film, on stage, and in the rising statistics of divorce, prostitution, venereal disease, and crime in general.[2] Twelve years later, Kittel decided that Adolf Hitler represented a return to traditional values. He joined the National Socialist Party in 1933 and became one of the leading members of Walter Frank's heavily anti-Semitic Institute for the History of the New Germany.[3]

In the 1920s and 1930s, German theologians also developed a nationalistic, *völkisch* theology that fit comfortably within the Third

---

[2]Gerhard Kittel, *Die religiöse und die kirchliche Lage in Deutschland. Vortrag, in Schweden gehalten* (Leipzig: n.p., 1921) 4, 7.
[3]For the story of Kittel, see Ericksen, *Theologians under Hitler*, 28–78.

Reich. Paul Althaus, a widely respected Lutheran theologian, cultivated a *völkisch* point of view that led him to greet the rise of Hitler
in 1933 as a "gift and miracle from God."[4] Two years later he added
this comment:

> As a Christian church we bestow no political report card. But in
> knowledge of the mandate of the state, we may express our
> thanks to God and our joyful preparedness when we see a state
> which after a time of depletion and paralysis has broken through
> to a new knowledge of sovereign authority, of service to the life
> of the *Volk*, of responsibility for the freedom, legitimacy, and
> justice of *völkisch* existence. We may express our thankfulness
> and joyful readiness for that which manifests a will for the
> genuine brotherhood of blood brothers in our new order of the
> *Volk*. . . . We Christians know ourselves bound by God's will to
> the promotion of National Socialism, so that all members and
> ranks of the *Volk* will be ready for service and sacrifice to one
> another.[5]

These two Germans immediately came to mind as I read Gäbler's
discussion of the 1920s and 1930s in Switzerland. He notes a high
level of social unrest after the First World War, marked by a general
strike in 1918 and increasing antagonism over questions of national
identity in subsequent years. "Italian fascism and German national
socialism beckoned seductively," he acknowledges.

To represent this period Gäbler cites a group of speeches by Swiss
Catholic bishops on the Swiss Day of Prayer in 1929. Their attacks
against socialism and the "immorality" of culture in the 1920s seem to
echo Gerhard Kittel. Like him, they pleaded for traditional values and
love of fatherland. Their words, however, also included a warning
against chauvinism and contempt toward other nations, and they made
no claim for a special Swiss relationship to God or history. Gäbler
characterizes these speeches as a Catholic variation on Lavater's civil
religion, devoid of absolute claims to truth or God's attention.

---

[4]Paul Althaus, *Die Deutsche Stunde der Kirche* (3d ed.; Göttingen:
Vandenhoek & Ruprecht, 1934) 5.
[5]Paul Althaus, *Kirche und Staat nach lutherische Lehre* (Leipzig: Deichert,
1935) 29.

Gäbler then cites a lecture by Emil Brunner two weeks after the outbreak of the Second World War. Brunner reviewed the history of Switzerland, much as Zwingli and Lavater had, including references to freedom and justice and refuge for the persecuted. He also noted, however, that God set Switzerland in a special place on the source of the streams of Europe, as their guardian. So too should Switzerland protect the spiritual traditions of Europe by remaining a praying, believing, and God-fearing people. This was its "mission" among the peoples of the world.

Brunner's pride in being Swiss and his belief in the "mission" of Switzerland resonate with the words of Paul Althaus or Emanuel Hirsch. These men discussed the special mission of the German *Volk* and its relationship to God, the way in which Germans could be a model to the world. Althaus and Hirsch would have denied any aggressive intent in their focus on the relationship of Germans to God. They were merely considering their particular *Volk*, its history and its place in the world, with pride and concern. I believe that Brunner shared a similar pride and concern as he pondered the special place of Switzerland.

There are differences, however. An obvious difference is the lack of any Versailles Treaty that impacted Switzerland. Brunner felt none of the resentment over Versailles that was pervasive throughout Germany at the time. This bespeaks a much larger issue: Switzerland had neither a history of being a menace to its neighbors nor an inclination to be one. Therefore, Brunner's comments about Switzerland's mission fit comfortably within the rest of his lecture about justice, harmony, and other Swiss values. Gäbler is justified in concluding that this does not represent a Swiss tendency to claim to be a chosen people, even though Brunner emphasized *Volk*. The same words from a German theologian would bear a heavier burden.

As these comments indicate, I find Gäbler's paper careful and convincing. His contention that the Swiss have not claimed to be a chosen people seems accurate. This is correct despite the fact that Swiss national consciousness in the nineteenth and twentieth centuries, a Swiss sense of uniqueness, and a Swiss need to build a national myth and feel special all resemble attitudes found in more aggressive neighbor nations.

Some might argue that Gäbler's evidence refutes his own conclusions. Without using the words "a chosen people," Zwingli, Lavater, and Brunner considered the Swiss a unique people, selected by God to exhibit special qualities and play a distinctive role in history. Swiss intellectuals in the nineteenth century cultivated a Swiss national consciousness similar to the European pattern. Wherein lies the difference? Less in ideas than in behavior.

At a time when Western, Euro-American arrogance reached its peak in the late nineteenth century, when the "white man's burden" was taken seriously, and when anthropologists set out to prove the superiority of white-skinned races, the Swiss do not seem to have translated this into military or colonial mission. In this century, the Swiss have not played the dangerous game of contested borders and power politics that has led to so much destruction and so many deaths.

What explains this situation? Or, in our context, what explains Swiss resistance to fantasies of being a chosen people? Gäbler cites lack of a common ethnic heritage, a common religion, a common language, or a strong central government. These are helpful explanations, but I am not convinced that they provide the entire answer. Interestingly, these four factors also are missing, at least to some extent, in the United States. A common ethnic and religious heritage has never existed in the United States (though white Anglo-Saxon Protestant dominance must be acknowledged). A common language exists, of course, but with large exceptions early and late in American history; and strong central government is a fairly recent phenomenon. Despite these factors, American nationalism and its claim to chosen people status are assumed by Gäbler. Another problem is that even Germany lacks a common religious heritage.

I would suggest one obvious but necessary additional piece in the puzzle. To differentiate Switzerland from other nations, it is important to note geography. Switzerland's small size and mountainous, landlocked terrain significantly reduce any temptation toward expansionism and international power politics. Switzerland has been more interested in safe borders than in expanded ones. Lacking a history of aggressive war and celebrating, in fact, its own "small size and. . . neutrality," Switzerland never suffered anything like the Versailles

Treaty, which so affected Germans. When the nationalist theme developed in Switzerland in the nineteenth century and the *völkisch* theme emerged between the wars, they had no dangerous place to go. This factor is important. It does make a difference to grow up Swiss. Whether this is due primarily to the restraint of Zwingli, Lavater, and Brunner, and their emphasis upon justice and asylum rather than national arrogance, or whether it also grows out of geographical and historical circumstances seems to me an important question, especially since national pride and self-consciousness are not lacking in the Swiss cultural tradition.

Concluding Reflections— and a Glance Forward

Hartmut Lehmann
and
William R. Hutchison

*D*o some nations "still see themselves as the chosen people?"[1] It would seem that they do. On 7 March 1991, the American president, George Bush, signed a proclamation in which he declared three days in the following month to be National Days of Thanksgiving. Americans should "gather in homes and places of worship to give thanks to Almighty God for the liberation of Kuwait, for the blessings of peace and liberty, for our troops, our families, and our Nation." The United States and its coalition partners had been blessed with a swift and decisive victory: "We thank the Lord for His favor, and we are profoundly grateful for the relatively low number of Al-

---

[1]This chapter originated as Lehmann's response to the papers presented at the 1991 conference; the conception and most of the emphases are his. Revision for this volume, however, was a collaborative enterprise.

lied casualties, a fact described by the commanding general as 'miraculous.'" President Bush also expressed thanks for the "unity of our people throughout this conflict." Recalling words of President Woodrow Wilson at the end of the First World War, Bush reminded everyone to ask for forgiveness and to pray "for God's help and guidance on the way that lies ahead."[2]

Prayers answered, a people blessed by God, events miraculous, a people united, a plea for forgiveness: these are themes of chosenness elaborated in 1991. We are led to believe that the Iraqi minefields opened up like the Red Sea and that General H. Norman Schwarzkopf, the American commander, displayed the leadership qualities of Moses.

Americans were not alone at the end of the twentieth century in displaying elements of the ideology examined in this volume. Linda Colley, although she assures us that in the minds of most latter-day English citizens "God has ceased to be British," finds Britons clinging to the idea that they have "drawn the long straw" nonetheless. In an anecdote that neatly suggests the ubiquity of such ideas at differing social levels, she tells of a Lincolnshire grocer named Alfred Roberts who habitually vilified France—"corrupt from top to bottom"—by way of vaunting a superior British virtue. Colley suspects that Roberts passed such attitudes along "to his deeply serious and adoring elder daughter, the future Margaret Thatcher."[3]

In addition to this kind of posthistory of our topic, there is the prehistory frequently alluded to in the preceding essays: the flight of the Puritans across the Atlantic to the new Jerusalem they attempted to build in the New World; the Swedish king, Gustavus Adolphus, fighting like King David to save the new faith granted by God in the Reformation; the numerous groups of reborn Christians in the seventeenth and eighteenth centuries that claimed an exclusive divine warrant and assembled to build God's new kingdom.

Thus, in commenting on these essays one faces a dual challenge: not only to compare the findings of these researchers, but also to

---

[2]*United States Code Congressional and Administrative News: 102nd Congress—First Session, 1991* (3 vols.; St. Paul: West, 1992) 3. A26–27.

[3]Linda Colley, *Britons: Forging the Nation 1707–1837* (New Haven: Yale University Press, 1992) 374, 368.

place historically the theme of chosenness as it manifested itself in a particular era, in this case the decades between 1880 and 1920. We propose, before "glancing forward," to attempt another approach to the comparative issues, one that will complement that of the Introduction by taking its start from perceived commonalities in the experience of western European societies.

Religion, Politics, and Society: The View from Western Europe

In nineteenth-century European history it is possible to identify several waves of de-Christianization and secularization, which were more or less successful, and several waves of re-Christianization, which were at best partially successful. One sees also the rise of substitute religion (*Ersatzreligion*), especially in the form of socialism. In Europe we find, at least indigenously, a very low incidence of radical sectarian forms such as Mormonism and Seventh Day Adventism, but Europe like America experienced the triumph of the secular religion called nationalism.

In both America and Europe, nationalism held special significance for Christian groups, but in both places this took contradictory forms. On the one hand, nationalism was the chief rival of traditional Christianity, claiming to be able to give "last answers" to "last questions," defining the goals of life, demanding the ultimate sacrifice, and furthering a secularized view of the world. On the other hand, many in the middle and lower-middle classes embraced nationalism wholeheartedly while remaining devout Christians or at least nominal members of the church. In the eyes of most people, it would seem, nationalism and Christianity were partners rather than enemies.

The combination of nationalism and Christianity provided a potent, dynamic force that manifested itself in at least two ways. Nationalism gave Christianity an added sense of mission in the domestic political arena and, in Europe at least, nurtured the hope that religious forces could stem the tide of de-Christianization and secularization. Christianity, in turn, gave nationalism an added sense of mission in the foreign political arena and led to the belief that power politics vis-à-vis the non-European world were imbued with a special civilizing mission.

Nothing inspired this symbiosis of nationalism and Christianity more than the chosen people model as it was derived, accurately or not, from the Hebrew scriptures. Indeed, without such symbols as the "Old Testament" account of a chosen people, a people united under God, the frequently powerful union of nationalism and Christianity might well have been less feasible in nations like Great Britain, Germany, or the United States. This biblical narrative, as Conrad Cherry suggests, provided a mythical structure capable of defining the goals and aspirations of a nation.

We should, however, determine more precisely the period in which chosen people themes gained the most influence. If we survey the history of Christianity in the Protestant countries of Europe in the nineteenth century, we can observe that two waves of de-Christianization and secularization were followed by two waves of re-Christianization. Such periods cannot be sharply outlined; there are undercurrents and overlapping developments, as well as differences among the various Protestant countries. If we are not afraid to generalize a bit, however, we arrive at the following sequence. The decades from the 1780s until about 1815 were characterized by massive movements of de-Christianization and secularization. These were followed by a remarkably strong wave of re-Christianization in the years from 1815 until about 1848. Although the secularizing process resumed after 1848, the decades from the late 1870s until 1914 witnessed another wave of attempts to re-Christianize. Christian churches and leaders sought to win back lost ground.

As Lehmann has pointed out elsewhere, those who led the efforts of re-Christianization seem to have been influenced strongly by the advancing secularization that they had experienced in the preceding epoch.[4] Those who wanted to re-Christianize Protestant European society after 1878 intended to overcome the effects of liberalism in general and of the revolution of 1848 in particular. From this same liberalism, of course, they had inherited the idea of nationalism, but

---

[4]Hartmut Lehmann, "Neupietismus und Säkularisierung. Beobachtungen zum sozialen Umfeld und politischen Hintergrund von Erweckungsbewegung und Gemeinschaftsbewegung," *Pietismus und Neuzeit* 15 (1989) 40–58.

with the help of a chosen people ideology they could hope to reinterpret nationalism, to give it a new meaning that would be in complete agreement with Christian values. The Hebrew Bible provided ample illustrative material to this effect: God rewarding a people and God punishing, leaders explaining the will of God and defining behavior, leaders demanding political unity and pointing out those whom they considered enemies.

In the context of a policy of re-Christianization, ideas of chosenness helped on the domestic front as much as in foreign policy. Because the concept of a chosen nation was rather vague, it could be used to address different political groups in the hope that they would rally behind a common policy of Christian nationalism—a nationally defined Christianity. Nothing, therefore, gave the policy of re-Christianization more strength than its combination with nationalism. On the other side, the nationalist political course, which was supposed to overcome unwanted movements like socialism, was greatly strengthened by adding the ingredient of intense Christian conviction as it was expressed in the chosen people theme.

Developments in the Roman Catholic countries of Europe seem to have progressed in a different manner and at a different tempo from those in predominantly Protestant societies; they therefore exhibit still other variations of the linkage between nationalism and religion. Countries like divided Poland that maintained a strong sense of common historical destiny, and those like Ireland that were suppressed under foreign rule, may be placed in one category. Countries like Italy (in other words, first divided, then united to some extent by anticlericalism) and France (united, yet also divided between pro- and anti-Catholic forces) fall into another. In all instances, the sense of chosenness possessed a somewhat ambivalent character. While Catholic groups strongly supported a feeling of national uniqueness, they also viewed their respective nations as part of a larger unit, the Roman Catholic Church, which pursued its own special mission both in Europe and abroad. The powers given to the Pope by the First Vatican Council in 1870 can be understood as a conscious attempt to counterbalance the centrifugal forces of nationalism that were seen as virulently at work in Catholic countries.

Even more important were the differences between Europe and North America. While European Christianity was generally on the defensive, its American counterpart seemed constantly to be gaining ground despite the secularization evident in intellectual circles after 1870. Concepts such as de-Christianization, secularization, and re-Christianization are therefore of little use as categories for describing the vibrant, dynamic character of North American Christianity in the nineteenth and twentieth centuries. Even if one identifies the various waves of religious revival and awakening in the United States as essentially similar to re-Christianization,[5] it will still be the case that neither this term nor its antonyms are particularly helpful in the analysis of the chosen people ideology in American culture. Other components appear far more salient: the strong Puritan tradition beginning in the seventeenth century, national independence as a Christian experience, nineteenth-century domestic reform as a means to build God's kingdom in America, the Civil War explained as a struggle between the powers of progress and reaction, and the strong domestic influence of American foreign missions.

Pretensions to chosenness, however, along with attitudes that supported such pretensions did manage to bridge the Atlantic (or more precisely, the North Atlantic). This was true, in particular, of anti-Catholicism and Teutonism. At least since the age of Enlightenment, American and European Protestants had considered Catholicism their common enemy. As viewed by anti-Catholic writers on both sides of the Atlantic, Catholics appeared to be backward and incapable of contributing substantially to the modern world. As both American and European Protestants idolized Martin Luther and praised him as a founding father of the modern world, they linked Protestantism with progress and came to the conclusion that the future would belong to those countries where Protestantism shaped the course of events.[6]

---

[5]Among a number of noteworthy treatments of "Christianization" in the nineteenth-century American society, see especially Jon Butler, *Awash in a Sea of Faith: Christianizing the American People* (Cambridge, MA: Harvard University Press, 1990) 225–95.

[6]Hartmut Lehmann, "Anti-Catholic and Anti-Protestant Propaganda in Mid-Nineteenth Century America and Europe," *Pietismus und Neuzeit* 17 (1991)

This Protestant optimism was strongly influenced by the belief that the people of Teutonic origin were best equipped to carry civilization forward. Teutonism as a motivating force therefore supplemented and, in the minds of many (perhaps even Josiah Strong), seemed to outweigh the motive of Protestant solidarity. Through Teutonism, just as through anti-Catholicism, ideas of a common chosenness emerged that linked the United States with Great Britain and, not infrequently, linked these two countries with Germany and northern Europe.

When questions of power politics were at stake, however, the notion of a collaborative chosenness among Teutonic Protestant nations could not displace the conviction of an individual destiny to which each of these nations adhered. Both war alliances of 1914 therefore contained Protestant and Catholic powers that had aligned themselves as their national interest seemed to command. No clear-cut adversarial division existed, in 1914 or before, between Protestant and Catholic powers, even though some Protestant "Teutonists" hoped that such a division would eventually emerge and come to dominate political decision making.

Looking Forward: Topics Deserving Further Attention

When one asks what further work needs to be done on chosenness and ideas associated with it, the first and most obvious response is that scholars should examine the experience of cultures and subcultures not treated in this volume. A number of Western examples were mentioned in the Introduction, as was the desirability of extending inquiries beyond the West. Any such wish list must also highlight the need for more attention to popular thought and to the relations between chosen people ideologies and public policy.

Equally obvious, although perhaps more difficult to pursue, is the need to think not only of regional and ethnic subcultures, but also of entities defined by class, gender, and, for lack of a neater term, condition in relation to nationhood. Indeed, the distinctions we have utilized between "chosen nations" and those aspiring to national status,

---

121–34; idem, *Martin Luther in the American Imagination* (Munich: Fink, 1988) 176–93; idem, "Martin Luther als deutscher Nationalheld im 19. Jahrhundert," *Luther: Zeitschrift der Luther Gesellschaft* 55 (1984) 53–65.

or between stronger and weaker forms of group identity, cry out for further analyses in which intracultural strains of many kinds could be examined.

To be more specific, chosen people ideologies plainly supported and complemented, on the one hand, the policies of hegemonic powers such as Germany after 1870, Great Britain, or the United States; in these cases, to differing degrees, the claim of chosenness was made part of both the domestic and the foreign policy outlined by the ruling groups. In such cases the chosen people *topos* served as a means of legitimation for domination and as a tool of suppression for those who did not conform. On the other hand, the chosen people theme also gave political direction and inner strength to suppressed minorities struggling for liberation and emancipation.

The latter is what we see in the case of black Americans, and to a certain degree in the cases of Zionism and of the Norwegians alluded to in Knut Aukrust's response. In these cases, the belief in a group's chosen status served as a means of legitimation for resistance and as a tool of liberation from those who stood in the way of emancipation. For these suppressed or subordinated societies, the march through the Red Sea to the promised land lay ahead; their political leaders acted as prophets capable of guiding a struggling people. If the bid for liberation succeeded, and if it led to the formation of a homogenous state, the idea of chosenness could be blended easily into the new nation's definition of national identity.

There were also, of course, political developments and formations that seemingly were not driven by anything resembling a chosen people ideology. By the nineteenth century, political expansionism was but a faint memory for the Swedish, a part of the national past long overcome; few were ready to revive the crusade of the seventeenth century. In Switzerland, no one wanted to reactivate the militaristic spirit of the late Middle Ages; the myth of the pious forefathers who had created the Swiss confederacy lived on only in a transformed manner. If, as in the Swiss example, multiculturalism was part of the state doctrine, with no linguistic group possessing political hegemony and none striving for political liberation, chosenness provided neither ideological cement for those ruling nor ideological ferment for those not in power.

At the same time, in both countries there was widespread belief in a different kind of mission. Henri Dunant, the founder of the Red Cross, gave Switzerland a new role in international politics, namely, that of a country that stayed out of power conflicts but was deeply involved in solving these conflicts and helping unfortunate victims of war. In recent Swedish history, the martyred leader Olof Palme personified the double quest of a society that wished to claim both a redemptive role in international politics and a special ability, domestically, to create a just and equal society.

Mythic, Theological, and Comparative Agendas

In examining the cases already before us, and others to be considered, we should also ask whether, as Conrad Cherry suggests, we ought not to analyze most ideas of chosenness under the rubric of myth. This interpretive move places the legacy of the Hebrew Bible on the same level as, for example, the heritage of the Edda or Greek mythology; it establishes a broad framework for intercultural and comparative analysis.

The advantages of this approach are obvious, yet we should not be blind to the shortcomings of such terminology. Throughout the nineteenth century and well into the twentieth, most of those who spoke of national chosenness and believed in national chosenness were determined, devout Christians. For them, Christianity was not a myth like other myths, but God's manifest, revealed, pronounced truth. For them, the Old Testament heritage possessed a special quality, since it linked their lives and the destiny of their respective nations to the progress of salvation history. One can argue, therefore, that use of the term "myth" does violence to views that in fact were existentially central to these pious nationalists.

On a more general level, one can also remark that words like myth or ideology are so vague that every thought and every belief can be labeled as such; in short, myth is too broad a category and more differentiation is needed. The very least we should do is to call the chosen people theme a special myth with special theological implications.

Theologians and biblical scholars, however, may have reason to apply their own canons of criticism to modern appropriations of the chosen people concept. They may, for example, wish to take a closer look at the kind of revelation that is supposedly the basis for the belief in a new covenant in nineteenth-century Europe or America. After all, Paul's letters inviting Gentiles and Jews to join the Christian movement and follow Christ had provided a completely new theological setting, so that in the centuries that followed no single nation could claim exclusive redemption or a preferential status in the history of salvation. Yet clearly, among nineteenth-century Western nations and groups, many claimed to be chosen, and few of these were ready to accept that others might also be called by God to a special destiny. Indeed, at the very core of one nation's claim to legitimacy one is likely to find a conviction that this nation is exceptional and the recipient of God's unique attention and help.

Finally, comparative historians may wish to pursue and examine the proposition advanced in this chapter, namely, that in the decades between 1880 and 1920 secularization progressed in Europe more rapidly than in America. Is this the case, and if so, why?

It would seem, certainly, that on the two sides of the Atlantic accelerated industrialization and urbanization had produced quite different effects. In Europe, the new social forces had not only influenced the various societies, but had also caused them to drift further and further from traditional Christianity. Before 1914, attempts to curb de-Christianization and secularization and to re-Christianize specific European nations were not very successful, if they were successful at all. In the same decades, ideas of chosenness penetrated the political belief of European nations to such an extent that their leaders found it difficult to compromise in the moment of political crisis. In July 1914, rather than arriving at a diplomatic solution, nations accepted war, and God was invoked to bless one's own cause, one's own arms, one's own soldiers.

This is not meant to give a new explanation for the controversy concerning war guilt, the *Kriegsschuldfrage*. What is of interest here is the psychological situation at the beginning of the First World War, when highly industrialized, sophisticated societies returned to the means of war to resolve political differences. Those who believed they were chosen were convinced that God was on their side in the case of an armed conflict; if their cause was just, God would bless them with victory. When the United States entered the war in 1917, it was evident that a sense of mission also prevailed there.

If we look for the elements that contributed to the rise of total war, we can say that the industrialization of war production was one such element and the exploitation of the civilian population was another. Yet it was only with the help of ideas of chosenness that politicians could answer the question of why they demanded from a whole people the ultimate sacrifices that they did. In this respect the chosen people "theology" was secularized when it was combined with imperialistic politics of power and expansion. In Europe, the notion of national chosenness thus became part of the de-Christianization and secularization that it had been meant to defeat. In America, by contrast, the Christian sense of mission helped to transform the national cause into a universal one.

Some Models for Cultural Interpretation

If we analyze the broader cultural and intellectual context of chosen people notions, we should reckon with two competing models of interpretation. One of these is provided by the idea of romantic nationalism since Johann Gottfried Herder.[7] For those who supported romantic nationalism, "ideal" nations possessed an ideal shape and landscape, all of which was defined by God, who had endowed these nations with a particular character. Each possessed a special language and literature, identifiable national customs, and a unique destiny. Within this framework, the idea of chosenness as exemplified in the Hebrew Bible could serve two functions in particular. First of all, it could explain the ups and downs of national history better than any other explanation available in the nineteenth century. Second, the notion of chosenness could give special authority to those who wanted to lead their people into a better future. The people had to obey God's commands, the leaders explained, and of course it was these leaders who claimed to have the power to interpret God's will.

In the case of Germany, since the late eighteenth century and Herder's time, the canon of a national literature had been established,

---

[7]See the articles in J. C. Eade, ed., *Romantic Nationalism In Europe* (n.p.: Humanities Research Centre, Australian National University, 1983).

and historians had invented a unique national past. National monuments had been built and national rituals such as the *Sedantag* initiated.[8] (It is remarkable that the Germans could not agree on what
constituted the typical, the ideal German landscape. Many considered
the Rhine the embodiment of the essence of Germanness, since it was
linked with legends such as the *Lorelei* and national episodes such as
that involving Luther at Worms; others, however, gave prominence to
the German highlands, the *Teutoburger Wald*, or Thuringia, again
linking topography with legend and history.) If we follow ideas provided by romantic nationalism, we must put the notion of chosenness
into the context of cultural history and topography, thus giving specific traits to each variant of national chosenness—whether European
or American, and whether triumphalist in tone or adapted to a suffering people.

The other model of interpretation is provided by modernization
theory or, more precisely, by religious responses to modernization as
we find them in both Europe and America beginning in the eighteenth
century. Pietism and Methodism, revivals and awakenings, and, most
importantly, fundamentalist movements formed a sequence of religious developments that reinforced and strengthened the element of
overt or explicit Christianity within European and North American
culture.

Martin Riesebrodt's recent study of the fundamentalist phenomenon
illustrates some of the possibilities in a response-to-modernization
model.[9] He argues that what he is calling fundamentalism is characterized by Manichaeism—that is, by the conviction that the world is
the battleground between the powers of light and darkness—and by
xenophobia, religious nativism, theories of conspiracy, and the
demonization of female sexuality. Within such a framework, the re-
activation of the biblical heritage as exemplified in chosen people
ideas is one aspect of a crisis (or of a theory reflecting societal crises)

---

[8]Hartmut Lehmann, "Friedrich von Bodelschwingh und das Sedanfest. Ein
Beitrag zum nationalen Denken der politischen aktiven Richtung des deutschen
Pietismus im 19. Jahrhundert," *Historische Zeitschrift* 202 (1966) 542–73.
　[9]Martin Riesebrodt, *Fundamentalismus als patriarchalische Protestbewegung*
(Tübingen: Mohr, 1990).

that is rooted in the changing social-moral milieu in modern urban centers and that has far-reaching political consequences.

Examination of chosen people ideas becomes, in this context, another way of looking at what Riesebrodt calls religious nativism, a phenomenon for which he finds ample documentation in American fundamentalism especially in the 1920s. According to Riesebrodt, it was the influence of Calvinism and Presbyterianism that transformed Christian universalism in America into religious nationalism and elevated the United States, in the minds of Americans, to the status of "the greatest nation in history."

Riesebrodt also discusses Shiite fundamentalism in the 1960s and 1970s in order to arrive at a more general theory of what he calls the active, world-shaping variety of fundamentalism. We should acknowledge with gratitude that in many ways his juxtaposition of Protestant and Shiite traditions breaks new ground.[10] It seems evident, however, that some querulousness is in order. The combination in European countries of Lutheran or Catholic traditions with national exceptionalism, for example, escapes Reisebrodt's attention. Surely we should be cautious about simply equating the impact of the chosen people theme, either within the Western world or beyond it, with the impact of fundamentalism.

Chosenness and Democracy

One other sort of "juxtaposition" seems especially important to attend to in Western settings: the relationship between the idea of national chosenness and various forms of government. On the evidence now before us, we can see that this idea seems to have thrived in conjunction with both democratic and non-democratic polities. If we identify the basic values of democracy as the rule of law, the guaranteeing of personal rights and liberties, the principle of "no taxation without representation," the division of national governmental powers, and a broad-ranging system of checks and balances, we

---

[10]One could also argue that Riesebrodt reclaims a research agenda that Max Weber had opened up, but which had been lost after Weber's death in 1920.

must then ask how much, and in what ways, the notion of chosenness supports or weakens democratic rule.

Assumptions about some automatic synergy between chosen people ideas and democracy may seem easy to dismiss, yet such assumptions are not uncommon either in historical literature or in popular thought. Ideologies of chosenness have seemed indubitably linked to nationalism, and most definitions of modern nationalism have, in turn, presupposed some form of popular sovereignty.

The resulting two-part formula has indeed enjoyed powerful embodiments. In the American case, for example, a nation's struggle toward an exceptional status can be seen as rooted in the common law tradition as this was applied in early New England history.

Our comparative inquiry, however, has served to underscore tensions between chosenness and democracy that may deserve just as much attention. The political language of chosenness includes ideas such as that of one nation united under God, a nation punished by God if disobedient and rewarded if faithful. The notion of chosenness supports, in addition, a special sense of mission and a belief in one nation's unique task in domestic affairs as well as in foreign politics. Clearly, with regard to democracy such ideas are ambivalent. Historians should investigate more closely, therefore, the ways in which the chosen people theme has been connected to the emergence of the varying political systems of the modern West.[11]

Their doing so should, among other things, encourage study of similar conjunctions and disjunctions in our own time, and even provide some way of peering into the future. Ideologies of chosenness do survive today. We have reason to suppose they will survive and function in the world of tomorrow.

[11]In order to promote the comparative analysis of national myth, the German Historical Institute in Washington is organizing a series of five conferences on "The German and the American National Experience in the Age of Total War."

Index